PRESENTED TO

Evie

FROM

Mom

May the God and Father of our Lord Jesus Christ cause you to be born again to a living hope, and to an inheritance that is imperishable, undefiled, unfading, and kept in heaven for you.

(based on 1 Peter 1:3-4)

NEW TESTAMENT

SALLY MICHAEL
ILLUSTRATED BY FRED APPS

MORE THAN A STORY

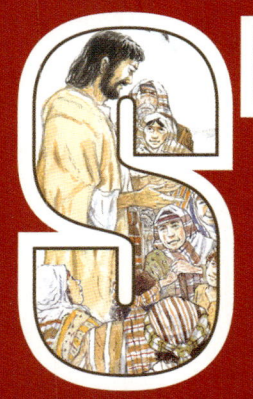

EXPLORING THE MESSAGE OF THE BIBLE WITH CHILDREN

Truth:78

More Than a Story: New Testament

by Sally Michael

Illustrated by Fred Apps
Art Direction and Design by Shannon Brown
Cover Design by Shannon Brown

Our vision at Truth78 is that the next generations know, honor, and treasure God, setting their hope in Christ alone, so that they will live as faithful disciples for the glory of God.

Our mission is to inspire and equip the church and the home for the comprehensive discipleship of the next generation.

We equip churches and parents by producing curricula for Sunday School, Midweek Bible, Intergenerational, Youth, and Backyard Bible Club settings; vision-casting and training resources (many available free on our website) for both the church and the home; materials and training to help parents in their role in discipling children; and the Fighter Verses™ Bible memory program to encourage the lifelong practice and love of Bible memory.

Copyright ©2021 Next Generation Resources, Inc. Illustrations Truth78. All rights reserved. No part of this publication may be reproduced in any form without written permission from Truth78.

First Printing 2021.

Published in the United States of America by Truth78.

Printed in China by Imago

ISBN: 978-1-952783-40-1

Truth:78

Toll-Free: (877) 400-1414
info@Truth78.org
Truth78.org

All Scripture quotations are from The Holy Bible, English Standard Version® (ESV®). Copyright © 2001 by Crossway, a publishing ministry of Good News Publishers. Used by permission. All rights reserved. ESV Text Edition: 2002, 2016.

Project Management: Brian Eaton, Steve Watters
Project Coordinator: Betty Dodge
Editing: Karen Hieb, Jill Nelson
Theological Review: Gary Steward
Proofing: Lois Greenlee Stück, Suzy Plocher, Anna Farthing

DEDICATIONS

Dedicated to my husband David, who has been a faithful and zealous partner in striving for the discipleship of the next generation for more than four decades.

May our children, grandchildren, and all our descendants be remembered by the LORD forever, and may your passion for the faith of the next generation be served through this book.

He established a testimony in Jacob and appointed a law in Israel, which he commanded our fathers to teach their children, that the next generation might know them, the children yet unborn, and arise and tell them to their children, so that they should set their hope in God and not forget the works of God, but keep his commandments; (Psalm 78:5-7)

Dedicated to John Piper, who taught me the theology in this book. May your God-centered, passionate teaching of the Word extend to generations beyond you through this book.

"Blessed are you, O LORD, the God of Israel our father, forever and ever. Yours, O LORD, is the greatness and the power and the glory and the victory and the majesty, for all that is in the heavens and in the earth is yours. Yours is the kingdom, O LORD, and you are exalted as head above all." (1 Chronicles 29:10b-11)

ACKNOWLEDGEMENTS

This book has been in my heart, mind, and prayers for decades. Throughout that span of time, there have been many individuals who have encouraged me to pursue a project like this. But chief among them has been my husband, David, who continually encouraged me to pursue my heart-burden to write a Bible story book for children and instilled in me the confidence that "God will help you." A close runner-up is my close friend and co-writer Jill Nelson, who has always given me honest feedback and strong encouragement.

There are so many others who have contributed to make this long-term dream a reality—my daughters who heard so many of these stories in some form or another growing up; my daughter Kristi, who patiently listened to story after story, stopping me when something needed to be reworded or suggesting better wording; my daughter Amy, who together with her children (my precious grandchildren) helped "test" these stories; my son-in-law, Gary Steward, who graciously checked for theological accuracy; Karen Hieb, who smooths my wording and corrects my grammar; Brian Eaton, who approved the project and brainstormed illustration ideas; Fred Apps, who came out of retirement to use his remarkable talents in pencil and paint to capture the heart of the text; the whole team at Truth78, who prayed, encouraged, and worked diligently to make computer files into a book; the many friends who have prayed consistently and fervently; and the financial contributors who gave sacrificially to make what was impossible for Truth78 a viable project.

The front cover of this book may have two names on it, but in reality, there are so many more names representing a host of people who have been associated with this book. Without their prayers and support, this book would not have happened. Their names may not be written on the cover, but they are written in my heart...and most importantly, they are written in the Lamb's Book of Life. Thank you, brothers and sisters.

TABLE OF CONTENTS

Preface 8
Introduction 9
A Note for Parents on Reading with Children 12

NEW TESTAMENT

Why does this book start with chapter 91? It's not a mistake. It's an intentional reminder that this is part of the bigger storyline of the Bible, which contains the full counsel of God. You will find the first 90 chapters in *More Than a Story: Old Testament*.

91 **God Speaks and Sends Good News!** (Gabriel Brings a Message to Zechariah and Mary–Luke 1:1-56) 16

92 **God Visits His People Again** (John the Baptist Is Born–Luke 1:57-80) 21

93 **Good News of Great Joy!** (The Birth of Jesus the Savior–Luke 2:1-35) 24

94 **Worthy of Worship** (The Wise Men Worship the King of the Jews, but Herod and the Jews Reject Him–Matthew 2) . . . 29

95 **He Has Spoken to Us by His Son** (Jesus Teaches in the Temple and Is Baptized by John– 33
Luke 2:40-52; Matthew 3:1-17; Luke 3:1-22)

96 **In Him There Is No Sin** (Jesus Has Victory over Temptation–Matthew 4:1-11) 38

97 **Greater Things than These** (Jesus Calls Five Disciples to See Greater Things; Jesus Turns Water into Wine– 42
John 1:19-2:11)

98 **Earthly Things and Spiritual Things** (Jesus, the True Temple, Cleanses the Earthly Temple; Nicodemus Hears 46
about Spiritual Birth –John 2:13-3:15)

99 **Living Water for All Peoples** (Jesus Offers Living Water to a Samaritan Woman–John 3:22-4:43) 51

100 **Anointed to Proclaim Good News** (Jesus Heals a Dying Son; Jesus Claims to be the Messiah– 56
John 4:46-54; Luke 4:16-30)

101 **Leaving Everything to Follow Jesus** (John the Baptist Is Imprisoned; Jesus Calls Fishermen to Be Fishers of Men– . . . 61
Matthew 4:18-20; Mark 1:14-20; Luke 5:1-11)

102 **Jesus Came to Be a Healer of Sinful Men** (Jesus Heals a Leper and a Paralytic; Jesus Calls Matthew– 66
Luke 5:12-32; Mark 2:1-12)

103 **Jesus Does His Father's Work on the Sabbath** (Jesus Heals on the Sabbath– 71
John 5:1-18; Matthew 12:9-14; Mark 3:1-6)

104 **True Followers of Jesus Have Changed Hearts** (Jesus Chooses His Disciples; the Kingdom Character 75
of a True Follower of Christ–Luke 6:12; Mark 3:13-19; Matthew 5)

The Beatitudes of the Sermon on the Mount (Matthew 5:3-12) 79

105 **Seeking Heavenly Treasures** (Jesus Teaches about Temporary Rewards and Lasting Treasure–Matthew 6) 82

The Lord's Prayer (Matthew 6:9-13) 86

106 **A Healthy Tree and a Diseased Tree** (Jesus Teaches about Seeking True Righteousness–Matthew 7) 89

107 **Who Is Jesus?** (Jesus Shows He Is the Promised One by Healing, Raising the Dead, and Forgiving Sin–Luke 7:1-50) . . . 93

108 **Hidden Truths in Kingdom Parables** (Jesus Teaches through Parables–The Sower, Treasure, Pearl, Rich Fool, Net– . . . 98
Matthew 13:1-23, 44-50; Luke 12:16-21)

109 **Jesus Stops Two Kinds of Storms** (Jesus Calms the Storm and Casts Out Demons–Mark 4:35-5:20) 102

110	**Do Not Fear, Only Believe** (People Respond to Jesus' Miracles in Faith, Unbelief, or Confusion—Mark 5:21-6:29)	106
111	**Jesus Is the Bread of Life that Satisfies Forever** (Jesus, the Bread of Life, Feeds Five Thousand—John 6; Matthew 14:13-21)	110
112	**Jesus Is God's Son Who Came to Die and Build His Church** (Jesus Foretells His Death and Describes a True Disciple; Jesus' Transfiguration—Matthew 16:13-17:13; Luke 9:28-36)	115
113	**Kingdom Greatness** (Jesus Teaches Humility through Children and Stories of the Pharisee and the Tax Collector, and the Good Samaritan—Mark 9:33-37; Matthew 18:1-6; Luke 18:9-14; Luke 10:25-37)	119
114	**Receiving Mercy and Showing Mercy** (Parable of the Unforgiving Servant; Jesus' Teaching on Forgiveness—Matthew 18:15-35; Luke 17:11-19)	124
115	**Jesus Welcomes People into His Kingdom** (Jesus Welcomes Children; the Parables of the Lost Sheep, Lost Coin, and Prodigal Son—Mark 10:13-16; Luke 15; Luke 17:11-19)	128
116	**Jesus and Two Kinds of Blindness** (Rich Young Ruler; Bartimaeus; Zacchaeus—Mark 10:17-31; Luke 18:35-19:10)	133
117	**Do You Believe in the Son of Man?** (Jesus Gives a Blind Man Physical and Spiritual Sight—John 9)	138
	I AM (Selected Scriptures)	142
118	**Jesus Is Glorified in Bringing a Dead Man to Life** (Jesus Visits with Mary and Martha; Jesus Raises Lazarus from the Dead—Luke 10:38-42; John 11:1-45)	144
119	**Hardened Hearts** (Jewish Leaders Plan to Kill Jesus; the Rich Man and Lazarus—John 11:45-57; Luke 16:19-31)	148
120	**Jesus Came to Glorify the Father** (Mary Anoints Jesus; Jesus Goes to Jerusalem Knowing His Destiny—Mark 14:3-9; John 12:1-19; Mark 11:1-10; Luke 19:29-44; Matthew 21:12-16)	152
121	**Jesus, the Perfect Prophet, Warns the Jews** (Jesus Teaches in the Temple; the Parable of the Tenants; the Woes to the Scribes and Pharisees—Luke 20:1-18; Matthew 21:33-22:14; Matthew 23:1-24:2)	157
122	**Be Ready** (Signs of the End of the Age—Matthew 24-25)	162
123	**Jesus Is the Perfect Passover Lamb** (Jesus Eats the Passover Meal with His Disciples—Luke 22:1-34; Matthew 26:1-35; John 13; Mark 14:1-31)	166
124	**Your Sorrow Will Turn into Joy** (Jesus Predicts Peter's Denial; Jesus Instructs His Disciples; Jesus' High Priestly Prayer—Luke 22:28-34; Matthew 26:30-35, John 14-17)	171
125	**Sad Betrayals and Willing Faithfulness** (Jesus Prays in the Garden and Is Arrested; Peter Denies Christ—Mark 14:32-72; Luke 22:39-71; Matthew 26:36-56; John 18:1-27)	175
126	**"Crucify Him!"** (Jesus Is Put on Trial —Matthew 27:1-33; Mark 15:1-22; Luke 23:1-31; John 18:28-19:17)	179
	Man of Sorrows (Isaiah 53)	185
127	**Father, Forgive Them** (Jesus Is Crucified—Matthew 27:34-44; Mark 15:23-32; Luke 23:32-43; John 19:18-27)	186
128	**"It Is Finished"** (Jesus Dies and Is Buried—Matthew 27:45-66; Mark 15:33-47; Luke 23:44-56; John 19:28-42)	190
	The Old Testament Pointed to Christ (Selected Scriptures)	194
129	**Imposter or the Son of God?** (Resurrection Appearances—Matthew 28:1-10, 16-20; John 20:11-29; John 21:1-17)	199
130	**You Will Receive Power** (The Holy Spirit Comes with Power—Acts 1-2)	205
131	**A Second Chance to Believe in Jesus and Be Saved** (A Lame Man Is Healed in Jesus' Name; Peter Preaches Boldly—Acts 3:1-4:31)	209
132	**The Holy Spirit Gives Believers Love and Courage** (The Church Grows in Love and in Number; Ananias and Sapphira Die; and the Apostles Preach—Acts 5)	213
133	**Full of Grace and Power** (Stephen Proclaims the Gospel and Is Martyred —Acts 6:1-8:3)	217
134	**You Will Be My Witnesses** (Simon's False Faith and an Ethiopian's True Faith—Acts 8)	222
135	**God's Chosen Instrument** (Jesus Saves Saul—Acts 9:1-31)	226

136 **Christ Welcomes All Peoples** (God Brings Peter and Cornelius Together—Acts 9:36-10:48) 230

137 **Two Kinds of Rescue** (The Gentile Church Grows; God Rescues Peter from Prison—Acts 11-12) 235

138 **God's Plan to Bless the Nations** (The First Missionary Journey—Acts 13-14) 239

139 **One Faith, One People** (The Jerusalem Council; the Macedonian Call—Acts 15:1-16:15) 244

140 **Great Rescues!** (God Rescues Paul, Silas, and a Jailer; Jesus Rescues Sinners in Greece—Acts 16:16-17:15) 249

141 **God Is Not Far** (Paul Teaches in Athens and Corinth—Acts 17:16-18:22) 253

    Loving Like Jesus Loves (1 Corinthians 13:1-13) 257

142 **Watching Over the Flock** (Paul Strengthens the Church on His Final Missionary Journey—Acts 18:23-21:16) 258

143 **"Away with Him!"** (Paul Is Imprisoned and Escapes Death—Acts 21:17-24:26) 263

144 **Take Heart and Trust God** (Paul Has Confidence in God in a Storm at Sea—Acts 24:27-27:44) 267

145 **An Ambassador in Chains** (God's Sovereign Plan for Paul in Rome—Acts 28) 271

    Dear Church 276

146 **An Awful Trade and a Wonderful Gift** (From Unrighteous to Righteous by Faith—Romans) 277

    The Bad News in Romans/The Good News in Romans 282

147 **Jesus Is Superior** (The Old Testament Foreshadows Jesus—Hebrews) 285

    The Great Faith Chapter (Hebrews 11) 290

148 **Wrong Thinking Leads to Wrongdoing** (Paul Corrects Error in the Corinthian Church—1 and 2 Corinthians) 294

149 **Salvation by Faith Alone** (By Faith in Christ God's Favor Is Poured out on the Gentiles—Galatians) 299

150 **Adopted by Faith to be Imitators of God** (Saved by Grace through Faith, Transformed by the Spirit —Ephesians) . . . 303

    The Whole Armor of God (Ephesians 6:10-13) 307

151 **Living Joyfully as Kingdom People** (Pictures of Christ and His Followers—Philippians and Colossians) 308

152 **Follow the Pattern of Sound Words** (Paul Instructs Timothy—1 and 2 Timothy) 312

153 **Doers of the Word** (Learning to Live in the Wisdom from Above—James) 317

154 **A Living Hope** (Hope for God's People in Persecution—1 and 2 Peter) 322

    Fellowship with God and One Another (Some Verses to Think about from 1 John) 327

155 **Let Him Hear** (Jesus' Message to the Seven Churches and to Us—Revelation 1-3) 329

156 **The King of Kings Reigns Forever!** (Jesus Will Return to Judge and to Bless—Revelation) 336

    Is He Worthy? 342

PREFACE

For whatever was written in former days was written for our instruction, that through endurance and through the encouragement of the Scriptures we might have hope. (Romans 15:4)

Long ago, at many times and in many ways, God spoke to our fathers by the prophets, but in these last days he has spoken to us by his Son, whom he appointed the heir of all things, through whom also he created the world. (Hebrews 1:1-2)

Page by page in our journey through thousands of years of Old Testament history, two stark realities stand out: the unchanging majestic character of God and the devastating effects of sin. These inescapable realities bring us to the threshold of the New Testament where we see the promise of deliverance fulfilled, unmerited redemption secured, and the glorious future for the redeemed revealed. It is a peculiar paradox and a staggering reality that God Himself rescues sinners from His own wrath. There is only one word that can describe it: GRACE. Amazing grace. Glorious grace—completely undeserved yet freely given.

This redemption repeatedly foreshadowed in the Old Testament is now revealed in the Person and work of God's own Son, Jesus—the second Adam, the Substitute Sacrifice, the Passover Lamb, the Mediator between God and man, the Perfect Law-Keeper, the Bread of Life, the Permanent High Priest, the Final Prophet through whom God has spoken, the Everlasting King from the line of David. By His miraculous birth in human form, His agonizing death on the cross, and His victorious resurrection, Jesus purchased salvation for sinners, fulfilling the promise of redemption made in the garden. Such a glorious rescue, such a deep and complete forgiveness cannot be comprehended in its glory without understanding the continual failings of the people of Israel generation after generation and the unfailing, secure light of the promise of the Messiah in the darkest and most wearisome of times. The New Testament does not stand alone. It is the continuing narrative of God's glorious provision for an undeserving remnant of humanity.

The New Testament reveals the unfolding plan of God to build the Church—His beloved children, from every tongue, tribe, and nation—to call out a peculiar people who act as salt and light in the darkness of this world...and to create a new heaven and a new earth when Jesus returns as King. He will establish His eternal Kingdom where His people can enjoy Him with unceasing praise. Will you be a part of that everlasting Kingdom of abundant life and profound joy?

As he was dying, former slave ship captain, redeemed sinner, faithful pastor, and writer of the hymn "Amazing Grace," John Newton whispered to a friend, "My memory is nearly gone. But I remember two things: that I am a great sinner, and that Christ is a great Saviour."

May this be the posture of your heart as you embark on this journey of reading through *More Than a Story: New Testament*.

...these are written so that you may believe that Jesus is the Christ, the Son of God, and that by believing you may have life in his name. (John 20:31)

INTRODUCTION

By Jill Nelson

For the past three decades, I have had the great privilege of teaching the Bible to children. I can honestly say that the longer I teach, the more I am absolutely stunned by the grandeur and power of God's written Word. The answer to every pressing question, every longing of the heart, every struggle of the will, and every hope of all-satisfying joy is found in the Bible. Therefore, there is no more pressing need than for our children to become fully acquainted with the Bible. Parents—and every believer—this is your sacred responsibility and privilege. Timothy's mother and grandmother knew this to be the case. Here is what the Apostle Paul wrote to Timothy:

> *"But as for you, continue in what you have learned and have firmly believed, knowing from whom you learned it and how from childhood you have been acquainted with the sacred writings, which are able to make you wise for salvation through faith in Christ Jesus. All Scripture is breathed out by God and profitable for teaching, for reproof, for correction, and for training in righteousness, that the man of God may be complete, equipped for every good work." (2 Timothy 3:14-17)*

Now more than ever, our children need to know, understand, and embrace the truths of Scripture. Toward that end, they also will benefit from solid Bible resources that not only reveal and explain the grand narrative of Scripture but also clearly help children understand the particular parts. Furthermore, they need Bible resources that serve to guide, challenge, and urgently impress upon them the need to wholeheartedly respond to God's Word with faith in Christ, resulting in love, honor, obedience, and worship of Him. I am delighted to say that *More Than a Story* is such a resource. It stands out as a unique discipleship tool for acquainting children with God's holy Word. Here are some distinguishing features that I deeply appreciate about this resource:

A Reverence for God's Holy Word

More Than a Story treats God's Word in the manner it rightly deserves. The clearest evidence of this is the sizable amount of biblical text included in every chapter and the meticulous care given to explain biblical truths clearly and accurately—nothing fanciful, exaggerated, silly, or speculative. Your child will be continuously reminded of the authority, clarity, necessity, and sufficiency of the Bible. God's Word is truly "more than a story"!

A Comprehensive Introduction to the Breadth and Depth of Scripture

By the time your children finish reading the Old and New Testament volumes of *More Than a Story*, they will have taken a chronological survey of the entire Bible from Genesis to Revelation. They will have discovered the Bible's many books and literary genres, as well as the major events, people, places, and themes. Additionally, your children will be exposed to the disciplines of biblical theology, systematic theology, and moral instruction, all grounded in the gospel.

Child-Appropriate without Compromising the Text

There is a great tendency when writing for children to take too much creative license in order to make the resource more "child-friendly"—fun and engaging. Sadly, children are often left with a delightful and memorable storyline but one that leaves out or minimizes essential biblical truths. This resource uses child-appropriate language to creatively convey biblical stories and truths, without compromising the nature or intent of the text.

A Clear Presentation of the Key Doctrines of the Christian Faith

Throughout *More Than a Story*, you will find numerous phrases and statements highlighted in bold font. These serve to develop a systematic theology for your children by highlighting key doctrines essential for the Christian life—doctrines concerning God, creation, man, the Fall, redemption, providence, the church, and many more.

A Serious and Sober Portrayal of the Problem of Sin

One of the unique features of *More Than a Story* is its depiction of the essence, pervasiveness, and problem of sin. Chapter after chapter your children will be confronted by the utter wretchedness of man's sin against a holy and righteous God. Rather than being distressed by this, consider it a great gift meant to point your children toward utter dependence on Christ. As D. A. Carson has stated:

> *There can be no agreement as to what salvation is unless there is agreement as to that from which salvation rescues us. The problem and the solution hang together: the one explicates the other. It is impossible to gain a deep grasp of what the cross achieves without plunging into a deep grasp of what sin is; conversely, to augment one's understanding of the cross is to augment one's understanding of sin.*
>
> *To put the matter another way, sin establishes the plot line of the Bible.*[1]

Grounded in the Gospel

Every chapter in this book is grounded in the glorious reality of the gospel. Every chapter points Christ-ward. However, in saying this, it is important to note that not every chapter in the Old Testament volume of *More Than a Story* overtly mentions Christ's redeeming work on behalf of sinful man. Rather, the author carefully lets the historical, progressive nature of Scripture unfold. This lays the crucial foundation on which to build true understanding and appreciation for the person and work of Christ. Where warranted, key connections to Christ are emphasized.

Guides Children in How to Study the Bible

Not only do children need to become acquainted with the actual text of Scripture, but they also need to be taught how to study the Bible. *More Than a Story* has been written

---

[1] D.A. Carson, "Sin's Contemporary Significance," Chapter 1 of *Fallen: A Theology of Sin*, edited by Christopher W. Morgan and Robert A. Peterson, (Wheaton, Ill.: Crossway, 2013), as republished on monergism.com

in an interactive manner that prompts children to observe and ask specific questions of a text in order to discover the meaning. This type of interaction not only encourages children to be eagerly and actively engaged, but it also develops critical thinking skills that will serve a lifetime of biblical study as they grow and mature.

Addresses the Mind, Heart, and Will

It isn't enough for a child to simply *know* the Bible—although that is the first step in the life of faith. God's Word must also be embraced by the heart and acted upon by the will. *More Than a Story* keeps all three realities in mind. Woven throughout every chapter are questions guiding your children to respond to what they read: How does God want me to respond? What should my heart feel and desire? What does God want me to think, be, and do?

Inspires Worship of God, for the Glory of God

Psalm 86 gives a beautiful summary of what biblical teaching is meant to inspire, fuel, and produce.

> [9]*All the nations you have made shall come*
> *and worship before you, O Lord,*
> *and shall glorify your name.*
>
> [10]*For you are great and do wondrous things;*
> *you alone are God.*
>
> [11]*Teach me your way, O LORD,*
> *that I may walk in your truth;*
> *unite my heart to fear your name.*
>
> [12]*I give thanks to you, O Lord my God, with my whole heart,*
> *and I will glorify your name forever.*

More Than a Story has been written with this glorious, God-centered goal in mind. Every chapter clearly and readily shines forth the incomparable greatness and worth of God, inspiring children to eagerly and whole-heartedly worship Him as their greatest treasure and delight!

In conclusion, *More Than a Story* is a wonderfully engaging discipleship tool for parents, grandparents, teachers, and anyone else who cares for the faith of the next generations. But bear in mind that it is also a serious tool, one conveying weighty truths that require our utmost attention. Will it be worth the added effort? Consider this thought and exhortation from John Piper:

> *The issue of earning a living is not nearly so important as whether the next generation has direct access to the meaning of the Word of God. We need an education that puts the highest premium under God on knowing the meaning of God's Book, and growing in the abilities that will unlock its riches for a lifetime...Lord, let us not fail the next generation!*[2]

---

2 John Piper, "A Compelling Reason for Rigorous Training of the Mind: Thoughts on the Significance of Reading," July 13, 2005, desiringgod.org/articles/a-compelling-reason-for-rigorous-training-of-the-mind

A NOTE FOR PARENTS ON READING WITH CHILDREN

There is a difference between reading *with* children and reading *to* children. Reading to children is when an adult reads and children listen; but reading with children is experiencing the story, the words, and the ideas together. It is an interactive exchange that takes place as the adult and the children discover meaning, wonder at the marvelous, mourn over the heartaches, ponder the incomprehensible, and rejoice in the beautiful together. Reading with children requires engaging your mind and heart in the text, letting your emotions overflow as you read together. It also takes a little bit of practice, a fair amount of abandonment, and, when reading to engage the heart and soul, a lot of prayer.

There are also some techniques we can employ in our quest to engage not only the minds of our children but also their hearts. Below are some suggestions to involve your children as you interact together to discover who God is, what He has done, and how we are to respond to Him.

- Pray briefly with your children before you begin reading. Ask God to open your minds and hearts and to show you who He is.

- Read with appropriate tone and emotion. The narratives and Scripture portions you will be reading warrant a response of enthusiasm, anger, sadness, joy, wonder—all kinds of emotions. Engage your heart in what you are reading and let your voice express that emotion.

- All the chapters include texts directly taken from the Bible itself. These are God's precious words meant to impart life, convict the soul, strengthen the weak, encourage the heart, inspire worship, warn the rebellious, comfort the fearful; so they should be read with understanding, feeling, and conviction. These are not emotionless scripts, but the words of the living God, which "[revive] the soul...[make] wise the simple...[and enlighten] the eyes." They should be read as such, for they are "more to be desired than gold...sweeter also than honey" (Psalm 19:7-10).

- Encourage your children to read some of the Bible texts so that they become familiar with God's Word.

- Involve your children in discovering the glorious truths in the chapter. Explain concepts or words your children do not understand. Encourage your children to ask questions. Engage your children by interacting with them and asking them to interact with the text. Ask them to read a portion of the text or to read a Bible verse. Stop and ask questions both to capture their wandering minds and to encourage them to think deeply about the truth. Some questions are included in the text itself. Some are rhetorical, but others, *in italics*, are meant to be answered. In some cases, these may be a springboard to further discussion. Don't feel tied to the text but add your own questions as you read.

- After asking a question for your children to answer...wait. Children need time to think. Sometimes they are intimidated and don't want to give the "wrong" answer. Encourage your children to be contributors by gently encouraging them and waiting patiently. Respond encouragingly, while still correcting, clarifying, or redirecting when needed.

- Examine the pictures and ask questions about them. Help your children to see the emotion and the realities expressed in the illustrations.

- The goal is not to "get through the chapter" but to encourage your children to discover who God is and ponder the eternal. It may take one sitting to finish a chapter, or it may take many sittings. Take your time and linger over discussions. Stop when your children are ready to stop and pick it up again later.

- Follow up after you finish the chapter or at a later time with some or all the ideas in the application boxes. It may take several sittings just to follow through on the application box.

- Apply the truths discovered in the chapter to everyday life. Be concrete and practical. How can the truth be lived out in your family, church, and community? Ask your children how God may want them to act on what they have learned.

- Discuss the verse in the application box. Explain unfamiliar words, talk about the meaning and application of the verse. Check the context when needed.

- Memorize key verses together and refer to them in everyday life, include them in your prayers, and encourage others with them.

As your hearts are drawn together through the shared experience of reading this book together, may your hearts be drawn to the One who "is the blessed and only Sovereign, the King of kings and Lord of lords, who alone has immortality, who dwells in unapproachable light, whom no one has ever seen or can see" (1 Timothy 6:15-16a).

BUT WHEN T
OF TIME HA
SENT FORT

...HE FULLNESS
...O COME, GOD
...H HIS SON...

CHAPTER 91
GOD SPEAKS AND SENDS GOOD NEWS!

Gabriel Brings a Message to Zechariah and Mary—Luke 1:1-56

…"I am Gabriel. I stand in the presence of God, and I was sent to speak to you and to bring you this good news." (Luke 1:19)

After hundreds of years of sin and failure, constant rejection of God and rebellious disobedience, the disappointment of waiting year after year for the Messiah to make things right, and then hundreds of years of God seeming to be absent…suddenly, the silence was broken! Not by God speaking through a prophet, but through a special messenger—an angel. This angel had two important messages from God. *To whom did the angel talk, and what did he say?*

The angel came to a priest named Zechariah first. Zechariah lived when Herod was king of Judea (Judah). Zechariah and his wife, Elizabeth, were godly older people who had no children—just like Abraham and Sarah.

One day, Zechariah was chosen to burn incense in the temple in Jerusalem. There was a crowd of people outside the temple praying. But Zechariah was alone at the altar of incense… until an angel appeared to him! *How do you think Zechariah reacted when he saw the angel?* Zechariah was surprised…and afraid!

But the angel said to him, "Do not be afraid, Zechariah, for your prayer has been heard, and your wife Elizabeth will bear you a son, and you shall call his name John. And you will have joy and gladness, and many will rejoice at his birth, for he will be great before the Lord. And he must not drink wine or strong drink, and he will be filled with the Holy Spirit, even from his mother's womb. And he will turn many of the children of Israel to the Lord their God, and he will go before him in the spirit and power of Elijah, to turn the hearts of the fathers to the children, and the disobedient to the wisdom of the just, to make ready for the Lord a people prepared." (Luke 1:13-17)

"In the spirit and power of Elijah"…These were familiar words. Could this be the messenger God promised through the prophet Malachi? How could Zechariah be sure that the message of the angel was true? How could he, an old man, and his wife, an old woman, have a baby? Who was this angel anyway? *And the angel answered him, "I am Gabriel. I stand in the presence of God, and I was sent to speak to you and to bring you this good news."*

But Zechariah doubted the angel's words. So Gabriel told Zechariah that he would not be able to speak until the promise was fulfilled. Sure enough, when Zechariah finally left the temple, he couldn't talk and had to "speak" by making signs. The people did not know exactly what had happened, but they realized that Zechariah had seen a vision in the temple.

Every word of God proves true. **Not one of His promises fails.** Just as God promised through the angel Gabriel, Elizabeth became pregnant. When Elizabeth was in her sixth month of pregnancy, Gabriel appeared again. But not to Zechariah. And not to Elizabeth.

He appeared to another woman, a young unmarried woman, a virgin named Mary. Mary was betrothed (promised in marriage) to a man named Joseph, who was of the royal line of David. *And he [Gabriel] came to her and said, "Greetings, O favored one, the Lord is with you!"* Just like Zechariah, Mary was troubled. What did his greeting mean?

And the angel said to her, "Do not be afraid, Mary, for you have found favor with God. And behold, you will conceive in your womb and bear a son, and you shall call his name Jesus. He will be great and will be called the Son of the Most High. And the Lord God will give to him the throne of his father David, and he will reign over the house of Jacob forever, and of his kingdom there will be no end." (Luke 1:30-33)

How could this be? Mary was not married to Joseph yet. She had never been with him or any man to have a baby. *And the angel answered her, "The Holy Spirit will come upon you, and*

the power of the Most High will overshadow you; therefore the child to be born will be called holy—the Son of God."

The Son of God—God's very own Son? The One who would crush the serpent under His heel? The promised Messiah, the eternal King from the line of David! This was the baby Mary would carry! Could God's glorious promises be coming true?

The angel had more surprising news for Mary. Her cousin, Elizabeth, was six months pregnant with a son. Elizabeth, who could have no children and now was old, was having a baby! How could this happen? This surely surprised Mary also, but **nothing is impossible with God. God is almighty; nothing is too hard for God.** He can give an old woman a baby with the spirit and power of Elijah to be God's special messenger…and He can give a young woman a holy child born through the miraculous power of the Holy Spirit!

What was Mary's response to the angel's message, to God's special but complicated plan for her life? And Mary said, "Behold, I am the servant of the Lord; let it be to me according to your word." She would do what God had called her to do. She was God's servant. She would willingly accept His plan for her and submit to God's will.

Who would understand these strange yet wonderful happenings? Mary decided to visit her cousin Elizabeth. When Elizabeth heard Mary's voice, the baby inside her leaped with great joy! *Why do you think this happened?* God's promise of a Messiah was being fulfilled! Elizabeth's baby rejoiced—he leaped for joy—in the presence of the unborn Savior. Mary saw with her own eyes the miracle of God—her cousin was having a baby in her old age. And that baby recognized that Mary's baby was God's own Son! How this must have encouraged Mary's faith in God's promise!

Elizabeth's baby was full of joy about Mary's special baby. *But how do you think Joseph felt when he heard that Mary was going to have a child?* He knew he was not the father. What should he do? He knew the punishment Mary could receive according to the Mosaic Law. If he made it known that Mary was pregnant and he was not the father, Mary could have been stoned to death. Joseph, *being a just man and unwilling to put her to shame, resolved [firmly decided] to divorce her quietly.* He would just quietly get out of the marriage agreement in front of two or three witnesses without raising a charge against her.

However, before Joseph did this, while he was still thinking about it, an angel came to him in a dream saying, *"Joseph, son of David, do not fear to take Mary as your wife, for that which is conceived in her is from the Holy Spirit. She will bear a son, and you shall call his name Jesus, for he will save his people from their sins."*

Mary's baby was formed by the Holy Spirit. The baby was the Son of God, the Savior. More than seven hundred years before this, the prophet Isaiah had foretold the birth of Jesus, and now Joseph and Mary were seeing the fulfillment of that glorious promise!

> *Therefore the Lord himself will give you a sign. Behold, the virgin shall conceive and bear a son, and shall call his name Immanuel. (Isaiah 7:14)*

Immanuel means, "God with us." The baby was God Himself coming as a man. This was the promised sign in Isaiah's prophecy that a child would be born, a Son would be given, *and his name shall be called Wonderful Counselor, Mighty God, Everlasting Father, Prince of Peace (Isaiah 9:6).* God was coming, not to live in the tabernacle, not to live in the Most Holy Place, but to live among men! God was coming in the flesh as a man to be among His people! He was coming to save them at last!

When Joseph woke from his dream, He accepted God's plan for his life, just as Mary did. He took Mary, who was carrying the Son of God, as his wife. They would be the earthly parents of the Messiah.

The eternal Son of God left heaven—a place of perfect love, peace, and goodness to be born as a baby into this sinful and broken world. Does the news of God sending His Son cause your heart to leap for joy? Are you amazed at a God who keeps His promises? Do you rejoice that God sent a Savior to come and live among us as fully God and fully man—the Son of God and the son of Mary?

> The true light, which gives light to everyone, was coming into the world. (John 1:9)

> ...though he [Christ Jesus] was in the form of God, did not count equality with God a thing to be grasped, but emptied himself by taking the form of a servant, being born in the likeness of men. (Philippians 2:6-7)

THAT YOU MAY BELIEVE

What does this chapter tell us about God?

Talk about and apply the **biblical truths** in **bold** text. Make them personal and apply them to what is happening in your family, church, community, or the world today.

Read Luke 1:46-55. What does this tell you about who God is?

Talk About: *...though he [Christ Jesus] was in the form of God, did not count equality with God a thing to be grasped, but made himself nothing, taking the form of a servant, being born in the likeness of men. (Philippians 2:6-7)*

Read Luke 1:1-4. Why did Luke write this story of God's miraculous work?

Pray: Thank God for keeping His promise to send a Savior. Praise Him that nothing is impossible for Him. Ask God to give you a heart to be His servant and to accept His plan for your life joyfully.

Think About: *Why is it so amazing that God sent His Son to come and live on earth?*

CHAPTER 92

GOD VISITS HIS PEOPLE AGAIN

John the Baptist Is Born—Luke 1:57-80

"Blessed be the Lord God of Israel, for he has visited and redeemed his people." (Luke 1:68)

Just as the angel Gabriel had foretold, there was "joy and gladness"! Elizabeth had given birth to a son in her old age! It was a wonderful miracle! Elizabeth's neighbors and relatives "rejoiced with her." Surely, the family thought, the baby should be named Zechariah, after his father. But Elizabeth disagreed with them. The baby should be named John.

John? Why John? No one in the family was named John. Elizabeth must be mistaken. The family would ask Zechariah to name the baby. What they did not know is that God had already named this special baby, and Gabriel had given his name to Zechariah. The family wondered what name Zechariah would give this special baby. Since Zechariah could not speak, he wrote on a tablet, "His name is John."

Do you know what happened then? God freed Zechariah's mouth and tongue, and he spoke! *What were his first words?* Before he was struck silent, Zechariah's last words to the angel were words of doubt, unbelief, and questioning. Now, his first words were words of praise to God!

News spread throughout Judea that this was a special child, and the people wondered who he would be, *for the hand of the Lord was with him.* But long ago, God had already let His people know about this child through the words of the prophets Malachi and Isaiah. His father, Zechariah, was filled with the Holy Spirit and foretold or prophesied about God's purpose using some of the words of these prophets.

*"**Blessed be the Lord God of Israel, for he has visited and redeemed his people and has raised up a horn of salvation for us** in the house of his servant David, as he spoke by the mouth of his holy prophets from of old…to show the mercy promised to our fathers and to remember his holy covenant, the oath that he swore to our father Abraham…that we… might serve him without fear, in holiness and righteousness before him all our days. And you, child, will be called the prophet of the Most High; for you will go before the Lord to prepare his ways, to give knowledge of salvation to his people in the forgiveness of their sins, because of the tender mercy of our God, whereby the sunrise shall visit us from on high to give light to those who sit in darkness and in the shadow of death, to guide our feet into the way of peace." (Luke 1:68-79)*

John was God's prophet or messenger. After 400 years of silence, God was speaking to His people again! An animal's horn was a symbol of its power. *Who was this "horn of salvation" that John was to prepare the way for—this powerful person who would redeem or deliver God's people?* The "horn of salvation" was the promised Messiah, the descendant of David, the promised Son of God spoken of by the angel to Mary.

God had broken the years of silence. He was fulfilling the promise made in the Garden of Eden thousands of years ago to crush the serpent's head—the promise made to Abraham of an offspring who would be a blessing to all nations, the promise made to David of an eternal King coming from his royal line, the promise made through the prophets that God would send a Redeemer to restore His people. Now, He had sent "the messenger to prepare the way," the voice crying in the wilderness, "prepare the way of the LORD."

Even though you are not a prophet like John the Baptist, you can tell others about the good news of God sending a Savior. You can pray that God will turn the hearts of those who resist Him to repent and be saved.

> "...for you will go before the Lord to prepare his ways, to give knowledge of salvation to his people in the forgiveness of their sins, because of the tender mercy of our God..." (Luke 1:76b-78a)

> "And he will turn many of the children of Israel to the Lord their God, and he will go before him in the spirit and power of Elijah, to turn the hearts of the fathers to the children, and the disobedient to the wisdom of the just, to make ready for the Lord a people prepared." (Luke 1:16-17)

THAT YOU MAY BELIEVE

What does this chapter tell us about God?

Talk about and apply the **biblical truths** in **bold** text. Make them personal and apply them to what is happening in your family, church, community, or the world today.

How does the birth of John the Baptist show God's mercy to His people?

Why would God send a prophet to His people before Jesus started His ministry?

Talk About: *"Blessed be the Lord God of Israel, for he has visited and redeemed his people." (Luke 1:68)*

Who can you tell about Jesus? What will you say?

Pray: Praise God for being a powerful, promise-keeping God. Ask Him to give you the heart to tell others about Jesus.

Think About: *Why would God be silent to His people for 400 years?*

CHAPTER 93
GOOD NEWS OF GREAT JOY!
The Birth of Jesus the Savior—Luke 2:1-35

..."Fear not, for behold, I bring you good news of great joy that will be for all the people. For unto you is born this day in the city of David a Savior, who is Christ the Lord." (Luke 2:10b-11)

The Old Testament prophets gave more than 300 hints, signs, or prophecies about Jesus. They spoke hundreds of years before the birth of Jesus. How could one person fulfill all these prophecies? No one could ever fulfill all the prophecies by mere chance. It would be utterly and completely impossible...apart from the all-powerful hand of the sovereign God.[3]

Joseph and Mary lived in Nazareth, ninety miles from Bethlehem, where the prophet Micah said the Savior would be born. Did the prophet make a mistake? Did God forget this detail? **God never forgets His word. He is omniscient—all-knowing.** God's plan was to show His greatness and worth. He loves to show His glory through "impossible situations," like Elizabeth having a baby in her old age, and having His Son born in Bethlehem, and fulfilling more than 300 other prophecies. *How would God get Joseph and Mary to Bethlehem so the prophecy would be fulfilled?*

About the time that John was born, the ruler of the Roman Empire, Caesar Augustus, made a law that all the peoples should be "registered." They needed to have their names recorded so the Romans could collect taxes from them. This had to happen in each person's hometown. Since Joseph was from the line of King David, Joseph had to go to Bethlehem, the birthplace of his ancestor

24

David. So Joseph and a very pregnant Mary left the town of Nazareth in the region of Galilee (northern Israel) to go to Bethlehem.

Why did the registration happen at this time? Was it just Caesar's idea? And why did Caesar decide that all the people had to go to their hometown? God gave Caesar this idea. It was all part of God's plan to fulfill the prophecy given through Micah:

> *But you, O Bethlehem Ephrathah, who are too little to be among the clans of Judah, from you shall come forth for me one who is to be ruler in Israel, whose coming forth is from of old, from ancient days. (Micah 5:2)*

Bethlehem was crowded because of the registration, and there was no room for Joseph and Mary. So Mary gave birth to baby Jesus, "the Son of the Most High," not in a palace, but in a place where animals were kept. Mary's baby was wrapped not in fine clothing but in "swaddling cloths," and the eternal King from the royal line of David was laid in a manger—a feeding trough for animals! What a humble and lowly way for the Messiah, the King of kings, to enter the world.

Mary and Joseph named the baby Jesus, the name given to them by God through the angel Gabriel. *Do you know what Jesus means?* Jesus is the Greek form of the Hebrew name Joshua, which means, "Yahweh is salvation." *Why is this a good name for God's Son?* Just as Joshua had led God's people into the Promised Land years ago, this "Joshua" would lead God's people into the land of eternal salvation.

God's plans never fail. Every word of God proves true. God always does what He says He will do. The long-promised Savior had come! He was born in Bethlehem, just as God had said He would be. Did anyone notice His birth? In a field near Bethlehem, there were some shepherds watching over their sheep during the night. To them, it was probably just an ordinary night, watching their sheep to make sure they were safe from wild animals and didn't wander away. But it became a very extraordinary night! For an angel of the Lord appeared in the dark night sky, "and the glory of the Lord shone around" the shepherds. What a magnificent display of light, glory, and greatness! It filled the shepherds with great fear.

> *And the angel said to them, "Fear not, for behold, I bring you good news of great joy that will be for all the people. For unto you is born this day in the city of David a Savior, who is Christ the Lord. And this will be a sign for you: you will find a baby wrapped in swaddling cloths and lying in a manger." And suddenly there was with the angel a multitude of the heavenly host praising God and saying, "Glory to God in the highest, and on earth peace among those with whom he is pleased!" (Luke 2:10-14)*

Was this true? Had the promised Savior finally come? After waiting for hundreds of years, was this the Messiah? The shepherds believed the amazing message of the angel. They were excited and decided to go to Bethlehem to see what "the Lord [had] made known to them." So they hurried away and found Mary, Joseph, and "the baby lying in a manger." It was just as the angel had told them! The shepherds spread the word about what they had heard and seen. Those who heard their words were amazed. *And the shepherds returned, glorifying and praising God for all they had heard and seen, as it had been told them.*

Why would the angels appear to shepherds? Why didn't they appear to the religious leaders or to the rulers of Judea? In the time of Abraham, Isaac, and Jacob it was good to be a shepherd—shepherds were valued and respected. After many years, the people of Israel began to consider shepherding a lowly job. Although David had been a shepherd, shepherds were looked down on at the time of Jesus' birth—they were treated as some of the least important people in Judea.[4] *So why would the angels appear to this unimportant, despised class of people?* Jesus didn't come with good news just for the rich and powerful. God's Son and His salvation is for all kinds of people, from the very highest to the very lowest.

Forty days after Jesus was born, Joseph and Mary brought Jesus to Jerusalem to present or dedicate Him to the Lord—just as Moses instructed in the Old Testament Law. They offered a sacrifice of two turtledoves (pigeons)—an offering allowed in the Old Testament for those who could not afford a lamb. *What does this tell you about Joseph and Mary?* Mary and Joseph were not rich or important people either. They were ordinary in many ways...but they were chosen by God to be the earthly parents for His Son.

Israel had waited so long for God to send the Messiah. For hundreds of years, they heard the prophets tell of God's promise to send a savior. People lived and died without seeing the coming of the Messiah. In Jerusalem, there was a godly man named Simeon who had waited all his life, trusting in God's promise. The Holy Spirit had revealed to Simeon that he would see the deliverance of God's people before he died. What a wonderful promise to Simeon! But how would Simeon recognize the Messiah? Would he be dressed as a king...or a priest? Simeon went to the temple the day Mary and Joseph brought Jesus there to dedicate him. There were all kinds of people in the temple. But when Simeon saw Jesus, he knew this was the One for whom he had long awaited. This tiny baby was the great, glorious, mighty Savior! Simeon took Jesus in his arms and praised God saying:

"Lord, now you are letting your servant depart in peace, according to your word;
for my eyes have seen your salvation that you have prepared in the presence of all peoples,
a light for revelation to the Gentiles, and for glory to your people Israel." (Luke 2:29-32)

Joseph and Mary were in awe of what this man said. God was making a way of salvation from sin! This was salvation not only for the Jewish people, but for all who would believe—for ordinary shepherds, for a godly old man, for men like Joseph and women like Mary, for young and old, for Jews and Gentiles (non-Jews), for people long ago, and for people today.

God has made a way for you, too. *Will you believe that Jesus is God's Son, the Promised Savior? Will you receive Jesus with joy as Simeon did?*

> For to us a child is born, to us a son is given; and the government shall be upon his shoulder, and his name shall be called Wonderful Counselor, Mighty God, Everlasting Father, Prince of Peace. (Isaiah 9:6)

> And the Word became flesh and dwelt among us, and we have seen his glory, glory as of the only Son from the Father, full of grace and truth. (John 1:14)

THAT YOU MAY BELIEVE

What does this chapter tell us about God?

Talk about and apply the **biblical truths** in **bold** text. Make them personal and apply them to what is happening in your family, church, community, or the world today.

Think about all that had to happen for Jesus to be born in Bethlehem. What does this tell you about God's sovereign plans and His power?

Talk About: *And the Word became flesh and dwelt among us, and we have seen his glory, glory as of the only Son from the Father, full of grace and truth. (John 1:14)*

Why would God have His Son come as a baby? Why couldn't he just have come as a grown man? What does it mean that Jesus was "fully God" and "fully man"?

Pray: Thank God for sending Jesus the Savior for sinners. Confess your sinful heart desires and ask God for His forgiveness.

Think About: *Why did the angel bring his message to lowly shepherds? Why didn't he announce Jesus' birth to the king and rulers, or the religious leaders?*

---

[3] Note of Interest: According to a professor of mathematics and astronomy, Peter W. Stoner, the chances of just eight prophecies coming true by sheer chance is 1 in 10^{17} (100,000,000,000,000,000). That would be equivalent to covering the whole state of Texas with silver dollars two feet deep *and then expecting a blindfolded man to walk across the state and* **on the very first try find the ONE coin** *you marked*...The chance that only forty-eight prophecies would be fulfilled is 1 in 10^{157} (static1.squarespace.com/static/54fda9aae4b0c72416a43fb8/t/598df751d2b8571265362ab5/1502476116977/Mathematical+Proof+for+the+Existence+of+Jesus+by+Prophecies+Fulfilled.pdf). We know that God providentially guided every one of these prophecies to fulfillment, which is naturalistically impossible.

[4] Randy Alcorn, "Shepherd's Status," Eternal Perspectives Ministries. In the time of Abraham, Isaac, and Jacob, it was noble to be a shepherd. But then Joseph moved his family to Egypt. The Egyptians didn't eat sheep. They thought sheep were worthless for food and sacrifices, and they despised anyone who was a shepherd. They also hated their Arab neighbors, who were shepherds. The Israelites spent 400 years in Egypt, and eventually the people of Israel also began to consider shepherding a lowly job. At the time of the birth of Jesus, shepherds were looked down on. They were treated as some of the least important people in Judea. *Why would God send angels to lowly shepherds?* (epm.org/resources/2008/Mar/11/shepherds-status/)

CHAPTER 94
WORTHY OF WORSHIP

The Wise Men Worship the King of the Jews, but Herod and the Jews Reject Him—Matthew 2

..."Where is he who has been born king of the Jews? For we saw his star when it rose and have come to worship him." (Matthew 2:2)

What was that light in the sky? Was it a star, a meteor, a comet, or something else? Whatever it was, wise men from the east saw it in the sky and figured out that it was over the land of Judea. Who were these wise men? They were not Jews. They were from the east, maybe from Persia.[5] They were educated and important men who advised kings. They studied the stars, planets, and the position of the sun and moon. So they knew this light was something extraordinary—it was new and different. They believed that a new light in the heavens was a sign or announcement that an important person had been born. This new light must mean that a king had been born in Judea, the land of the Jews.

The wise men left home and traveled to Jerusalem. When they got there, they started looking for the child, *"Where is he who has been born king of the Jews? For we saw his star when it rose and have come to worship him."* This should have been good news, wonderful news for the Jews! God had sent the Messiah, the Savior! But when King Herod heard this, *he was troubled and all Jerusalem with him.*

Herod was terrified at the thought of losing his throne. He was not a descendent of David and had no right to be king. He was not even a descendant of Jacob.[6] Herod was a cruel ruler, who actually had some of his own wives and children put to death because he thought they were plotting against him. He had to find out about this "king of the Jews"! So Herod called

29

the religious leaders and asked them where the prophets said the Christ, the Messiah was to be born.

The news was alarming. The prophesied birthplace of the Messiah was Bethlehem, a small town just about five miles from Jerusalem. Could this child, whose star the wise men had seen, actually be the Messiah? Herod quizzed the wise men. When did they see the star? How long ago had it appeared in the sky? Their answer revealed that the child could not be more than two years old.

Herod would take care of this threat to his throne! He had a sly plan. Herod sent the wise men to Bethlehem with a lie, *"Go and search diligently for the child, and when you have found him, bring me word, that I too may come and worship him."*

When the wise men left Jerusalem, the light appeared again and led them right to the place where the child Jesus was.

> *When they saw the star, they rejoiced exceedingly with great joy. And going into the house they saw the child with Mary his mother, and they fell down and worshiped him. Then, opening their treasures, they offered him gifts, gold and frankincense and myrrh. (Matthew 2:10-11)*

These wise and educated men, these important men who were not Jews, recognized the true King of the Jews… and they fell down and worshiped Him. Though Jesus was just a child, the wise men knew they were in the presence of a great king. They offered Him very expensive gifts—gifts fit for a king. They brought gold, frankincense, and myrrh to honor Jesus. We know that gold is a precious metal. *But what are frankincense and myrrh?* Frankincense and myrrh were both made from dried resin (like tree sap). Frankincense was a fragrant perfume sometimes used in worship or in healing illnesses. Myrrh was a spice with a strong sweet smell sometimes used to prepare bodies for burial. All these gifts were expensive and appropriate for a king.

When the wise men left, they returned to their countries without passing through Jerusalem. *Why did they do this?* God had warned them in a dream not to return to Herod. An angel appeared to Joseph in a dream and warned him, too. The angel told Joseph to take Mary and Jesus and flee to Egypt because Herod would soon be searching for Jesus. *Why would Herod want to find Jesus? Did he want to worship Him as he had said?* The angel told

Joseph that Herod wanted to destroy Jesus! So Joseph got up and left with Mary and Jesus at night to travel to Egypt.

Were the angel's words true? **God's word is always true.** Just as the angel had said, murderous Herod was furious when he realized that the wise men had tricked him. They had not returned to tell him where the child king was. Then Herod did something absolutely despicable and horrifically evil. He sent his soldiers to kill all the male children—all the boys—in Bethlehem and nearby who were two years old or younger. He would get rid of this King of the Jews and hang on to his throne! But God had protected Jesus, who by now was no longer in Bethlehem or anywhere near Jerusalem. **No one can defeat God's purposes**—not even powerful kings, not even Satan, who works through evil kings. God knew about Herod's evil plan...and had predicted it hundreds of years earlier through the prophet Jeremiah:

> "A voice was heard in Ramah [a city near Jerusalem], weeping and loud lamentation, Rachel [Jewish mothers] weeping for her children; she refused to be comforted, because they are no more." (Matthew 2:18; quoting Jeremiah 31:15)

But wicked King Herod did lose his throne. About three years later he died. Once again, an angel of the Lord appeared to Joseph in a dream telling him to leave Egypt with Mary and Jesus to return to Israel. Those who wanted to kill Jesus were now dead. As Joseph arrived in Israel, he learned that Herod's son was ruling over Judea, so he was afraid to go there. Again, God was faithful and sent an angel to warn Joseph. So Joseph took his family to Nazareth, a town in the Northern Kingdom of Israel.

And he went and lived in a city called Nazareth, so that what was spoken by the prophets might be fulfilled, that he would be called a Nazarene. (Matthew 2:23)

Most Jews despised Nazareth. This was where the Roman soldiers for the northern parts of Galilee were based. (Galilee was a region in Israel). The Jews hated the Romans because the Romans ruled over them. They saw the Romans as their enemies. Anyone living in Nazareth was seen as mixing or joining with the enemy. To "be called a Nazarene" was an insult. Someone from Nazareth was unimportant, lowly, and scorned.

So Jesus, the true King of the Jews, was rejected by powerful King Herod, despised by the Jews as a Nazarene, yet worshiped by foreign wise men. *What about you? What does Jesus mean to you? Is He the King of your heart—worthy of your full worship? What does it look like to make Jesus most important in your life?*

The true light, which enlightens everyone, was coming into the world. He was in the world, and the world was made through him, yet the world did not know him. He came to his own, and his own people did not receive him. But to all who did receive him, who believed in his name, he gave the right to become children of God, (John 1:9-12)

THAT YOU MAY BELIEVE

What does this chapter tell us about God?

Talk about and apply the **biblical truths** in **bold** text. Make them personal and apply them to what is happening in your family, church, community, or the world today.

What were the different responses to Jesus? What is so strange about this?

Talk About: *The true light, which enlightens everyone, was coming into the world. He was in the world, and the world was made through him, yet the world did not know him. He came to his own, and his own people did not receive him. But to all who did receive him, who believed in his name, he gave the right to become children of God, who were born, not of blood nor of the will of the flesh nor of the will of man, but of God, (John 1:9-13)*

Why were gold, frankincense, and myrrh especially appropriate gifts to bring Jesus?

How did God provide for Joseph to care for his family in Egypt? Can you see that, at every step in this true story, God took care of Joseph, Mary, and Jesus? Explain. What does this tell you?

Pray: Thank God for sending Jesus to be the true Light. Ask Him to open your eyes to the beauty of who Jesus is and give you a heart to truly worship Him.

Think About: *Why is it significant that wise men "from the east" came to worship Jesus? What does this tell you about God's plan of salvation?*

---

5 They were probably from what is now Iraq, Iran, Saudi Arabia, or Yemen.
6 Herod was a descendent of Jacob's brother, Esau.

CHAPTER 95

HE HAS SPOKEN TO US BY HIS SON

Jesus Teaches in the Temple and Is Baptized by John— Luke 2:40-52; Matthew 3:1-17; Luke 3:1-22

Long ago, at many times and in many ways, God spoke to our fathers by the prophets, but in these last days he has spoken to us by his Son, whom he appointed the heir of all things, through whom also he created the world. (Hebrews 1:1-2)

How horribly heartbreaking it is that evil Herod killed the baby boys under two years old. Again, the sin that came into the world caused death. But God's plan to rescue sinners could not be stopped. God had spared His own Son to be the Savior. Jesus grew up in Nazareth in the home of Mary and Joseph. *And the child grew and became strong, filled with wisdom. And the favor of God was upon him.*

Joseph worked as a carpenter to support his family and probably taught Jesus how to work in his woodshop. But Joseph and Mary also taught Jesus the Law of God. They were very dedicated followers of God. Every year, they traveled to Jerusalem to celebrate the Passover. *Do you remember what the Jews celebrated during Passover?* The Passover was a time for the Jews to remember their rescue from slavery in Egypt and God's protection of their firstborn sons from death. The blood of a perfect lamb painted on the top and sides of their doors was a sign to the angel of death to "pass over" their houses during the tenth plague in Egypt.

When Jesus was twelve years old, Joseph and Mary again made their yearly trip to Jerusalem to celebrate the Passover. After the Passover celebration, they started the long four to five day trip home. At the end of the first day of traveling, Joseph and Mary began searching for Jesus. But they couldn't find him. Jesus was missing! He was not among their relatives and friends who had journeyed together with them. Where could He be? Was He still in Jerusalem? Joseph and Mary had to return to find Him.

They traveled the whole next day back to Jerusalem to look for Jesus. Can you imagine how worried they must have been? On the third day, they found Jesus. *Do you know where they found him?* They found Jesus in the temple. Twelve-year-old Jesus was sitting among the teachers in the temple, "listening to them and asking questions." *And all who heard Him were amazed at his understanding and his answers.* His wisdom and understanding astonished the best religious leaders of Israel! God had broken the years of silence. Now He was speaking, not through the prophets, but through His Son! Even Jesus' parents were amazed when they saw

Him. Did they still not really understand the wonder of who Jesus is?

They explained to Jesus how frantic and worried they had been when they discovered He was missing. Now it was time for Jesus to wonder at how little they understood about why He came to earth and about His relationship with God, the Father—*"Why were you looking for me? Did you not know that I must be in my Father's house?"* Jesus had important work to do in helping people understand God's Word and His plan of salvation. Still, He obeyed His earthly parents and returned to Nazareth with them. There He continued to grow in wisdom and favor with God, living in Nazareth for most of His life.

Jesus' cousin, John the Baptist, also *grew and became strong in spirit.* John lived in the wilderness for years wearing clothing made from camel's hair and eating locusts and wild honey. *What do you think it would be like to live in the wilderness and eat locusts?* John stayed in the wilderness until God called him out of the wilderness to be *the prophet of the Most High* to *go before the Lord to prepare his ways, to give knowledge of salvation to his people in the forgiveness of their sins.* In those days, when a king or another very important person went on a journey, people went ahead of him to clear things out of the way, fix holes, and make the road smooth. In a way, this is what John did for Jesus.

> *For this is he who was spoken of by the prophet Isaiah when he said, "The voice of one crying in the wilderness: 'Prepare the way of the Lord; make his paths straight.'"* (Matthew 3:3)

John was preparing the way for Jesus' message of salvation. He traveled from place to place, calling people to repent from sin and to seek God's forgiveness. John's message was a message of salvation through repentance—a heart change of hating sin, turning away from it, and asking God's forgiveness. Crowds of people came to John to confess their sins and be baptized. John baptized people by immersing them under water in a lake or river, and then raising them out of it. This was a sign that they had repented of sin and wanted to live a pure life of obedience to God.

Many of the Pharisees and Sadducees came to see John's baptism. When John saw them, he exclaimed:

> "You brood of vipers! Who warned you to flee from the wrath to come? Bear fruit in keeping with repentance. And do not presume to say to yourselves, 'We have Abraham as our father,' for I tell you, God is able from these stones to raise up children for Abraham. Even now the axe is laid to the root of the trees. Every tree therefore that does not bear good fruit is cut down and thrown into the fire." (Matthew 3:7b-10)

The Jews were proud to be God's people—even though they had often turned away from God. They thought that, because **God is faithful to keep His promises**, they would be blessed as the descendants of Abraham. But just being a Jew does not make a person a member of the true family of God. Salvation does not come from being born as a descendant of Abraham. The Jews could not escape God's fierce anger toward sin just by being Jewish. **Salvation does not come through birth, but by repentance and faith.**

Why do you think John called the Pharisees and Sadducees a "brood of vipers"? He called them a brood of vipers—a family of snakes—because they were dangerous deceivers. Pretending to be godly, they were very proud and unrepentant. They were proud of acting in obedience to the law—showing off their outward obedience to strict rules and laws that they added to the Law of Moses. They trusted in keeping these laws for their salvation and expected others to follow these laws, too. They rejected John's message to admit they were sinners and trust in God's mercy toward repentant sinners. Because they did not truly repent from sin, they could not *bear fruit in keeping with repentance*; they could not show the true loving actions that come from a changed heart.

> *And the crowds asked [John], "What then shall we do?" And he answered them, "Whoever has two tunics is to share with him who has none, and whoever has food is to do likewise." Tax collectors also came to be baptized and said to him, "Teacher, what shall we do?" And he said to them, "Collect no more than you are authorized to do." Soldiers also asked him, "And we, what shall we do?" And he said to them, "Do not extort money from anyone by threats or by false accusation, and be content with your wages." (Luke 3:10-14)*

True repentance from selfishness means sharing what you have with others. Repentance from greed means tax collectors would not cheat people but only collect the amount of money a person should pay for taxes. Repentance from pride and bullying is shown by refusing to use power to get what you want. True repentance that comes from a true heart change is shown by a change in behavior.

As John was baptizing, Jesus came to John to be baptized. But John didn't want to baptize Jesus. *Do you know what John said to Him?* *"I need to be baptized by you, and do you come to me?"*

Jesus was sinless—He had no need to repent. John the Baptist was a sinner. Why should a sinner baptize the perfect, sinless Son of God? But Jesus told John to baptize Him, *"Let it be so now, for thus it is fitting for us to fulfill all righteousness."* **Jesus was fully God, and He was also fully human.** He would do what God required of men. He would be baptized because it was the right thing to do. Even though Jesus was not a sinner, He would join fallen sinners and be baptized.

And when Jesus was baptized, immediately he went up from the water, and behold, the heavens were opened to him, and he saw the Spirit of God descending like a dove and coming to rest on him; and behold, a voice from heaven said, "This is my beloved Son, with whom I am well pleased." (Matthew 3:16-17)

Now there was no question who Jesus is—Jesus is God's Son. God Himself announced this! John would continue to preach his message of repentance and faith…faith in Jesus, the Son of God. John the Baptist would tell the "good news"—the gospel—that the Savior had come!

Do you rejoice in the good news that Jesus is the Savior? In what do you trust? Do you trust in being born into a Christian home, or being a "good person" in order to be saved? Do you trust in going to church and doing religious things like the Pharisees and Sadducees did? Or do you truly understand that you are a sinner who needs to repent and trust in Jesus, God's Savior to take away your sins?

…"The time is fulfilled, and the kingdom of God is at hand;
repent and believe in the gospel." (Mark 1:15)

THAT YOU MAY BELIEVE

What does this chapter tell us about God?

Talk about and apply the **biblical truths** in **bold** text. Make them personal and apply them to what is happening in your family, church, community, or the world today.

Explain what true repentance is. How can you tell if you have truly repented from sin?

Talk About: *"Bear fruit in keeping with repentance. And do not presume to say to yourselves, 'We have Abraham as our father,' for I tell you, God is able from these stones to raise up children for Abraham. Even now the axe is laid to the root of the trees. Every tree therefore that does not bear good fruit is cut down and thrown into the fire." (Matthew 3:8-10)*

Why is Jesus called "the Lamb of God"?

Pray: Admit that you are a sinner and confess your sin to God. Ask God to give you a truly repentant heart. Thank Him for sending Jesus to die on the cross for the sins of men.

Think About: *In what am I truly trusting? Am I trusting in Christ alone for the forgiveness of sin?*

CHAPTER 96
IN HIM THERE IS NO SIN
Jesus Has Victory over Temptation—Matthew 4:1-11

You know that he appeared to take away sins, and in him there is no sin. (1 John 3:5)

Look around you. What effects of sin do you see? All the sadness, sickness, brokenness, hatred, selfishness, deception…all the evil in the world is the result of the Fall. Adam and Eve failed in the garden. They listened to Satan, gave in to temptation, trusted their own wisdom instead of God's wisdom, and disobeyed God. Adam's sin spread to all men… all men but One. Jesus was fully man, and He was fully God, too. Would Jesus, the Son of Man, be another Adam, giving in to sin? Or would He be a new Adam, without sin?

The Spirit of God[7] led Jesus into the wilderness to be tempted by Satan. Satan would try to get Jesus to do what is wrong. He would tempt Jesus to sin. Would Jesus obey God perfectly, or would He fail like Adam, Israel, and all other people? Just as Satan came to Adam and Eve in the garden, he came to Jesus in the wilderness. He had no new tricks. Once again, he came with lies and false promises. In the garden, Adam and Eve could eat the fruit of any tree but one. In the wilderness, Jesus did not eat, but fasted for forty days and forty nights. Satan knew that Jesus was hungry. After all, Jesus was a man with the same need for food as all men. Satan, "the tempter," said to Jesus, *"If you are the Son of God, command these stones to become loaves of bread."* Wouldn't bread seem pretty good to a starving man? Satan was tempting Jesus through His appetite, His desire for food, through "the desires of the flesh"—with what His physical body wanted. Would Jesus turn the stones into bread and eat it, like Adam and Eve ate the fruit that looked so good?

> But [Jesus] answered, "It is written, "'Man shall not live by bread alone, but by every word that comes from the mouth of God.'" (Matthew 4:4)

Jesus trusted God's Word and God's wisdom. He stood firm on the truth and did not listen to Satan's suggestion to give in to temptation and sin.

Do you think Satan gave up? No, **Satan is very determined. He hates God and loves to tempt men to sin.** How He would love to spoil God's plan to redeem men through the Savior! So the devil took Jesus to a high place on the temple in Jerusalem. Again, Satan spoke his evil suggestion...and this time, he even used God's own promise, which he twisted to use wrongly. *"If you are the Son of God, throw yourself down, for it is written, 'He will command his angels concerning you,' and 'On their hands they will bear you up lest you strike your foot against a stone.'"* Satan was tempting Jesus to test God's promise to protect Him. Now Satan was telling Jesus to purposefully jump from the top of the temple to see if God would really do what He promised. Could God really be trusted? Satan succeeded in getting Adam and Eve to doubt God's Word, but Jesus did not doubt God's Word. He would not follow this evil suggestion. He would not force God to prove His truthfulness.

> Jesus said to him, "Again it is written, 'You shall not put the Lord your God to the test.'" (Matthew 4:7)

Again, Jesus the Son of Man would not give in to sin. But Satan had still another temptation. He would tempt Jesus with pride, power, and greed. Satan took Jesus up to a high mountain where he showed Jesus "all the kingdoms of the world and their glory"...

and said to him, "To you I will give all this authority and their glory, for it has been delivered to me, and I give it to whom I will. If you, then, will worship me, it will all be yours." (Luke 4:6-7)

What a temptation this was! Satan was trying to deceive or fool Jesus. God has given Satan some temporary power and rule over this world. But God promised that His Son would rule an eternal Kingdom! Do you remember the words of the prophet Daniel?

"I saw in the night visions, and behold, with the clouds of heaven there came one like a son of man, and he came to the Ancient of Days and was presented before him. And to him was given dominion and glory and a kingdom, that all peoples, nations, and languages should serve him; **his dominion is an everlasting dominion**, *which shall not pass away, and his kingdom one that shall not be destroyed." (Daniel 7:13-14)*

This was what God promised His Son. Someday all nations would bow before Him...but Satan was tempting Jesus to make this happen His own way. Abraham had tried to make God's promise come true his own way by having a son with Sarah's slave, Hagar. Jacob and Rebekah tried to get the blessing, the promise that the elder would serve the younger, their own way, and they deceived Isaac. Would Jesus do the same thing? Or would He wait for God, the Father, to keep His promise His way, in His own time? Would Jesus trust His heavenly Father...or trust Satan's suggestion like Adam and Eve had done? Would He sin and break the first commandment to worship God alone, or would He resist the sins of pride, power, and greed?

With complete trust in His Father and perfect obedience to Him, Jesus boldly stood up to Satan.

Then Jesus said to him, "Be gone, Satan! For it is written, 'You shall worship the Lord your God and him only shall you serve.'" (Matthew 4:10)

Jesus would not rebel against God. He would not worship any other, and He would not sin. **In all these temptations, Jesus did not sin.** Jesus, the Son of God, would fulfill His Father's plan for Him on earth. He would be the perfect sacrificial lamb, the Lamb of God, the Messiah, the Savior. Satan would not win!

Then the devil left him, and behold, angels came and were ministering to him. (Matthew 4:11)

Jesus, the Son of God, defeated Satan and evil in the wilderness, and **someday Jesus will crush the serpent's head forever! Jesus came to earth to fulfill the purposes of His heavenly Father.** Jesus came to do what no one else could do—to perfectly keep God's Law and be the perfect sacrifice for sin. Satan could not turn Jesus away from God's plan to save man through the sinless Lamb of God.

Jesus never sinned...not when He was tempted in the wilderness or at any time throughout His entire life on earth. He perfectly obeyed the Law of God. Because Jesus was perfectly obedient, He has perfect righteousness. But, unlike Jesus, we are sinners who cannot perfectly obey God. Jesus is the Perfect Law-Keeper, who can give sinners what we could never earn—perfect righteousness. Only by trusting in Jesus can you receive perfect righteousness. Do you trust in your own righteousness? Or do you trust in God's solution for your sin problem?

> Therefore, just as sin came into the world through one man, and death through sin, and so death spread to all men because all sinned...For as by the one man's disobedience the many were made sinners, so by the one man's obedience the many will be made righteous. (Romans 5:12, 19)

THAT YOU MAY BELIEVE

What does this chapter tell us about God?

Talk about and apply the **biblical truths** in **bold** text. Make them personal and apply them to what is happening in your family, church, community, or the world today.

Talk with your father or mother about how Satan tempts you. What are some ways you can fight that temptation with God's powerful Word?

Talk About: *Therefore, just as sin came into the world through one man, and death through sin, and so death spread to all men because all sinned...For as by the one man's disobedience the many were made sinners, so by the one man's obedience the many will be made righteous. (Romans 5:12, 19)*

How are believers saved through Jesus' perfect obedience?

Pray: Ask God to give you a heart that loves Him more than you love the world. Thank Him for sending Jesus to defeat Satan. Confess your sin to God, and thank Him for making a way for sinners to have perfect righteousness through trusting in Jesus.

Think About: *What in my life shows that I love God, or that I love the world? (See 1 John 2:15-17.)*

---

7 Remember that God is a triune God—He is three Persons in one God: God the Father, God the Son, and God the Holy Spirit. These three are one God.

CHAPTER 97
GREATER THINGS THAN THESE

Jesus Calls Five Disciples to See Greater Things; Jesus Turns Water into Wine—John 1:19-2:11

"Behold, the Lamb of God, who takes away the sin of the world!" (John 1:29b)

Do you like to be first? Do you like to come in first in a race, win a game, or be the best at something? It is part of our human nature to want to be the most important. John the Baptist had many followers—many who listened to his teaching and went to his baptisms. But John knew he was not the most important. He was not the promised Messiah; he was the "voice crying in the wilderness" to prepare the way of the Lord. John was a true messenger of God and faithfully pointed away from himself to Jesus as the Messiah, the Savior, and the Son of God. When John was asked, "Who are you?" he did not exalt himself. He was a humble servant of God.

He confessed, and did not deny, but confessed, "I am not the Christ."...So they said to him, "Who are you?...What do you say about yourself?" He said, "I am the voice of one crying out in the wilderness, 'Make straight the way of the Lord,' as the prophet Isaiah said...I baptize with water, but among you stands one you do not know, even he who comes after me, the strap of whose sandal I am not worthy to untie." (John 1:20, 22-23, 26-27)

John didn't think he was worthy even to untie the straps of Jesus' sandals! He recognized the greatness and worth of Jesus, the Son of God. John knew he was a sinful man chosen to be God's messenger, and he would not claim to be greater than he was. The next day, John was with two of his disciples when he saw Jesus coming toward him, and he said:

"Behold, the Lamb of God, who takes away the sin of the world! This is he of whom I said, 'After me comes a man who ranks before me, because he was before me.' I myself did

not know him, but for this purpose I came baptizing with water, that he might be revealed to Israel." (John 1:29b-31)

John came to show Israel who Jesus is. He called Jesus, "the Lamb of God who takes away the sin of the world." No one; not Adam or Eve, Abraham, Isaac, Jacob, or the Israelites could keep God's commands and His covenant. They continually broke God's Law. But God was making a new covenant, not sealed by the blood of animals but by the blood of the Lamb of God, Jesus. In this new covenant, there is salvation by grace through faith in Jesus alone. It does not come about by a covenant of works, by keeping the Law. It comes about by a **covenant of grace—by undeserved favor received through faith in Christ.**

The two disciples with John followed Jesus. One of them, Andrew, went to find his brother Simon to tell him, *"We have found the Messiah."* When Andrew brought Simon to Jesus, Jesus looked at Simon and gave him a new name. Can you remember anyone else whose name God changed? Do you remember the importance of names in the Bible? Names told something about the person's character or purpose. Jesus changed Simon's name to Peter, which means "rock." Does that seem strange? Later, we will find out why Jesus changed Peter's name.

The next day, Jesus went to Galilee. There he found a man named Philip, *and said to him, "Follow me."* Just as Andrew did, Philip went and found someone to tell about Jesus. He found Nathanael and said to him, *"We have found him of whom Moses in the Law and also the prophets wrote, Jesus of Nazareth, the son of Joseph."* Do you know how Nathanael responded? Did he get excited? Did he ask Philip to take him to Jesus? No, Nathanael doubted this could be true and said, "Can anything good come out of Nazareth?"

But Philip told Nathanael to "come and see." So, Nathanael went with Philip to see Jesus. When Jesus saw them coming, He greeted Nathanael with the words, *"Behold, an Israelite indeed in whom there is no deceit!"* He knew Nathanael had spoken frankly—he had said just what he thought, with no pretending. That surprised Nathanael! He wanted to know how Jesus knew this. He was even more surprised when Jesus answered, *"Before Philip called you, when you were under the fig tree, I saw you."* This was enough to convince Nathanael—*"Rabbi [teacher] you are the Son of God! You are the King of Israel!"* Nathanael was convinced about who Jesus was because Jesus knew about him...but Jesus told Nathanael that he would see even greater things than that. He would see that Jesus is the link between earth and heaven.

One of these greater things happened at a wedding that Jesus attended with the five disciples. Wedding feasts in those days sometimes lasted a week or longer. How much food and drink it must have taken to feed the guests for all that time! This feast must have taken more than the bridegroom thought it would because, during the wedding feast, the servants ran out of wine to serve the guests. This was a very embarrassing situation! What in the world could they do about it?

But Mary knew what to do—she turned to Jesus. Jesus would know what to do and would solve the problem. The disciples were about to see one of those greater things Jesus talked about. Six large stone water jars were there. These were very large jars. Each held 20 to 30 gallons. The Jews used the water in these jars for "purification rites"—for washing before and after meals.[8] They did not use these jars for drinking water. No Jew would drink that water.

But Jesus told the servants to fill the jars with water. What would Jesus do with gallons and gallons of water? The servants filled the jars to the very top. Then Jesus told them to take some to the master of the feast. But what the servants poured out of these jars was not water, but wine! What does this tell you about Jesus? **Jesus is God, the Creator**, who turned water into wine! He did what no merely human person can do. Can you change water into milk or orange juice? Only Jesus can do a miracle like changing water into wine. But Jesus did more than just change the water into wine…

When the master of the feast tasted the wine that Jesus made, he was amazed. This did not make sense. Most people served the good wine first and then, after people had plenty to drink, they would serve the poor wine—the wine that wasn't very good. That way, the people really wouldn't notice how poor the wine was. The master of the feast was amazed. This was the finest wine! He thought that the bridegroom had saved the best wine to serve last. He didn't know that Jesus had created this fine wine. But the disciples knew about it.

This, the first of his signs, Jesus did at Cana in Galilee, and manifested his glory. And his disciples believed in him. (John 2:11)

Jesus' miracles showed that He was not just a mere man. **Jesus is God. He is the Messiah, who would** do greater things and **bring a better covenant.** He would not purify His people through a "rite of purification," making them clean with water. The Old Testament laws for cleansing or washing were just a sign of what God wanted for His people—pure hearts. Jesus would pour out His blood as the Lamb of God to purify them from sin. He would be their Bridegroom, who would give only the very best—He would give Himself. This is the greater thing that Jesus would do. God saves the best for last!

Do you believe that Jesus is the Son of God who offers the very best? What greater things are coming for those who trust in Jesus? Do you believe that real, true wonderful life comes through believing in Jesus?

Now Jesus did many other signs in the presence of the disciples, which are not written in this book; but these are written so that you may believe that Jesus is the Christ, the Son of God, and that by believing you may have life in his name. (John 20:30-31)

THAT YOU MAY BELIEVE

What does this chapter tell us about God?

Talk about and apply the **biblical truths** in **bold** text. Make them personal and apply them to what is happening in your family, church, community, or the world today.

God gave us the Bible so that we would believe in Him. What does it mean to "believe"? Is this just knowing about Him, or is it more than that?

Talk About: *Now Jesus did many other signs in the presence of the disciples, which are not written in this book; but these are written so that you may believe that Jesus is the Christ, the Son of God, and that by believing you may have life in his name. (John 20:30-31)*

What are some other signs that Jesus did? What do they tell you about Jesus? (We will discover more and more of these signs as we continue through our stories.)

Pray: Praise God for sending Jesus to be "the Lamb of God who takes away the sins of the world." Confess your doubts to God. Ask God to give you a true heart of belief and trust in Jesus. Pray for those who do not trust in Jesus.

Think About: *How can I tell if I really believe in Jesus?*

---

8 The Jews believed that many things were "unclean," and touching or being around those things would make them unclean—not unclean like being dirty, but unclean like being unholy or impure. Eating with tax collectors and sinners, touching a dead body or a leper (person with a skin disease called leprosy) would make them unclean. To become clean again, they had to follow certain instructions or "purification rites."

CHAPTER 98

EARTHLY THINGS AND SPIRITUAL THINGS

Jesus, the True Temple, Cleanses the Earthly Temple; Nicodemus Hears about Spiritual Birth—John 2:13-3:15

For in him all the fullness of God was pleased to dwell, and through him to reconcile to himself all things, whether on earth or in heaven, making peace by the blood of his cross. (Colossians 1:19-20)

Oxen, sheep, and pigeons! That's what Jesus saw at the temple when He went to Jerusalem for the Passover. He was thirty years old. He understood that these animals were used for sacrifices in the temple. But these people were not bringing the animals to sacrifice; they were selling them. Other people were exchanging money. Travelers would come from other parts of the Roman Empire with their money to pay their offering or temple tax or to buy an animal to sacrifice. They may have had Roman money and needed to trade it—for a price—for Jewish money. The temple courtyard looked like a marketplace!

God's temple was meant to be a place to humbly ask forgiveness for sin through sacrificing an animal. It was a place of prayer—a place to meet with God and worship Him. God was present in a special way in the Most Holy Place. But this courtyard didn't look like the courtyard of a place of spiritual worship. It looked like an earthly place to buy and sell things—a market! *What do you think Jesus thought of that?*

Jesus was rightly angry. They were disrespecting His Father's house! They were dishonoring God. Jesus could not stand by and watch that happen. So He began to cleanse the temple. He overturned the tables and poured out the coins. He made a whip to clear out God's house. Bird cages crashed to the floor. Oxen ran in all directions. Sheep crashed into each other. Coins rolled around on the floor. People scurried to get out of the way…as Jesus drove them all out of the temple.[9] *"Take these things away; do not make my Father's house a house of trade."*

What do you think the Jews thought of what Jesus did? They demanded a sign or a miracle. What right did Jesus have to treat them like this? Who did Jesus think He was? He had better prove that He was someone special! *Do you know how Jesus answered them?*

Jesus answered them, "Destroy this temple, and in three days I will raise it up." (John 2:19)

The Jews thought this was ridiculous! It had taken forty-six years to build the temple. Did Jesus actually think He could destroy it and raise it back up in three days? But they were thinking of earthly things, not spiritual things. They were only thinking about what they could see or about the ordinary meaning of things. However, Jesus wasn't talking about God's presence in a stone and wood temple. Jesus was talking about a different temple—His body. The temple was the place where God promised to dwell with His people—to be with them in a special way. But **Jesus is the living, eternal God**. *For in him all the fullness of God was pleased to dwell.* God's presence was with His people through His Son. God was not *just* present in a special way in the Most Holy Place, but also in the Messiah who would make a way for His people to worship God and be with Him always. The temple that would be destroyed would be Jesus' body, which would die upon the cross...but He would "raise it up" in three days. Jesus would also destroy the Jewish religious system of temple sacrifices because **Jesus would be the final sacrifice for sin.**

But the Jews did not understand the spiritual meaning of what Jesus said. They didn't understand that Jesus is the way to the Father. They could only think in earthly ways. Jesus did many signs while he was in Jerusalem that showed He is God...and "many believed in Him." But Jesus knew they didn't really believe as true disciples who would follow Him faithfully. They just liked the miracles He did. They were still thinking in earthly ways.

A Pharisee named Nicodemus was someone who thought in earthly ways. Nicodemus was an important religious leader and ruler of the Jews. One night, he came to Jesus to ask a question. *"Rabbi,"* he said, *"we know you are a teacher come from God, for no one can do these signs that you do unless God is with him."* Nicodemus was also a teacher...a teacher who wanted to talk to "a teacher come from God." *Do you think that Nicodemus fully understood who Jesus is?* Jesus is not just "a teacher from God"—He *is* God!

Jesus answered him, "Truly, truly, I say to you, unless one is born again he cannot see the kingdom of God." (John 3:3)

Do you know how Nicodemus responded to this? He asked how a person could be born when he is old. *"Can he enter a second time into his mother's womb and be born?"* Nicodemus was thinking in earthly ways. He was thinking about being physically born—coming from his mother's body. But Jesus was talking about spiritual things. He wasn't talking about being born physically but being born spiritually. **Spiritual birth is a work of the Spirit of God, which makes a person a child of God.** No one can be alive to spiritual things unless he is born again.

Even though Nicodemus was a religious teacher, he did not understand what the Old Testament prophets taught about the new covenant God would make with His people.

I will sprinkle clean water on you, and you shall be clean from all your uncleannesses, and from all your idols I will cleanse you. And I will give you a new heart, and a new spirit I will put within you. And I will remove the heart of stone from your flesh and give you a heart of flesh. And I will put my Spirit within you, and cause you to walk in my statutes and be careful to obey my rules. (Ezekiel 36:25-27)

Jesus was giving Nicodemus an earthly example of a spiritual truth. Everyone knows what it means to be born physically. Jesus was telling Nicodemus that being born as a person is not enough. **Every person is born with a sinful heart and needs a new heart**…a new heart that only God can give them by "being born again"—by being born spiritually. Then Jesus gave Nicodemus another picture of what this new spiritual birth meant.

> *"And as Moses lifted up the serpent in the wilderness, so must the Son of Man be lifted up, that whoever believes in him may have eternal life." (John 3:14-15)*

Do you remember when Moses made the bronze serpent? Why did he make it? Snakes had come into the Israelite camp because of Israel's disobedience, and people were dying of snakebites. God told Moses to make a bronze serpent and put it on a pole. Everyone who looked at the snake would be healed. *Did the bronze serpent make them well?* No, they were healed by faith in God—faith that God would heal them, faith that what God said was true.

Jesus was telling Nicodemus that the one who has spiritual birth and a new heart looks to Jesus with faith. He trusts in Jesus, the Messiah, who would also be put on a pole or a cross. **The Holy Spirit gives a new heart that empowers a person to understand spiritual truth and trust in Jesus. Faith in Jesus, not law-keeping, was the new covenant that God was making with His people.**

Earthly things are easy to understand. But spiritual things can only be understood when the Holy Spirit gives a person a mind to understand them and the heart to accept them. *Do you want to understand spiritual things? Have you been born again through true faith in Jesus? Will you ask God to open your mind and heart to understand and accept the spiritual truth of who He is?*

> "For God so loved the world, that he gave his only Son, that whoever believes in him should not perish but have eternal life." (John 3:16)

THAT YOU MAY BELIEVE

What does this chapter tell us about God?

Talk about and apply the **biblical truths** in **bold** text. Make them personal and apply them to what is happening in your family, church, community, or the world today.

Why didn't the Jews understand Jesus' teaching? Why were they drawn to the miracles, rather than to the miracle-maker? What does this tell you about earthly understanding and spiritual understanding? Read and explain John 2:23-25.

Talk About: *"For God so loved the world, that he gave his only Son, that whoever believes in him should not perish but have eternal life." (John 3:16)*

What does it mean to be "born again"? How do born-again people respond to Jesus? How was the bronze serpent a picture of Jesus?

Pray: Thank God for being present with His people everywhere, all the time through the work of Jesus. Ask God to give you spiritual understanding and the heart to accept His Word. Ask God to show you your need for a Savior.

Think About: Read John 2:17. *Do I have a zeal for the honor of God?*

Memorize: John 3:16

---

9 There is disagreement among scholars as to whether there were two cleansings of the temple or one. In *More Than a Story: New Testament*, the cleansing of the temple is mentioned at the beginning of Jesus' ministry and again briefly during the Passion Week with the recognition that the theological truths are pertinent regardless of the number of incidents.

CHAPTER 99
LIVING WATER FOR ALL PEOPLES

Jesus Offers Living Water to a Samaritan Woman—
John 3:22-4:43

"...whoever drinks of the water that I will give him will never be thirsty again. The water that I will give him will become in him a spring of water welling up to eternal life." (John 4:14)

Have you ever heard the words, *"No fair! He has more than I do"*? What does this attitude show? John's disciples had the same jealous attitude. More people were going to Jesus to be baptized than were going to John the Baptist. John's disciples did not like this, and they complained to John about it. But John the Baptist had a different attitude. He knew that God was drawing people to Jesus' ministry. He knew that *"A person cannot receive even one thing unless it is given him from heaven."* John was full of joy about Jesus. He was excited that people were going to Jesus and believing in Him. So John told his disciples, *"He must increase, but I must decrease."* What did John mean by this?

The Pharisees didn't have the same attitude as John. They were jealous. They didn't want anyone to have more religious authority, power, or popularity with the people than they did. Jesus knew this, but He didn't come to argue with them. He came to do the work His Father sent Him to do. So Jesus left Judea to go to Galilee.

There were two routes or ways that Jesus could travel. Both went through areas where

51

Gentiles lived, who were thought of as "unclean" by the Jews. Jesus chose the route that went through Samaria. *Do you remember who the Samaritans were?*

After the Assyrians conquered the Northern Kingdom of Israel, they took the Jews and sent them to parts of the Assyrian Empire. Then they sent other conquered peoples to live in Samaria, a part of the Northern Kingdom. These people brought their gods and their religion with them. Before long, they added Yahweh as another of their gods. Some of them married the Jews who were left in Israel and, in time, many of them worshiped Yahweh alone. But the Jews of Jesus' day hated the Samaritans because they were not "pure Jews." They were "half-breeds"—partly Jewish and partly some other nationality.

The walk from Judea to Galilee was long. It took about three days, and Jesus became very tired. Remember, Jesus was fully human, so He got tired, hungry, thirsty, and sleepy like anyone else. Jesus sat down beside Jacob's Well in Samaria to rest while His disciples went into town to buy food. But Jesus also had another reason to wait there. His Father had an appointment for Jesus at the well.

Most people got water from the well in the morning and evening, before and after the heat of the afternoon sun. It was a social time—a time to meet together as they were getting water. But it was noon, and along came a Samaritan woman, alone, to get water from the well. *What does this tell you about this woman?* She was not welcome at the well with the other women, because they knew about the many sinful things she had done, and they didn't want to be around her.

Meeting the Samaritan woman at the well would be a problem for most Jewish men— the Jews hated the "unclean" Samaritans, and men didn't talk to women in public. But Jesus wasn't like other Jews. **Jesus loves all peoples**—Jews, Gentiles, Samaritans, sinners. So Jesus talked to the woman and asked her for a drink of water. Why would Jesus speak to this "unclean" Samaritan woman? Certainly, the woman was curious about this. She asked Jesus why He, a Jew, would ask for a drink from a Samaritan woman. Jesus answered her in a most unusual way.

> *Jesus answered her, "If you knew the gift of God, and who it is that is saying to you, 'Give me a drink,' you would have asked him, and he would have given you living water." (John 4:10)*

Water is very precious in Israel because it only rains a few months of the year. So there isn't much fresh water. But what is "living water"? What could Jesus be talking about? *Do you remember what Jesus meant when He told Nicodemus that he must be born again?* Jesus often talked about spiritual things, but other people thought He was talking about earthly or physical things. The Samaritan woman couldn't understand what Jesus was talking about. He didn't have a bucket or rope to get water from the well. How could He get water, and why would He call it living water? Was He greater than their ancestor Jacob, who had dug the well?

> *Jesus said to her, "Everyone who drinks of this water will be thirsty again, but whoever drinks of the water that I will give him will never be thirsty again. The water that I will give him will become in him a spring of water welling up to eternal life." (John 4:13-14)*

Jesus offers new spiritual life—a life that refreshes forever. He was offering the Samaritan woman cleansing from sin. Again, the Samaritan woman did not understand that Jesus was talking about spiritual things. She wanted physical water so she would not be thirsty or have to make the trip to the well to get water again. But Jesus knew she had a greater problem than getting water. She had a sin problem, just like every person. **Jesus cares about the souls of people and pursues them.** So Jesus uncovered her sin by asking about her husband. Her husband? She didn't have a husband and told Jesus so. Jesus already knew this and said to her, *"You are right in saying, 'I have no husband'; for you have had five husbands, and the one you now have is not your husband. What you have said is true."* Jesus praised her for speaking truthfully. But He had pointed out her sin. She had had many husbands and was living wrongfully with someone who wasn't even her husband. She would have to admit her sin to receive salvation and the eternal life Jesus was offering.

Instead of confessing her sin, the woman changed the subject. She asked about the right place to worship God. Jesus did not come to talk about *where* to worship but rather about *what* true worship is. He was not concerned about a place, but about the heart.

> *"But the hour is coming, and is now here, when the true worshipers will worship the Father in spirit and truth, for the Father is seeking such people to worship him. God is spirit, and those who worship him must worship in spirit and truth." (John 4:23-24)*

True worshipers are born again through the Holy Spirit. Where they worship is not important. What is important is that they have changed hearts—they have the desire to honor and trust God. How could this woman understand this? Well, she said that she knew the Messiah was coming, and He would explain everything. She probably did not expect Jesus' answer: *"I who speak to you am he."* **Jesus is the Messiah who offers salvation to all peoples**—not just to the Jews.

When the disciples returned, they were amazed that Jesus was talking to a woman…to a *Samaritan woman!* But the woman left her jar and went back to town. She had news to tell, *"Come, see a man who told me all that I ever did. Can this be the Christ?"*

The disciples urged Jesus to eat the food they brought. Again, instead of giving an earthly response, Jesus gave them a spiritual response: *"I have food to eat that you do not know about."* What? Did someone bring Jesus food? The disciples did not understand the spiritual meaning of what Jesus said. So Jesus explained it to them.

> *Jesus said to them, "My food is to do the will of him who sent me and to accomplish his work. Do you not say, 'There are yet four months, then comes the harvest'? Look, I tell you, lift up your eyes, and see that the fields are white for harvest." (John 4:34-35)*

Jesus was more concerned about lost people—sinners in need of forgiveness and salvation—than He was about eating lunch. God sent Him to earth to tell of His great salvation. Many of the Samaritans believed in Jesus because of what the woman at the well told them. So they asked Jesus to stay with them and teach them. **Jesus seeks the lost** and wants sinners to repent and believe. So He stayed with them two more days, and many more believed in Jesus. *They said to the woman, "It is no longer because of what you said that we believe, for we have heard for ourselves, and we know that this is indeed the Savior of the world."*

Jesus is still offering "living water." He is offering salvation to whoever believes in Him.

Have you received Jesus' gift of salvation? Do you truly worship God in your heart? Do you treasure God more than anything—more than food, water, or life itself?

Whoever believes in the Son has eternal life; whoever does not obey the Son shall not see life, but the wrath of God remains on him. (John 3:36)

As a deer pants for flowing streams, so pants my soul for you, O God. My soul thirsts for God, for the living God. (Psalm 42:1-2a)

THAT YOU MAY BELIEVE

What does this chapter tell us about God?

Talk about and apply the **biblical truths** in **bold** text). Make them personal and apply them to what is happening in your family, church, community, or the world today.

Why would the religious leaders be jealous of Jesus? What does this tell you about their hearts and what they truly treasured most?

Talk About: *Whoever believes in the Son has eternal life; whoever does not obey the Son shall not see life, but the wrath of God remains on him. (John 3:36)*

What was Jesus' response to the Samaritan woman's sin? What does this tell you about the heart of Jesus?

Pray: Thank God that He keeps His promises. Thank Him for sending Jesus and the Holy Spirit to change sinful hearts. Ask God to give you a heart that thirsts for Him and an understanding of spiritual things.

Think About: *What does it look like to thirst after God?*

CHAPTER 100

ANOINTED TO PROCLAIM GOOD NEWS

Jesus Heals a Dying Son; Jesus Claims to be the Messiah—
John 4:46-54; Luke 4:16-30

"The Spirit of the Lord is upon me, because he has anointed me to proclaim good news to the poor. He has sent me to proclaim liberty to the captives and recovering of sight to the blind, to set at liberty those who are oppressed, to proclaim the year of the Lord's favor." (Luke 4:18-19)

Why did Jesus come to earth? Most importantly, Jesus came to save sinners—offering salvation for all who will believe in Him. But He also came to set people free from some of the effects of the Fall—to lessen suffering, to heal the sick, to free people from the lies of the devil. He came to show the compassionate heart of His Father.

So when a government official heard that Jesus was in Cana in Galilee again, he left his home in Capernaum. Even though he was a Gentile and not a Jew, he went to find Jesus. This man's son was desperately sick—in fact, he was close to dying. The father had heard that Jesus was healing the sick. Maybe Jesus would heal his son! This worried father found Jesus and asked Him to come to Capernaum and heal his son. In answering him, Jesus spoke not only to the man but to the whole crowd, *"Unless you see signs and wonders you will not believe."* This seems like a strange response. The official wasn't talking about believing. But Jesus knew that people were seeking Him out not because they believed in Him and wanted to honor Him, but because they wanted to see His miracles.

Jesus understood the son was seriously ill. But He knew that the official's condition was even more desperate than his son's. The man needed faith; he needed to believe in Jesus, the Son of God. However, the official's concern was for his son, and he said to Jesus, *"Sir, come down before my child dies."* This man wasn't seeking Jesus. He was seeking healing. Yet Jesus treated this man with grace. *Jesus said to him, "Go; your son will live."* Just go? Your son will live? That's it? Jesus just spoke? Yes, that is it. Jesus didn't need to go to Capernaum to heal the boy. **Jesus is God Almighty!** And the Bible says, the *man believed the word that Jesus spoke to him and went on his way.* The man *believed* Jesus—without seeing any miracle or sign. This was the greatest grace of all. God had given this man the faith to believe in Jesus.

On his way home, the man's servants met him on the road. They told him that his son was getting better. What time did the son start getting better? At the seventh hour the day before, the fever left—the same time, the exact time that Jesus told the man, *"Your son will live."* Jesus healed the official's son without even going to him—just by speaking! And as soon as Jesus spoke, the boy was healed. What an amazing miracle! But Jesus did an even greater miracle. The greater miracle was that Jesus gave the man faith to believe His word. The man and "all his household" believed—they believed that **Jesus heals, Jesus has compassion, Jesus is the Son of God.**

Jesus continued traveling, and as He met people along the way He told them, *"Repent, for the kingdom of heaven is at hand."* And some of them, like the official with the dying son, believed. God's word through the prophet Isaiah was being fulfilled:

> *The people who walked in darkness have seen a great light; those who dwelt in a land of deep darkness, on them has light shined. (Isaiah 9:2)*

The Jews were living in spiritual darkness. They had tried to be right with God through keeping the law, but they failed. They did not honor God or worship Him from the heart. But **Jesus had come to set them free from sin and death.** He came so they could receive living water and be born again through the work of the Holy Spirit. **Only Jesus can change hearts**.

As He traveled, Jesus came to Nazareth where he grew up. On the Sabbath, as He usually did, He went to the synagogue. *Do you remember what a synagogue is?* A synagogue is like a church. During the Babylonian captivity, the people could not go to the temple to worship. So they built synagogues where they could go to worship God and hear the Word of God. By the time Jesus was a man, there were synagogues in most large towns. The people could go there on the Sabbath to hear the Old Testament, to pray, and to hear preaching and teaching.

Jesus was a well-known teacher by the time He went to Nazareth. So He stood to read the Scripture in the synagogue. After He was handed the scroll of the prophet Isaiah, he unrolled it and found the verses He wanted to read:

The Spirit of the Sovereign LORD is on me, because **the LORD has anointed me to proclaim good news** *to the poor. He has sent me to bind up the brokenhearted, to proclaim freedom for the captives and release from darkness for the prisoners, to proclaim the year of the LORD's favor... (Isaiah 61:1-2a NIV)*

Then Jesus rolled up the scroll and sat down. The Jewish custom was to read the Scripture while standing out of respect for God's Word. But then the teacher sat down to explain the Scripture that was read. So when Jesus sat down, He was expected to explain the passage. All were looking at Jesus, and He simply stated, *"Today this Scripture has been fulfilled in your hearing."* The verses in Isaiah were about the Messiah who would bring God's promised Kingdom. So by saying that the Scripture was fulfilled, **Jesus** was stating that He **is the Messiah!**

Those who heard Jesus' claim were stunned. They were amazed at His words. What Jesus had read from Isaiah was good news! God was sending the Messiah to bring spiritual healing and freedom from the power of sin. Jesus was bringing forgiveness and blessing to those who recognized their need for Him! Jesus was the Messiah sent by God to bring salvation to His people. This should have been wonderful news to the Jews! They should have rejoiced and thanked God for sending His Son. But then they began to wonder about Jesus' claim. Wasn't Jesus the son of Joseph? This was the boy who grew up in Nazareth in the home of a carpenter. How could He be the Messiah?

Jesus knew what they were thinking. He knew that often a prophet was not honored in his own hometown; people doubted that someone they knew could actually be a prophet. So Jesus reminded them of two Old Testament prophets the Jews did not accept. One was the prophet Elijah, who lived during a time of great famine. There were many Jewish widows who lived during that famine, but it was to a Gentile widow that God sent Elijah for food. God did a miracle for her. *Do you remember what the miracle was?* Her jar of flour and jug of oil did not run out until the famine was over.

The other prophet was Elisha. There were many lepers in Israel while Elisha was a prophet, but none of them were healed. Only Naaman, a Syrian—a Gentile—was healed. Naaman and the widow were Gentiles who received God's blessing, while the Jews rejected the prophets.

When the men in the synagogue heard these words from Jesus, they "were filled with wrath." They crowded around Jesus and drove him outside the town right to the edge of a cliff. They were furious— so furious that they were going to throw Jesus over the cliff! But Jesus passed right between them. He left Nazareth and went to Capernaum where He began to teach again.

Remember the official whose son was healed? He was not a Jew either but a Gentile. The official and his whole Gentile household believed in Jesus, the Messiah, the Son of God. But the Jews who knew God's Word and His promise did not believe that Jesus is God's anointed Son who came to bring God's message and His blessing to His people. How very, very sad is this?

The Bible shows us it does not matter that you have grown up hearing the Word of God

if you do not truly believe it in your heart. Do you believe that God's Word is true—that every promise in it will be fulfilled, that God's Law and His way are best? Do you truly believe that Jesus is God's Son who gives eternal life to all who have faith in Him? Does your faith show in the way you live your life? Will you be like the Gentile official who believed or the religious Jews who rejected Jesus?

> "Truly, truly, I say to you, whoever hears my word and believes him who sent me has eternal life. He does not come into judgment, but has passed from death to life." (John 5:24)

> "You search the Scriptures because you think that in them you have eternal life; and it is they that bear witness about me, yet you refuse to come to me that you may have life." (John 5:39-40)

THAT YOU MAY BELIEVE

What does this chapter tell us about God?

Talk about and apply the **biblical truths** in **bold** text. Make them personal and apply them to what is happening in your family, church, community, or the world today.

What does Luke 4:18-19 tell us about why Jesus came? Explain.

Talk About: *"Truly, truly, I say to you, whoever hears my word and believes him who sent me has eternal life. He does not come into judgment, but has passed from death to life." (John 5:24)*

What is spiritual blindness? How can someone who reads or hears the Bible be blind to the truth? What things keep a person from truly believing in Jesus and honoring Him?

Pray: Thank God for His compassionate heart. Thank Him for the many blessings in your life. Ask God to give you spiritual understanding and a believing heart. Confess that you are a sinner in need of grace.

Think About: *How do I know that I believe in my heart, not just in my head? What evidence is there in my life of genuine trust and faith in Christ?*

CHAPTER 101

LEAVING EVERYTHING TO FOLLOW JESUS

John the Baptist Is Imprisoned; Jesus Calls Fishermen to Be Fishers of Men—Matthew 4:18-20; Mark 1:14-20; Luke 5:1-11

And when they had brought their boats to land, they left everything and followed him. (Luke 5:11)

What is repentance? Repentance is admitting your sin, sincerely grieving over your sin, and turning away from it. John the Baptist preached the good news of the coming of the Lamb of God to take away sin. He preached about faith in the Son of God, but he also preached about repentance.

Not everyone liked John's message. One person who definitely did *not* like John's message was Herod, a ruler in Galilee. John was bold in his preaching and sure in the truth of God's Word. He was not afraid to call sin "sin"—and that is what got him in trouble with Herod. Herod had divorced his wife and then had wrongly taken his brother's wife, Herodias, to be his own wife. John would not ignore this, and he told Herod that he had sinned against God. *How should Herod have responded?* Herod should have admitted his sin and repented. *But do you know what he did instead?* He threw John in prison!

But John's message of faith and repentance was still being preached. *Now after John was arrested, Jesus came into Galilee, proclaiming the gospel of God, and saying, "The time is fulfilled, and the kingdom of God is at hand; repent and believe in the gospel."* Simon Peter, Andrew, James, and John were already followers of Jesus who had heard Him tell the good news of repentance and faith. But they were also fishermen who spent many hours at night catching fish. Now Jesus was going to show them greater things and call them to follow Him as His special disciples. How did this happen?

Jesus had a big crowd around Him as He was teaching near the lake of Gennesaret (or the Sea of Galilee). The crowd was pushing to get closer to Jesus. There were so many people that those in the back could not see or hear Jesus. But Jesus knew what to do. Jesus saw two empty boats in the water. The fishermen had already been fishing all night and were cleaning and fixing their nets—pulling off weeds and sticks, washing off sand and pebbles, and mending any torn parts.

Jesus got into Simon's boat and asked Simon to push the boat out into the water, not far from shore. This way, Jesus could teach the people, and they all could see and hear Him. When Jesus was done teaching, He told Simon, *"Put out into the deep and let down your nets for a catch."* This did not make sense! *Why didn't this make sense?* The best time to fish is at night when the fish are closer to the surface. During the day, fish hide deeper down in the water and are harder to catch. Simon knew this. He was an experienced fisherman. So were his partners Andrew, and James and John, the sons of Zebedee. They all knew that this was not the right time to fish. Besides, they had just cleaned their nets. They wouldn't want to clean them again!

And Simon answered, "Master, we toiled all night and took nothing!" These men were tired. They had been fishing all night. They were probably discouraged too as they had no fish after all their hard work. But Peter respected and followed Jesus, calling Him "Master." He had already seen Jesus heal his mother-in-law of a high fever. Jesus commanded the fever to leave her...and it left! Simon had also seen others healed. He had seen Jesus command Satan's demons to come out of tormented people. Simon saw that Jesus had authority and power over sickness and evil spirits. Simon could trust in his knowledge of fishing, or he could trust Jesus and follow Him. What would Simon do? He answered Jesus, *"But at your word I will let down the nets."* Simon would trust and obey Jesus. He would honor Jesus as Master.

So the fishermen threw their nets back into the water. *And when they had done this, they enclosed a large number of fish, and their nets were breaking. They signaled to their partners in the other boat to come and help them. And they came and filled both the boats, so that they began to sink.* Their nets were full of all kinds of fish—big, little, skinny, fat, brown, green, silver...so many fish that the nets were starting to break! They filled two boats with fish—so full the boats began to sink! There were fish everywhere! *Why was there such an enormous catch of fish?* Jesus was not a fisherman, but **Jesus is the Lord and Master** of fish and of all things! The fishermen were amazed at the number of fish in the nets! This didn't just happen! This was a miraculous act! Who was this Jesus?

> But when Simon Peter saw it, he fell down at Jesus' knees, saying, "Depart from me, for I am a sinful man, O Lord." (Luke 5:8)

Simon Peter recognized who Jesus is—**Jesus is the holy Son of God**. He knew that Jesus was worthy of His worship. Simon, a sinner, was not worthy to be in the presence of Jesus. But **Jesus came to save sinners.** *And Jesus said to Simon, "Do not be afraid; from now on you will be catching men."*

Jesus was calling Simon and his partners to travel with him and preach the good news—the good news that God was bringing salvation to His people. The four hundred years of silence

64

had been broken. God was making a new covenant with His people; a covenant of **salvation by faith alone**. Instead of throwing out their nets and catching fish, these fishermen would "throw out" the good news of the gospel and "catch" people to believe in Jesus. *How did these simple fishermen respond to Jesus' invitation to follow Him?*

> *And when they had brought their boats to land, they left everything and followed him. (Luke 5:11)*

Simon, Andrew, James, and John left everything—their fishing business, their families, their friends, their homes…they left everything to follow Jesus. What would they see and what would they learn following Jesus? How would they be changed? What cost would they have to pay to follow Jesus? Would they end up in prison like John the Baptist? Would the sacrifices be worth it to follow Jesus? It would take faith to follow Jesus.

You, too, can follow Jesus wholeheartedly. It will not always be easy. There will be sacrifices. Others may make fun of you for doing what God says is right. How important is following Jesus to you? Are you the kind of person who will say, "At your word, I will…"?

> **Indeed, I count everything as loss because of the surpassing worth of knowing Christ Jesus my Lord. (Philippians 3:8a)**

THAT YOU MAY BELIEVE

What does this chapter tell us about God?

Talk about and apply the **biblical truths** in **bold** text. Make them personal and apply them to what is happening in your family, church, community, or the world today.

John's boldness to speak the truth caused him to be put in prison. What does this tell you about what John treasured most? Are there times you have been afraid to speak the truth? Explain.

Talk About: *Indeed, I count everything as loss because of the surpassing worth of knowing Christ Jesus my Lord. (Philippians 3:8a)*

How could the disciples leave all to follow Jesus? What does this tell you about Jesus? Though Simon knew morning was not the right time to fish, he trusted Jesus enough to obey Him. *("But at your word I will let down the nets.")* Do you trust Jesus enough to follow His Word even when things don't make sense to you?

Pray: Praise Jesus for His mighty acts. Confess to God that you are a sinful person. Thank Him for sending His Son to be a friend of sinners and to rescue sinners. Ask God to give you a heart that treasures Him more than anything else. Ask Him to give you a heart that is submissive to Him as your Master.

Think About: *What is hard for me to give up for the sake of Christ?*

CHAPTER 102

JESUS CAME TO BE A HEALER OF SINFUL MEN

Jesus Heals a Leper and a Paralytic; Jesus Calls Matthew—Luke 5:12-32; Mark 2:1-12

..."Those who are well have no need of a physician, but those who are sick. I have not come to call the righteous but sinners to repentance." (Luke 5:31-32)

Do you remember when Jesus told Nathanael that he would see "greater things"? What were some of the "greater things" Jesus' followers saw? One greater thing was what Jesus did for a leper. *Do you remember what leprosy is?* Leprosy is a disease that affects the skin. People who had leprosy were called "lepers," and they were considered "unclean." They were diseased and could not live with the rest of the people but had to live alone or with other lepers. If someone touched a leper, that person was also "unclean" until it was shown that he had not caught the disease. The Law of Moses instructed that a person had to show his skin to the priest, who would decide if the person was "clean" or free from the disease. *What would it be like to have this disease? How would a person's life change?*

While Jesus was traveling with His disciples, a man "full of leprosy" was there. *And when he saw Jesus, he fell on his face and begged him, "Lord, if you will, you can make me clean."* This man was desperate; he was begging to be free from his disease. He showed respect for Jesus by falling on his face and calling him "Lord." What would Jesus do? This man was unclean.

Jesus stretched out his hand and touched him. People didn't touch lepers! They would be made unclean if they did. But Jesus came to *proclaim liberty to the captives and recovering of sight to the blind, to set at liberty those who are oppressed.* When Jesus touched the leper, He said, *"I will; be clean." And immediately the leprosy left him.* When Jesus touched the leper, Jesus didn't become unclean; instead, the leper became clean at Jesus' touch! Jesus came to *bind up the brokenhearted, to proclaim freedom for the captives.*

Then Jesus told him not to tell anyone about being healed. He instructed the man to show himself to the priest as proof that he had been made clean and to make an offering. But the news about what Jesus did spread, and crowds of people came to hear Jesus and be healed. There were crowds around Jesus constantly. Everyone wanted something from Jesus. Yet Jesus wanted to find a place to be alone and pray. Although He was fully God while on earth, He was also fully man. Jesus needed time to rest and have time alone with His Father. These times alone with God the Father refreshed Jesus to do the work God sent Him to do…the work of setting people free from sin and sickness; *to proclaim good news…*

One day, Jesus was teaching in a house—proclaiming good news. As usual there was a big crowd of people, including Pharisees and teachers of the law. These men had come from "every village of Galilee and Judea and from Jerusalem." Jesus was becoming well-known, and many came to hear him and see His miracles. *And the power of the Lord was with him to heal.*

While Jesus was teaching, four men brought a paralyzed friend to be healed by Jesus. *Do you know what paralyzed means?* It means that something can't move or can hardly move. This man's legs couldn't move, so his friends brought the man on a mat-like bed. But the four men couldn't even get near the doorway. How could they bring their paralyzed friend to Jesus? *Do you know what they did?* They climbed to the top of the house and started taking off part of the roof. They were determined! If they couldn't get through the door, they would get through the roof!

When they had made a big enough hole, they lowered the paralytic down on his mat... right in front of Jesus. These men obviously had faith that Jesus could heal!

And when Jesus saw their faith, he said to the paralytic, "Son, your sins are forgiven." Does this seem like a strange thing for Jesus to say? The man was brought to Jesus to be healed—he couldn't walk. But Jesus saw his greater need, the need for forgiveness of sin. And **Jesus, the Son of God, came to set sinners free**, to heal sinful hearts.

What did the religious leaders think of this? They were angry! Who was this man to say the paralytic's sins were forgiven? Only God can forgive sin. How dare Jesus tell the man his sins were forgiven! They didn't say what they were thinking...but Jesus knew what was in their hearts and what they were thinking. *How could Jesus know this?*

Jesus is God...and God knows everything. He is omniscient or all-knowing. So Jesus said to them, *"Why do you question in your hearts? Which is easier, to say, 'Your sins are forgiven you,' or to say, 'Rise and walk'? But that you may know that the Son of Man has authority on earth to forgive sins"—he said to the man who was paralyzed—"I say to you, rise, pick up your bed and go home."*

How could the people know the man's sins were really forgiven? They couldn't see it with their eyes. So Jesus did a miracle of healing to show that **He is God and has the authority to heal...and to forgive sins**. Jesus healed the man's legs. Everyone could see what Jesus did when the man immediately got up and walked away! He just picked up his mat and went home, "glorifying God." Everyone was filled with wonder! It was a glorious miracle!

And amazement seized them all, and they glorified God and were filled with awe, saying, "We have seen extraordinary things today." (Luke 5:26)

What was most amazing was not that Jesus could heal paralyzed legs, but that he could heal a sinner's heart. He had the power to forgive sin and declare a man clean before God! **Jesus is God the Son who came to save sinners...** all kinds of sinners. Even...tax collectors.

Tax collectors were hated by the Jews. They often cheated people, so the Jews knew that they were definitely sinful men. But all men are sinners. Just as lepers were unclean and could not come near other people, all people are sinful or "unclean" and cannot come near to a holy God. Our leprosy is not a skin leprosy but a kind of "leprosy of the heart." *But do you remember what happened to the leper when Jesus touched him? Jesus didn't become unclean; instead, the leper became clean!* **Jesus came to be a healer of sinful men**—to cleanse sinful hearts, to call sinners to repent and believe in Him, to make sinful men acceptable to a holy God. So when Jesus walked by and saw a tax collector sitting at his booth, He stopped. He looked at Levi, the tax collector, and said to him, *"Follow me."* **Jesus welcomes sinners and invites them to come to Him!** Just as Simon Peter, Andrew, James, and John had done, Levi (also known as Matthew) left everything...and followed Jesus.

Levi made a great feast—a wonderful meal—at his house and invited many people to the feast. *What kind of friends do you think Levi had?* Many of Levi's guests were tax collectors. *Do you think Jesus was bothered by this?* Jesus sat and ate with Levi and his guests. But the Pharisees were indignant—they were upset, angry, irritated! Why would Jesus eat with these people—these *sinners*? The Pharisees and their scribes asked Jesus' disciples, *"Why do you eat and drink with tax collectors and sinners?"* Do you think they really wanted to understand why Jesus would eat with Levi and his friends?

The Pharisees were criticizing Jesus. They would not eat with or be friends with such obvious sinners. Why would Jesus? What was He thinking? Didn't Jesus know any better?

And Jesus answered them, "Those who are well have no need of a physician, but those who are sick. I have not come to call the righteous but sinners to repentance." (Luke 5:31-32)

What was Jesus telling them about why He came to earth? Jesus came to be a healer of sinful men—to cleanse sinful hearts, to ask sinners to repent. **Jesus came to forgive sin and save sinners.**

Do you think you are better than others? You probably go to church and try to be a good person. But you are still a sinner who needs to repent and be forgiven. Jesus came to save sinners like you. Will you repent and accept Jesus' offer to cleanse, heal, and forgive your sinful heart?

> for all have sinned and fall short of the glory of God, and are justified by his grace as a gift, through the redemption that is in Christ Jesus. (Romans 3:23-24)

> But to all who did receive him, who believed in his name, he gave the right to become children of God. (John 1:12)

THAT YOU MAY BELIEVE

What does this chapter tell us about God?

Talk about and apply the **biblical truths** in **bold** text. Make them personal and apply them to what is happening in your family, church, community, or the world today.

Most people avoided lepers and tax collectors, but not Jesus. What does this tell you about Jesus?

Talk About: *for all have sinned and fall short of the glory of God, and are justified by his grace as a gift, through the redemption that is in Christ Jesus. (Romans 3:23-24)*

Why can Jesus forgive sins? What does this tell you about Jesus? Why would Jesus call a tax collector to follow Him? Why were the Pharisees indignant (upset)? What does it tell you about them?

Pray: Praise God for accepting all kinds of people. Thank Him for His grace toward sinners. Confess your sin and ask God to forgive your sin and cleanse your sinful heart.

Think About: *Am I prideful? Do I think I am better than I am? Do I truly see that I have a sinful heart and that I need God's forgiveness and grace?*

Memorize: Romans 3:23-24

CHAPTER 103

JESUS DOES HIS FATHER'S WORK ON THE SABBATH

Jesus Heals on the Sabbath— John 5:1-18; Matthew 12:9-14; Mark 3:1-6

…"My Father is working until now, and I am working." (John 5:17)

We know that the Pharisees and other religious leaders were already upset at Jesus for eating with tax collectors and sinners. But then Jesus did something else that made them even more upset…

It happened when Jesus went to Jerusalem for a Jewish feast. In Jerusalem, there was a pool called the Pool of Bethesda, which had five porches or "porticos" around it. The porches had roofs held up by columns. These porches were a popular place for sick people to rest. On the Sabbath day, Jesus went to the Pool of Bethesda. There He saw blind, lame, and paralyzed people lying in the porches. How sad it must have been to see so many sick people. One man who was there had been sick for thirty-eight years! *When Jesus saw him lying there and knew that he had already been there a long time, he said to him, "Do you want to be healed?"* How would you answer Jesus if you were this man?

Instead of saying, "Yes!" the man explained that he had no one to bring him to the pool "when the water is stirred up." Why would he say this? The Jews had a strange and wrong idea that an angel would come at times and stir up or swish around the water. The first person in the pool would be healed. Maybe the man thought Jesus would bring him to the water when it was stirred. But Jesus didn't put the man in the water. Jesus is the true Healer, and He just said to the man, *"Get up, take up your bed, and walk." And at once the man was healed, and he took up his bed and walked.* He was instantly healed! *What must this have been like after being sick for thirty-eight years?* He could now walk, and run, and maybe even jump with joy! He was no longer sick but healed by the powerful word of Jesus.

This was a very happy thing! It should have caused much celebration! But it didn't for the Jews. They couldn't rejoice in the wonderful miracle of grace and goodness. Instead, they were *angry*. They told the man it was "not lawful" to pick up and carry his bed on the Sabbath. Seriously? They were angry about their Sabbath law instead of being amazed and joyful that the man was healed. The Jews had many laws. Some of them were God's good Law given through Moses, like keeping the Sabbath holy. But they also added their own laws to God's Law. The Pharisees thought they could earn their own righteousness by strictly keeping these laws. But they really didn't understand the heart of God. **God's Laws are good and right. God's ways bring joy to those who keep them.** God's Sabbath Law for the Jews wasn't just a law about what to do and not do on the Sabbath, it pointed to a future eternal rest that God would bring about through Jesus, the Lord of the Sabbath.

When the Jews found out that Jesus was the one who had healed the man, they were angry at Him for healing on the Sabbath. Instead of recognizing Jesus' kindness and power, and worshiping Him as the Son of God, they insulted Him. *But Jesus answered them, "My Father is working until now, and I am working."* **Jesus was doing the work of God. He was not acting by Himself**, on His own—He was doing what the Father wanted Him to do. This only made the Jews angrier! They were so angry they wanted to kill Jesus!

> *This was why the Jews were seeking all the more to kill him, because not only was he breaking the Sabbath, but he was even calling God his own Father, making himself equal with God. (John 5:18)*

The same thing happened on another Sabbath day. When Jesus went to the synagogue, He saw a man with a "withered" or shriveled up, weak hand. *And the scribes and the Pharisees watched him, to see whether he would heal on the Sabbath, so that they might find a reason to accuse him.* The scribes and Pharisees were hoping Jesus would heal the man…not so they could rejoice at the healing, but so they could accuse Jesus of breaking their law. Sadly, they cared more about the laws they made than they did about having compassion on suffering people.

Jesus knew exactly what the scribes and Pharisees were thinking. **Jesus knows everything**, and He knew what was in their hearts. But Jesus did not walk away and ignore the suffering man. He didn't do the safe thing. Instead, He told the man with the withered hand to come to Him. Jesus looked around. He saw the accusing scribes and Pharisees. And He said,

> *"I ask you, is it lawful on the Sabbath to do good or to do harm, to save life or to destroy it?" (Luke 6:9)*

But the scribes and Pharisees wouldn't answer Jesus. *And he looked around at them with anger, grieved at their hardness of heart.* Then Jesus gave them an example to show them how foolish and hard-hearted they were.

> *He said to them, "Which one of you who has a sheep, if it falls into a pit on the Sabbath, will not take hold of it and lift it out? Of how much more value is a man than a sheep! So it is lawful to do good on the Sabbath." (Matthew 12:11-12)*

Then Jesus told the man to hold out his hand... and when the man did, it was perfectly formed! It was whole and healthy, just like his other hand! *How do you think this man felt? How do you think the Pharisees felt?*

Jesus had compassion and healed a suffering man. He healed on the Sabbath, doing the good work His Father wanted done. He was not afraid of what others might think—He would honor and please His Father. Jesus perfectly kept the Sabbath law. He kept the Sabbath holy by doing the will of His Father, not by keeping man-made laws.

Seeing a man being healed should have made the Pharisees worship Jesus as the Son of God. They should have realized that **Jesus is God and Lord of the Sabbath**. They should have rejoiced at the kindness of Jesus. Instead, the Pharisees were furious! They left and made plans of how they would destroy Jesus. No wonder Jesus was so grieved at their hardness of heart. They did not truly honor the Sabbath. They loved their man-made laws more than they loved the heart of God. They loved their strict rules more than they loved having compassion on others. They were prideful, thinking they were righteous because of their rule-keeping.

It is good to keep God's good Laws meant for our joy and protection. But keeping the Law cannot make anyone acceptable to God... because no human person can perfectly keep the Law! We need a better way of salvation. We need to trust Jesus as God's Son—the Perfect Law-Keeper—sent to save sinful men. Do you rejoice in Jesus' kindness to undeserving sinners?

yet we know that a person is not justified by works of the law but through faith in Jesus Christ, so we also have believed in Christ Jesus, in order to be justified by faith in Christ and not by works of the law, because by works of the law no one will be justified. (Galatians 2:16)

For whoever keeps the whole law but fails in one point has become accountable for all of it. (James 2:10)

THAT YOU MAY BELIEVE

What does this chapter tell us about God?

Talk about and apply the **biblical truths** in **bold** text. Make them personal and apply them to what is happening in your family, church, community, or the world today.

What do you see in these stories that shows you that Jesus has authority? What does that tell you about Jesus?

Talk About: *yet we know that a person is not justified by works of the law but through faith in Jesus Christ, so we also have believed in Christ Jesus, in order to be justified by faith in Christ and not by works of the law, because by works of the law no one will be justified. (Galatians 2:16)*

Why were the Pharisees so angry? What was in their hearts? Do you have any of these sinful attitudes in your heart? Can you keep God's commands perfectly? How did you disobey God this week?

Pray: Praise God for His authority over sin and sickness and all the works of the devil. Thank Him for His compassion. Ask God to show you your sinful heart and your need for a Savior.

Think About: *Do I keep God's good commands because I love God and His ways, or am I trying to gain God's favor?*

CHAPTER 104

TRUE FOLLOWERS OF JESUS HAVE CHANGED HEARTS

Jesus Chooses His Disciples; the Kingdom Character of a True Follower of Christ—Luke 6:12; Mark 3:13-19; Matthew 5

"Blessed are the poor in spirit, for theirs is the kingdom of heaven." (Matthew 5:3)

The religious leaders were "filled with fury" at Jesus for healing on the Sabbath. They were so angry that they began plotting how they would get rid of Jesus. Jesus knew about their hard hearts, and He knew the day would come when He would be taken away. It was time for Jesus to choose twelve men to be His special followers or disciples. These men would continue to preach the good news of salvation by faith when He was gone. Whom should He choose? He had many followers. *How would Jesus know who to choose to be His closest friends? He went out to the mountain to pray, and all night he continued in prayer to God.* Jesus asked for wisdom from His Father. What was the Father's will? Whom had His Father created to be these special disciples?

Jesus prayed all night. Then *he appointed twelve (whom he also named apostles) so that they might be with him and he might send them out to preach and have authority to cast out demons.*

> *The names of the twelve apostles are these: first, Simon, who is called Peter, and Andrew his brother; James the son of Zebedee, and John his brother; Philip and Bartholomew; Thomas and Matthew the tax collector; James the son of Alphaeus, and Thaddaeus; Simon the Zealot, and Judas Iscariot, who betrayed him. (Matthew 10:2-4)*

Jesus came down with His disciples to a level place on the mountain where there was a great crowd of people from many towns *who came to hear him and to be healed of their diseases.*

And those who were troubled with unclean spirits were cured. And all the crowd sought to touch him, for power came out from him and healed them all.

Then Jesus preached His most famous sermon. *Do you know what it is called?* It is called the Sermon on the Mount. Jesus started it by describing a true disciple of His. A true follower of Jesus is "poor in spirit." He understands he is a sinner and cannot fix his sin problem. He needs God's mercy. This leads him to deep sorrow over sin and a deep desire to turn away from sin and turn to God. He humbly accepts God's will for his life.

Have you ever been really, really hungry or thirsty? When? A person who is truly "born again" is very hungry and thirsty too…but not for food and drink. He is "hungry and thirsty" to be right with God. He is eager to have a close relationship or friendship with God and to get rid of the sin that separates him from God. Because he has received God's forgiveness and a new heart, a true believer in Jesus is merciful or kind to those who don't deserve kindness or are suffering. He will want to have a pure mind, heart, and will, and he follows Jesus with his whole heart.

Because of our sin nature, we find it very easy to be angry with others or to argue and fight. But when someone trusts in Jesus as his Savior, Jesus gives him a new heart that wants to live peacefully with others. He wants to be a "peace maker" not a "peace breaker."[10]

Do you remember how the Pharisees treated Jesus? They were trying to figure out how to kill Jesus. *What did Jesus do that made them so mad?* Jesus said that He is God, and He did the things that pleased His Father—healing the sick, freeing people from demons (evil spirits), and teaching about God's Kingdom. The followers of Jesus will also be hated by those who don't want to hear the truth and don't love God. They will be hated just because they are followers of Christ. They will be treated wrongly for doing what is right. But they will be "blessed" by God—God will accept them and reward them in heaven. Followers of Jesus will receive mercy and be called sons of God!

So even though other people or friends may not understand or agree, God's people are to be like "salt" and "light" in this world. *Can you tell if something you eat has salt on it?* Just like you notice the salt, if you are a true believer in Jesus, it should be very easy for others to see that you follow Christ. The "light" of love, joy, peace, patience, kindness, goodness, faithfulness, gentleness, and self-control should flow out of your heart to others.

The Pharisees had many rules they followed, but the light of God's goodness and kindness did not flow out of their hearts. They were concerned about *doing* the right thing, but they were not concerned about *being* righteous. **Jesus wanted to teach people that it is not just actions that are important, but having a right heart is most important—a heart that has been changed by true faith in Jesus.** So Jesus gave some examples in his sermon.

> "You have heard that it was said to those of old, 'You shall not murder; and whoever murders will be liable to judgment.' But I say to you that everyone who is angry with his brother will be liable to judgment; whoever insults his brother will be liable to the council; and whoever says, 'You fool!' will be liable to the hell of fire." (Matthew 5:21-22)

What was Jesus saying? Jesus was saying that if a person is angry with someone, he is sinning. Sin is not just the wrong things we do, but sin is also the wrong attitudes in our hearts. It is wrong to murder, but it is also sinful to hate someone. The Pharisees cared about the rules a person broke or kept, but Jesus cared about what is in a person's heart.

In the Sermon on the Mount, Jesus told the people some surprising things—like don't try to get even when someone treats you wrongly. Instead, Jesus said, the heart of the true follower loves and forgives…just like God does. The Kingdom of God is a Kingdom of forgiveness, love, and kindness. To be a follower of Jesus is to have the kind of heart God has.

> "You have heard that it was said, 'You shall love your neighbor and hate your enemy.' But I say to you, Love your enemies and pray for those who persecute you, so that you may

be sons of your Father who is in heaven. For he makes his sun rise on the evil and on the good, and sends rain on the just and on the unjust. For if you love those who love you, what reward do you have? Do not even the tax collectors do the same? And if you greet only your brothers, what more are you doing than others? Do not even the Gentiles do the same? You therefore must be perfect, as your heavenly Father is perfect." (Matthew 5:43-48)

God's heart is very different from our sinful human hearts. And life in God's Kingdom is very different from life among sinful men. But those who are trusting in Jesus for forgiveness have received a new heart. Their attitudes and actions show others what the Kingdom of God is like—not perfectly, but sincerely. If you are a follower of Jesus, you will have a heart that loves what He loves and hates what He hates. You will still sin. There will be times when you get angry with others and times when you are unkind, but a true follower of Jesus will have deep sorrow over his sin and repent. **True believers in Jesus are perfect in God's eyes because Jesus' blood on the cross has given us His perfect righteousness.** But until Christians get to heaven, they will not have sinless hearts. Do you truly see that you have a sin problem and mourn over your sin? Are you convinced that you cannot solve your sin problem, and you need God's mercy and forgiveness? How can you love like God loves and be salt and light in this sinful world? What will it be like for true followers of Jesus to live forever in God's Kingdom?

> Therefore, if anyone is in Christ, he is a new creation. The old has passed away; behold, the new has come. (2 Corinthians 5:17)

> I have been crucified with Christ. It is no longer I who live, but Christ who lives in me. And the life I now live in the flesh I live by faith in the Son of God, who loved me and gave himself for me. (Galatians 2:20)

THAT YOU MAY BELIEVE

What does this chapter tell us about God?

Talk about and apply the **biblical truths** in **bold** text. Make them personal and apply them to what is happening in your family, church, community, or the world today.

Read Matthew 5:13-16. How can Christians be "salt" and "light"? How can your family be salt and light to those around you? Be very practical in your answer.

Talk About: *Therefore, if anyone is in Christ, he is a new creation. The old has passed away; behold, the new has come. (2 Corinthians 5:17)* (You may also want to discuss Galatians 2:20.)

Pray: Thank God for His forgiving and loving heart. Confess your sin to God. Ask Him to show you what is truly in your heart and if you are a true follower of Jesus.

Think About: *What has been in my heart this week? Have I lived like a follower of Jesus this week?*

Memorize: 2 Corinthians 5:17

---

10 An excellent guide for peacemaking in your family is Ken Sande's book, *Peacemaking for Families* (Colorado Springs, Colo.: Focus on the Family, 2002).

THE BEATITUDES[11] OF THE SERMON ON THE MOUNT

In Matthew 5:3-12, Jesus described the heart and life of a person who is a true disciple of Jesus. A true disciple or Christian desires to live in obedience to Jesus' rule over him. He wants to be like Jesus—to have the heart attitudes of Jesus, to treat others in loving ways, and to spread the good news of salvation. Christians are not perfect; we still have a sin nature. But the true Christian is daily growing to *become* more and more like Christ.

The true born-again Christian is **blessed**—he has God's approval, and he is accepted by God—which brings great happiness.[12]

"Blessed are the poor in spirit, for theirs is the kingdom of heaven."

To be poor in spirit is to truly understand that you are a sinner and cannot fix your sin problem. You are hopeless and helpless. You are spiritually poor, and you know that you do not deserve God's mercy—His kindness—and you desperately want His mercy. The Kingdom of heaven belongs to those who know they need God's mercy. *Do you truly see that you cannot fix your sinful heart?*

"Blessed are those who mourn, for they shall be comforted."

If you are a true Christian, you will have great sadness or grief about your sinful heart. Your deep sorrow over your sin will cause you to repent, to turn away from sin, and to turn to God for forgiveness. God will comfort those who turn to Him to repent. *Do you truly hate your sin?*

"Blessed are the meek, for they shall inherit the earth."

To be meek does not mean that you are weak. It means that you accept Jesus' right to rule over you. You know you do not deserve God's kindness, and you trust that what God brings into your life is for your good; you trust God's wisdom and His plan. If you are meek, your reward will be satisfaction or contentment with your life on earth, and someday you will rule with Jesus forever. *Do you truly trust God and humbly accept what He brings into your life?*

"Blessed are those who hunger and thirst for righteousness, for they shall be satisfied."

Being hungry and thirsty are powerful urges that we have every day. If you are hungry and thirsty for righteousness, you have a powerful desire to be righteous—to have a changed heart and to obey God's good commands. You know that sin separates you from God, and you truly want to be in a good and right relationship with Him. True believers will be made perfectly righteous when Jesus returns. *Do you truly want to have a right heart and live in obedience to God's good commands?*

"Blessed are the merciful, for they shall receive mercy."

If you truly understand that you do not deserve God's mercy, your heart will overflow with mercy toward others. You will want to help suffering and sinful people; you will forgive those who have sinned against you. God will be merciful toward merciful people. *Do I truly care about those who are suffering and try to help? Am I critical toward others (do I look for their faults, criticize and condemn them), or do I have sympathy for others?*

"Blessed are the pure in heart, for they shall see God."

Being pure in heart means that your mind, heart, and will (actions) turn away from evil. Jesus has given you a new heart with new godly desires. You want to follow Jesus with your whole heart. You love who God is, and you can see His work in your life and in the world. Someday you will see Him face to face in heaven. *Do you strive (make great effort, work hard) to have a pure mind, heart, and will?*

"Blessed are the peacemakers, for they shall be called sons of God."

Jesus' death on the cross has made a way for sinners to be at peace with God. If you are trusting in Jesus to be your Savior, you are a child of God and a peacemaker. A peacemaker "makes peace" by not picking fights, helping others to get along with each other, forgiving others, not being offended easily, not saying unkind things to others or about others…and by being kind, and encouraging others to be kind. *Do you get angry with others, or do you try to live peacefully with others?*

> "Blessed are those who are persecuted for righteousness' sake, for theirs is the kingdom of heaven."

True followers of Jesus will be persecuted for being Christians. They will be misunderstood and mistreated for wanting to live godly lives and standing up for what is right. But this life on earth is very short, and someday all true believers in Jesus will live forever in God's Kingdom.

> "Blessed are you when others revile you and persecute you and utter all kinds of evil against you falsely on my account. Rejoice and be glad, for your reward is great in heaven, for so they persecuted the prophets who were before you."

There are different kinds of persecution—being made fun of or insulted, being treated wrongly, having unkind lies said about you, maybe even being killed just because you follow Jesus. This is not being mistreated because you did something foolish, rude, unkind, or wrong, but being treated badly because you belong to Jesus and follow Him. We are told to rejoice when we are mistreated for being a Christian because it shows that we are like Christ and belong to Him. We can also rejoice because we will have a wonderful reward in heaven. *Are you willing to suffer and to be treated wrongly for being a follower of Jesus?*

---

11 Adapted from the Leader's Edition of Sally Michael's youth curriculum titled, *Teach Me Your Way: A Study for Youth on Surrender to Jesus and Submission to His Way* (Minneapolis, Minn.: Truth78, 2009), 85-152.

12 Parents, you may want to intentionally talk through each of these Beatitudes. Give practical examples from your life or the lives of others and help your child to make real-life application to your child's life. It may take several occasions to talk through these pages, but the Beatitudes will give your child a good understanding of the character of the Kingdom, which is only possible through a relationship with Jesus. Make sure your child understands that though believers already exhibit Kingdom character, we are still in the process of being changed and will not perfectly reflect the character of Christ in this life.

CHAPTER 105

SEEKING HEAVENLY TREASURES

Jesus Teaches about Temporary Rewards and Lasting Treasure—Matthew 6

"For where your treasure is, there your heart will be also." (Matthew 6:21)

Have you heard of the word "beware"? It means to be careful of something. It is a warning that there is danger. Jesus also gave some warnings in His Sermon on the Mount. His warnings were not about getting too close to the edge of a cliff or eating something poisonous. Jesus warned the crowd about doing the right thing…for the wrong reasons.

"Beware of practicing your righteousness before other people in order to be seen by them, for then you will have no reward from your Father who is in heaven." (Matthew 6:1)

It is right to do what is right. But if your *heart* is wrong, you are doing the right thing for the wrong reason. Jesus was explaining that God is not pleased with a wrong heart—even if the behavior is right. Then Jesus gave a few examples so the people would understand just what He meant.

"Thus, when you give to the needy, sound no trumpet before you, as the hypocrites do in the synagogues and in the streets, that they may be praised by others. Truly, I say to you, they have received their reward. But when you give to the needy, do not let your left hand know what your right hand is doing, so that your giving may be in secret. And your Father who sees in secret will reward you." (Matthew 6:2-4)

Do you know what a hypocrite is? A hypocrite is like an actor playing a part. He is pretending to be someone he isn't. *Can you think of an actor?* Is the role he plays who he really is? Maybe he plays the part of a doctor, but he isn't a real doctor. He is just pretending.

People can pretend to be righteous too. They can do the right thing, but it is an act. A hypocrite is a person who *acts* rightly, but in his heart, he doesn't *love* what is right. A person who gives money or help to a poor person but only does it because he wants other people to think he is a nice person is a hypocrite. He is not helping the person because he is compassionate and caring. He is only pretending to care about the person. The person he really cares about is *himself*.

Jesus taught that when a person helps a poor person "in secret"—without making a big show of it—because he has a heart that loves God and truly cares about others, God will be pleased, and God will reward that person. True righteousness comes from a pure heart. The right reason for doing good works is to show others the goodness of God.

Jesus also gave an example about praying. Hypocrites pray just to be heard and seen by others. *What reward do they get?* They can fool some people. Their reward is that those people admire them. But God is not pleased. Jesus taught the people not to be hypocrites. He said, *"when you pray, go into your room and shut the door and pray to your Father who is in secret. And your Father who sees in secret will reward you."*

Was Jesus saying that you can never pray with others? What was He teaching? Jesus was explaining that praying from a humble and right heart is what pleases God. The heart of a true follower of Jesus prays with a pure, humble heart full of faith in God's fatherly love, goodness, power, and authority. Praying with the right heart brings a great reward.

What kind of rewards can men give? What kinds of rewards does God give? Which reward is better—the rewards that men can give or the rewards that God gives? Why? Jesus saw the crowd of people before Him, and He just wanted them to desire what is spiritual. He wanted them to treasure a relationship with God more than loving money or things or the praise of others.

> *"Do not lay up for yourselves treasures on earth, where moth and rust destroy and where thieves break in and steal, but lay up for yourselves treasures in heaven, where neither moth nor rust destroys and where thieves do not break in and steal. For where your treasure is, there your heart will be also." (Matthew 6:19-21)*

Money is easily lost. Possessions like baseball gloves, games, the kind of shoes that are popular, or the latest phone wear out, get broken, go out of style, or get old. They don't last. But spiritual treasures—the blessings of being a child of God and receiving God's love and forgiveness of sin; growing in love, joy, peace, patience, kindness, goodness, faithfulness, gentleness, self-control; a friendship with God and life in heaven with Jesus—last forever! Spiritual treasures can never be taken away from the true believer in Jesus. When you have Jesus, you have everything! **Jesus is the greatest treasure!**

Jesus looked at the crowd and saw their worries, their fears. He saw the pain and sadness caused by sin, greed, and everything that is in the hearts of those who depend on themselves because they don't know God. Many of them were looking for everything the world had for them instead of searching for God. But Jesus had a better way for them. Jesus came to show them who the Father is—to show them what God is like. To let them know that they can trust God.

"Therefore I tell you, do not be anxious about your life, what you will eat or what you will drink, nor about your body, what you will put on. Is not life more than food, and the body more than clothing? Look at the birds of the air: they neither sow nor reap nor gather into barns, and yet your heavenly Father feeds them. Are you not of more value than they? And which of you by being anxious can add a single hour to his span of life? And why are you anxious about clothing? Consider the lilies of the field, how they grow: they neither toil nor spin, yet I tell you, even Solomon in all his glory was not arrayed like one of these. But if God so

clothes the grass of the field, which today is alive and tomorrow is thrown into the oven, will he not much more clothe you, O you of little faith? Therefore do not be anxious, saying, 'What shall we eat?' or 'What shall we drink?' or 'What shall we wear?' For the Gentiles seek after all these things, and your heavenly Father knows that you need them all. But seek first the kingdom of God and his righteousness, and all these things will be added to you." (Matthew 6:25-33)

Jesus knew what these people needed to hear. They needed to hear the truth about who God is and how He can be trusted to care for everything in His world. They needed to put their faith in God and "**seek first the kingdom of God.**"

This is the same truth you need today. Every day you will make choices of whether to seek God and the joys of spiritual treasures or to seek the world and its temporary treasures. Do you want earthly rewards or heavenly rewards? How can you seek heavenly treasures and live to bring glory to God?

> "But seek first the kingdom of God and his righteousness, and all these things will be added to you." (Matthew 6:33)

THAT YOU MAY BELIEVE

What does this chapter tell us about God?

Talk about and apply the **biblical truths** in **bold** text. Make them personal and apply them to what is happening in your family, church, community, or the world today.

Read Matthew 6:1-6, 16-18. What is the difference between a hypocrite and a sincere Christian? What are some practical examples of hypocrisy you can think of?

Talk About: *"Do not lay up for yourselves treasures on earth, where moth and rust destroy and where thieves break in and steal, but lay up for yourselves treasures in heaven, where neither moth nor rust destroys and where thieves do not break in and steal. For where your treasure is, there your heart will be also." (Matthew 6:19-21)*

What are some tempting earthly treasures? What does it mean to "serve two masters"? (Matthew 6:24) Why can't you serve two masters? Explain.

Pray: Ask God to show you any hypocrisy in your life—any way you pretend to be more spiritual than you really are. Ask Him to show you what captures your heart the most—what things you love most. Confess your sin to God and ask Him to give you the desire to seek Him with all your heart.

Think About: *What do I think about most? What makes me excited? What would I be angry about losing? What do I treasure most?*

THE LORD'S PRAYER

(Matthew 6:9-13)

Now Jesus was praying in a certain place, and when he finished, one of his disciples said to him, "Lord, teach us to pray, as John taught his disciples." (Luke 11:1)

Do you know the words to the prayer we call the Lord's Prayer?[13] It is a beautiful prayer Jesus told His disciples. But Jesus did not mean for this prayer to be repeated mechanically back to God. Rather, Jesus used it to teach His disciples and us *how* to pray. The Lord's Prayer is a *pattern* or a *model* of prayer for us. In it, Jesus is showing us what should be in our hearts when we pray. Let's look at this prayer and see what we can learn from Jesus.[14] *Pray then like this:*

"Our Father in heaven, hallowed be your name."

What do the first two words tell you?

If Jesus is your Savior, then God is your heavenly Father and you are His dear child. He is not a stranger or someone who is far away and uninterested in your life. God is someone you can have a relationship or friendship with. When Christians pray, we are spending time with our loving heavenly Father.

What do the next two words—"in heaven"—tell you?

"In heaven" is not telling us *where* God is. God is omnipresent. That means He is everywhere all the time. "In heaven" is telling us *who* God is. It is showing that God is the greatest authority who is in charge of the whole world! He is all-powerful, He knows everything, and He is eternal—He has no beginning and no end. So God is worthy of our respect. When Christians pray, our hearts should have love for our Father and respect for the Creator and Owner of the world. When God's children pray, we need to truly believe and trust that God is great enough to answer our prayers for all our needs.

What does "hallowed be your name" mean?

To "hallow" is to honor or have great respect for someone or something. Every follower of Jesus should have a heart that desires God be honored and respected above all, and that God's name would be shown as great. God and His purposes should be the center of our prayers, not "me" and what I want. We should pray that God's name would be honored *by* us and *because* of us.

"Your kingdom come,"

What do these words show about what a Christian should have in his heart when he prays?

Every follower of Christ should have a great desire for His return. "Your kingdom come" shows a greater longing for heaven than for the things of this world.

"your will be done, on earth as it is in heaven."

The true believer wants all his desires to be godly desires. He longs for God to rule completely and perfectly on earth just like He does in heaven. A Christian should come to God in prayer wanting what God wants—not just what he wants. He should have an obedient heart that is willing to do whatever has to be done for God's purposes and plan to be accomplished. It is like saying to God, "I will do whatever You want me to do. Your purposes are more important to me than any plan of my own."

"Give us this day our daily bread,"

Why should we ask God for what we need if He already knows everything and knows what we need? When we pray for our needs, we are admitting that we need God every day and reminding ourselves that everything we have comes from Him. Telling God about our needs is also a way of showing Him that we trust Him to take care of us. A follower of Christ prays with the heart of faith, knowing that God is able and willing to answer prayer, but understanding that God sometimes answers "yes," sometimes "no," and sometimes "wait." However God answers the prayers of His children, His answer is always good and right.

"and forgive us our debts, as we also have forgiven our debtors."

What does the word, "debts" mean? Our debts are our sins. Our sin separates us from God and His answers to our prayers. So when we come to God in prayer, we should come with a desire to confess our sin that has separated us from God and to restore our broken relationship with God. Confession involves naming specific sins (like lying or anger), not just saying, "Forgive me for my sins." Even though God's children are free from the eternal punishment for sin, our sin grieves the God we love. We need to ask God's forgiveness for offending Him with our sin.

We should also have a heart attitude of being willing to forgive others because we know we have been forgiven of so much. Jesus warns us that if we are not willing to forgive others, God will not forgive our sins (Matthew 6:14-15).

"And lead us not into temptation, but deliver us from evil."

What does this phrase show us about the Christian's heart? The true follower of Jesus has a humble heart that recognizes he has a weakness for sin. Our hearts want to do what is good and right ("the spirit is willing"), but our sin nature pulls us toward sin ("the flesh is weak").[15]

Problems can make us strong, but they can also tempt us to sin. When we pray, "lead us not into temptation," we are asking God to protect us from sinning in our trials. We are also admitting that we need God because without His grace we would do all kinds of evil. We need His protection from our sin nature. We must depend on God to do for us what we cannot do for ourselves. (See 1 Corinthians 10:13.)

SUMMARY

True prayer is focused on God and flows out of a relationship with God. The heart of a true follower of Jesus desires to come to prayer with a pure, humble heart full of faith in God's fatherly love, goodness, power, and authority. We pray because we desperately need a pure heart and understand that our faith is weak. We know only God can change our hearts and give us the will and strength to honor Him and bless others.

---

13 Adapted from the Teacher's Guide of Sally Michael's intergenerational curriculum, *Lord, Teach Us To Pray: A Study for Children and Adults on Prayer* (Minneapolis, Minn.: Truth78, 2020), 132-15.

14 Take your time in talking through this pattern for prayer and lead your child in prayer through each section. This will take several sittings. When you pray together daily with your child, use Jesus' model for prayer to get beyond, "Thank You for the nice day..."

15 Romans 7:18-25

CHAPTER 106
A HEALTHY TREE AND A DISEASED TREE

Jesus Teaches about Seeking True Righteousness—Matthew 7

"Thus you will recognize them by their fruits." (Matthew 7:20)

What kind of fruit does an apple tree produce? Apples, of course! *Can a thorn bush grow apples?* Of course not! *If you hung apples on a thorn bush, would it be an apple tree?* No, it would still be a thorn bush that could not produce real fruit.

So what do an apple tree and a thorn bush have to do with the Bible? The Pharisees were the religious leaders in the time that Jesus was on earth. They knew the Law, but they didn't really understand it. When the Pharisees did good works, it was often for the wrong reasons—for the praise and admiration of others. Their hearts were not right. They were prideful, thinking they were righteous rather than sinners in need of God's grace. They were judgmental—critical and condemning of others—thinking they were better than others. They didn't have the true fruit of righteousness. They were like thorn bushes that scratch, not apple trees that produce delicious apples. They pretended to have good fruit (true good works), but they were really like thorn bushes that could not produce apples. So they taped "apples of good works" on their thorny branches. They were hypocrites who looked good on the outside, but their hearts were darkened. Following the teaching of the Pharisees led to death. Following Jesus leads to life.

Jesus continued to warn the crowd about being hypocrites in His teaching in the Sermon on the Mount. He taught about humility—seeing ourselves as sinners in need of God's grace. Instead of seeing the sin in others, Jesus taught that we should look at our own sinful hearts first and confess our sin. Then we can help others to repent.

"Why do you see the speck that is in your brother's eye, but do not notice the log that is in your own eye? Or how can you say to your brother, 'Let me take the speck out of your eye,' when there is the log in your own eye? You hypocrite, first take the log out of your own eye, and then you will see clearly to take the speck out of your brother's eye." (Matthew 7:3-5)

So how does a person get a humble heart? How can the heart of stone be replaced with a heart of flesh? **Only God can change a person's heart.** So Jesus told the crowd to pray…and to keep on praying…keep on asking…keep on seeking…keep on knocking. *"For everyone who asks receives, and the one who seeks finds, and to the one who knocks it will be opened."*

Jesus explained that God gives good things to those who ask Him. He did this by giving an example the people could understand.

"Or which one of you, if his son asks him for bread, will give him a stone? Or if he asks for a fish, will give him a serpent? If you then, who are evil, know how to give good gifts to your children, how much more will your Father who is in heaven give good things to those who ask him!" (Matthew 7:9-11)

God gives true good gifts—the best gifts! He gives the spiritual gifts of a humble heart, repentance, faith, and true good fruit that comes from a changed heart. Jesus was pleading with the people to seek "true religion"—true worship of God that comes from the heart and true good works that bring glory and praise to God.

It is easy to "act" righteous—to pretend to be a good person with a good heart. That is a "wide path" that is easy to follow. But to truly have a pure heart is impossible. To be the kind of person who treats others the right way—the way you would want to be treated—can only happen to those to whom God has given a new heart. Very few people follow the "narrow path" to seek true righteousness; the narrow path that leads to the "new birth" Jesus told Nicodemus about. The narrow path of seeking God leads to life because pretenders will be destroyed. Jesus said,

"A healthy tree cannot bear bad fruit, nor can a diseased tree bear good fruit. Every tree that does not bear good fruit is cut down and thrown into the fire." Then Jesus said something even more serious about pretenders or hypocrites.

"Not everyone who says to me, 'Lord, Lord,' will enter the kingdom of heaven, but the one who does the will of my Father who is in

heaven. On that day many will say to me, 'Lord, Lord, did we not prophesy in your name, and cast out demons in your name, and do many mighty works in your name?' And then will I declare to them, 'I never knew you; depart from me, you workers of lawlessness.'" (Matthew 7:21-23)

Do you know how Jesus ended His sermon? Jesus ended with a story—a story with a warning and a promise. The story was about two houses…but Jesus was really talking about two kinds of people. One kind of person hears Jesus' teaching and follows Him. This person obeys God's Word and seeks the true treasure of a relationship with Jesus, a pure heart, and spiritual blessing. The other kind of person hears the same words, but He does not seek spiritual life.

"Everyone then who hears these words of mine and does them will be like a wise man who built his house on the rock. And the rain fell, and the floods came, and the winds blew and beat on that house, but it did not fall, because it had been founded on the rock. And everyone who hears these words of mine and does not do them will be like a foolish man who built his house on the sand. And the rain fell, and the floods came, and the winds blew and beat against that house, and it fell, and great was the fall of it." (Matthew 7:24-27)

What is the promise in Jesus' story? What is the warning? We don't know how many people in the crowd were wise and how many were foolish. But the Bible does tell us that many of them were surprised: *And when Jesus finished these sayings, the crowds were astonished at his teaching, for he was teaching them as one who had authority, and not as their scribes.*

Jesus taught with authority because **Jesus is God**, the Supreme Ruler of the Universe. **Every word of God is true.** That means that Jesus' warning should be taken very seriously, and His promise should be seen as very precious. Not everyone who claims to be a Christian is a true Christian. Going to church, reading the Bible, and saying the right things does not make a person a Christian. Humbly seeking for God, admitting sin, trusting in Jesus' payment on the cross for sin, and treasuring God most of all is the good gift that God will give to those who keep asking, keep seeking and keep knocking.

Jesus knows those who are pretenders and those who have a true relationship with Him. What is the difference between following the wide path of just looking righteous and the narrow path that leads to Jesus and true righteousness? Do you know if you are a pretender or a true friend of Jesus?

For by grace you have been saved through faith. And this is not your own doing; it is the gift of God, not a result of works, so that no one may boast. (Ephesians 2:8-9)

THAT YOU MAY BELIEVE

What does this chapter tell us about God?

Talk about and apply the **biblical truths** in **bold** text. Make them personal and apply them to what is happening in your family, church, community, or the world today.

Read Matthew 7:1-5. Are you quick to see your own sin? When you have a problem with another person, do you look at your part in the problem first? What can we know about our hearts by the way we think about others?

Talk About: *For by grace you have been saved through faith. And this is not your own doing; it is the gift of God, not a result of works, so that no one may boast. (Ephesians 2:8-9)*

How can you tell if you are a pretender (hypocrite) or a true Christian?

Pray: Praise God for being the Giver of good gifts. Ask Him to show you your true heart. Ask Him to give you a heart to seek Him and to desire spiritual gifts.

Think About: *What am I really seeking?*

CHAPTER 107
WHO IS JESUS?

Jesus Shows He Is the Promised One by Healing, Raising the Dead, and Forgiving Sin—Luke 7:1-50

"...the blind receive their sight, the lame walk, lepers are cleansed, and the deaf hear, the dead are raised up, the poor have good news preached to them." (Luke 7:22b)

As Jesus became better known, more and more Jews began to ask, "Who is Jesus?" His teaching about true faith was so different from the Pharisees' teaching about religious duty and works. Was Jesus just a good teacher? Jesus healed people...but so did the prophets Elijah and Elisha. Was Jesus just a prophet? Or was Jesus more than this? Some people believed He was more...others were confused...and some were sure He was a fake or worse.

After teaching on the mountain, Jesus went to the town of Capernaum. Some Jewish leaders there went to find Jesus. They were sent by a centurion—that's a Roman soldier. The leaders asked Jesus to heal the centurion's servant, who was so sick that he was close to dying. They told Jesus the centurion had been good to the Jews and had even given money to help build their synagogue. Their opinion of the centurion was, *"He is worthy to have you do this for him."*

Jesus went with them, but when he got close to the centurion's house, friends of the centurion met Jesus with a message from him, *"Lord, do not trouble yourself, for I am not worthy to have you come under my roof. Therefore I did not presume to come to you. But say the word, and let my servant be healed."* The Jews thought the centurion was worthy or deserving of Jesus' kindness because he was "a good man." But the centurion realized he was unworthy to have Jesus enter his house. *Why would he think this?*

The centurion believed that Jesus was more than a good teacher and a prophet. He recognized Jesus' authority—Jesus could heal just by speaking a word. *When Jesus heard these things, he marveled at him, and turning to the crowd that followed him, said, "I tell you, not even in Israel have I found such faith."* Jesus saw greater faith in the non-Jewish, Gentile, Roman soldier than He saw in the Jews. Jesus was worthy of the centurion's faith in Him because **Jesus is God**. When the centurion's friends got to the centurion's house, they discovered that the servant was well! Jesus had healed him!

Soon after this, Jesus was entering the town of Nain and a funeral procession came by. The crowd had gathered to bury the only son of a widow. When Jesus saw the heartbroken mother, He had compassion on her and tenderly said to her, *"Do not weep."* Do you know what Jesus did next? He touched the special platform the coffin was sitting on and said, *"Young man, I say to you, arise."* Jesus had just healed a servant who was very sick, but this young man was *dead!* But at Jesus' word, *the dead man sat up and began to speak.* **Jesus has power over sickness and death! Sin brought death, but Jesus brings life!**

Imagine the overwhelming astonishment and joy the mother must have felt! But this is not how the others felt. *How do you think the other people felt? Fear seized them all, and they glorified God, saying, "A great prophet has arisen among us!" and "God has visited his people!"* The crowd knew that this was the work of God. They must have wondered, "Who is Jesus?"

What do you think happens with news of a dead man being made alive again? One person tells another...who tells another...who tells another...and the news of what Jesus did spread through all Judea and further. The news was even told to John the Baptist in prison. John sent two of his disciples to Jesus to ask Him, *"Are you the one who is to come or shall we look for another?"* Jesus did not tell them who He is, He showed them. *In that hour he healed many people of diseases and plagues and evil spirits, and on many who were blind he bestowed sight.* Do you know what Jesus told John's disciples?

> *..."Go and tell John what you have seen and heard: the blind receive their sight, the lame walk, lepers are cleansed, and the deaf hear, the dead are raised up, the poor have good news preached to them. And blessed is the one who is not offended by me." (Luke 7:22-23)*

Who is Jesus? **Jesus is the Son of God who has the authority to break the curse of sin.** Sin had brought sickness, suffering, and death into the world. But Jesus has the power over all things. **Jesus has the power to reverse the curse of sin. He is the promised Messiah!**

Sadly, most of the Jews did not understand who Jesus is. Some thought maybe He was another prophet sent from God. One of the Pharisees named Simon would see if Jesus was truly a prophet. So Simon invited Jesus to dinner. In those days, usually the host made arrangements for the guests' feet to be washed before dinner. *Does this sound strange?* We wash our hands before dinner. *Why would they wash their feet before dinner?* Most of the roads in Israel were dusty dirt roads, and most people wore sandals. So of course, their feet got very dirty as they walked from place to place. But Simon did nothing to make sure that Jesus' feet could be washed. He did not show common courtesy or respect to Jesus.

While they were at the dinner table, a woman came in with an expensive jar of perfume. She stood behind Jesus weeping, and her tears began to wet Jesus' feet. Then she used her hair to dry Jesus' feet, *and she kissed his feet and anointed them with the ointment.* Simon watched this with disgust. He was very offended. Simon knew this woman was a very sinful person. He thought to himself that if Jesus were really a prophet, He would know this woman was a great sinner. Why would Jesus even let her touch Him? But **Jesus knows everything.** And He knew exactly what Simon was thinking...and Jesus had something to say to Simon. He had something to teach Simon, but Jesus did it in a story.

> *"A certain moneylender had two debtors. One owed five hundred denarii, and the other fifty. When they could not pay, he cancelled the debt of both. Now which of them will love him more?" (Luke 7:41-42)*

Naturally Simon said the one who owed the most money and didn't have to pay it. Which, of course, was the right answer.

> *Then turning toward the woman he said to Simon, "Do you see this woman? I entered your house; you gave me no water for my feet, but she has wet my feet with her tears and wiped them with her hair. You gave me no kiss, but from the time I came in she has not*

ceased to kiss my feet. You did not anoint my head with oil, but she has anointed my feet with ointment. Therefore I tell you, her sins, which are many, are forgiven—for she loved much. But he who is forgiven little, loves little." (Luke 7:44-47)

Who loved Jesus more? Prideful Simon, who did not treat Jesus with honor and respect? Or the sinful woman, who washed Jesus' feet and used her precious perfume on Him? Simon, who thought his sins were few and unimportant...or the woman, who knew she was a great sinner and needed Jesus' forgiveness? The woman loved Jesus because she knew she was not worthy to be forgiven, respected, or loved. Yet Jesus had forgiven her and treated her with love and respect.

Jesus looked at her and said, *"Your sins are forgiven...Your faith has saved you; go in peace."* The other guests were puzzled. Who was Jesus? Who was this person who "even forgives sins"?

Who is Jesus? **Jesus is the Messiah who has the power and authority to forgive sins.** He is God's Promised One announced by John the Baptist. He is God the Son who came to earth as a man to show us the heart of His Father. He is the One who crushes the serpent's head. **Jesus brings life and light and healing and love.**

Who is Jesus to you? Is He just someone you read about in the Bible or hear about in church? Or is He your Savior and Friend? Is He someone whose authority you respect and whose heart you trust? Is He someone whose feet you would wash and anoint with expensive perfume?

"And blessed is the one who is not offended by me." (Luke 7:23)

For with the heart one believes and is justified, and with the mouth one confesses and is saved. For the Scripture says, "Everyone who believes in him will not be put to shame." (Romans 10:10-11)

THAT YOU MAY BELIEVE

What does this chapter tell us about God?

Talk about and apply the **biblical truths** in **bold** text. Make them personal and apply them to what is happening in your family, church, community, or the world today.

How do Jesus' miracles show us who He is?

Talk About: *For with the heart one believes and is justified, and with the mouth one confesses and is saved. For the Scripture says, "Everyone who believes in him will not be put to shame." (Romans 10:10-11)*

How would you describe your relationship with Jesus?

Pray: Praise God for keeping His promise and sending Jesus. Ask God to show you what is in your heart. Ask God to show you how you can grow in your relationship with Jesus. Thank Jesus for coming to save sinners.

Think About: *Am I more like Simon or like the woman who washed Jesus' feet?*

CHAPTER 108

HIDDEN TRUTHS IN KINGDOM PARABLES

Jesus Teaches through Parables—The Sower, Treasure, Pearl, Rich Fool, Net—Matthew 13:1-23, 44-50; Luke 12:16-21

..."To you it has been given to know the secrets of the kingdom of heaven, but to them it has not been given." (Matthew 13:11b)

Sometimes people put a message in secret code so that only the person who receives the message can understand it. *How can you read a message if it has been written in a secret code?* If you know the secret code—the symbol the message writer used for each letter—you can easily figure out the message. But if you don't know the code, the message is hidden and looks very confusing. Jesus sometimes taught using "hidden messages" in stories called parables. The parables Jesus told were stories about things in the real world that have a hidden spiritual meaning. Only with the help of the Holy Spirit can a person truly understand and accept Jesus' teaching in parables. In a way, the Holy Spirit "gives them the code" to understand the truth. But other people are blind to the great truths of Jesus' stories.

Why do you think that Jesus sometimes used parables? Stories are easy to remember, and they create emotions in our hearts. But parables are stories that also make us think and force us to try to figure out spiritual truth. The parables show truth to those who are seeking God, and they hide truth from others. Sometimes Jesus used stories because He knew it was better for people to be confused than to deliberately reject the truth.

What are some of the parables Jesus told? One parable is about a sower and seeds. A man scattered his seeds. Some fell on the path, some landed on rocky ground, some fell into the thorns, and some landed on good soil. *What happened to each of these seeds?* The seeds on the path were eaten by birds. The seeds on rocky ground grew up quickly, but since there wasn't much dirt, they couldn't form strong roots. When the sun came up, the plants dried out and withered away. The seeds in the thorns were choked out by the thorns. But the seeds on the good dirt grew into strong, fruitful plants.

Jesus' disciples could not understand why Jesus taught in parables. Why didn't He just teach in easy, plain language? Jesus told them that God had given them the gift of knowing the secrets of the Kingdom—spiritual truth. But for others, *"seeing they do not see, and hearing they do not hear, nor do they understand."* Even though these people heard the parables, they just didn't understand the spiritual meaning of them; the spiritual meaning was hidden from them.

Jesus did not always explain His parables, but He did explain the Parable of the Sower to His disciples. The hidden truth in the parable is this: the seed is God's Word; the different soils describe different people who hear God's Word. This is how Jesus described them:

People who are like the "path"—*"When anyone hears the word of the kingdom and does not understand it, the evil one comes and snatches away what has been sown in his heart."*

People who are "rocky ground"—*"this is the one who hears the word and immediately receives it with joy, yet he has no root in himself, but endures for a while, and when tribulation or persecution arises on account of the word, immediately he falls away."*

People who are "thorns"—*"this is the one who hears the word, but the cares of the world and the deceitfulness of riches choke the word, and it proves unfruitful."*

People who are "good soil"—*"this is the one who hears the word and understands it. He indeed bears fruit."*

God's Word is truth, but the hearts of the people who hear it can be very hardened…and they turn away. They don't love life with God. They don't love His ways or see Him as the most important treasure in life. Other people have hearts that receive God's Word and let it grow in their hearts so that it changes them.

Jesus also told two parables about how valuable it is to live in the Kingdom of God. God's Kingdom is where God's family lives joyfully forever under God's perfect rule.

> **"The kingdom of heaven is like treasure** hidden in a field, which a man found and covered up. Then in his joy he goes and sells all that he has and buys that field. Again, the kingdom of heaven is like a merchant in search of fine pearls,

who, on finding one pearl of great value, went and sold all that he had and bought it." (Matthew 13:44-46)

Being part of God's family is the greatest treasure a person could have—more valuable than everything a person has. But sadly, not everyone believes this. There are people who love the temporary things of this world more than they love the eternal things God offers. *Did Jesus care enough about these people to warn them?* Yes, so He used a parable to explain the danger of loving things more than loving God. It was about a landowner whose crops grew very, very well. In fact, he had so much food that it would not fit in his barns. *Do you know what he did?* He didn't share the extra crops he had. He didn't give them to poor or hungry people. Instead, he tore down his barns and built BIGGER barns in which to store his crops. He kept all his crops thinking that he had everything he needed for many years. He could relax and enjoy what he had.

But Jesus ended His story with this warning:

"But God said to him, 'Fool! This night your soul is required of you, and the things you have prepared, whose will they be?' So is the one who lays up treasure for himself and is not rich toward God." (Luke 12:20-21)

What good is a barn full of crops when a person is dead? What will happen to the person who treasures earthly things more than heavenly things? Jesus told another parable about what will happen when life on earth ends.

> *"Again, the kingdom of heaven is like a net that was thrown into the sea and gathered fish of every kind. When it was full, men drew it ashore and sat down and sorted the good into containers but threw away the bad. So it will be at the close of the age. The angels will come out and separate the evil from the righteous and throw them into the fiery furnace. In that place there will be weeping and gnashing of teeth." (Matthew 13:47-50)*

There are only two paths to follow in life—an earthly path, storing up temporary treasures here that don't last; or a heavenly path, storing up treasures in heaven that last forever. *What kind of treasure do you want?*

What kind of heart do you have? Is your heart like the hardened soil, the rocky soil, the thorns, or the good soil where the Word of God can grow and change you? You cannot change your heart and make yourself treasure God most of all. But you can pray that God will give you a heart of good soil, a heart that treasures Him and His ways and His Kingdom most of all. Will you pray for your heart?

Search me, O God, and know my heart! Try me and know my thoughts! And see if there be any grievous way in me, and lead me in the way everlasting! (Psalm 139:23-24)

Do not love the world or the things in the world. If anyone loves the world, the love of the Father is not in him. (1 John 2:15)

THAT YOU MAY BELIEVE

What does this chapter tell us about God?

Talk about and apply the **biblical truths** in **bold** text. Make them personal and apply them to what is happening in your family, church, community, or the world today.

Not everyone is given "spiritual hunger" (the desire to know God). What are some signs of spiritual hunger?

Talk About: *Search me, O God, and know my heart! Try me and know my thoughts! And see if there be any grievous way in me, and lead me in the way everlasting! (Psalm 139:23-24)*

Explain the Parable of the Sower (Matthew 13:3-9, 18-23) to your mother or father.

Pray: Ask God to give you a love for Him and a desire to know Him better. Ask Him to open your eyes and your heart to see and accept spiritual truth. Thank Him for His Word.

Think About: *Do I want "bigger barns" or spiritual treasure? What in my life shows this?*

CHAPTER 109

JESUS STOPS TWO KINDS OF STORMS

Jesus Calms the Storm and Casts Out Demons—Mark 4:35-5:20

..."Why are you so afraid? Have you still no faith?" (Mark 4:40)

Have you ever been really afraid? What happened that made you afraid? The disciples were afraid too—very afraid! Jesus had been teaching a crowd of people. When He was done, He and the disciples got in a boat to go to the other side of the lake. Jesus must have been very tired because He fell asleep in the boat. While He was sleeping a fierce storm came up. *What do you think it is like to be in a small boat in a big storm?*

The wind was blowing furiously, the waves were crashing into the boat...and water was pouring into the boat! Some of the disciples were fishermen so they were used to storms, but this storm scared them. The boat was rocking up and down and filing with water! This storm was fierce! The disciples were terrified, thinking they were going to die! Yet Jesus was peacefully sleeping in the back of the boat! So they woke Jesus by shouting, *"Master, Master, we are perishing!" "Teacher, do you not care that we are perishing?" "Save us, Lord; we are perishing."* The disciples were panicking! *What did Jesus do?*

And he awoke and rebuked the wind and said to the sea, "Peace! Be still!" And the wind ceased, and there was a great calm. He said to them, "Why are you so afraid? Have you still no faith?" And they were filled with great fear and said to one another, "Who then is this, that even the wind and the sea obey him?" (Mark 4:39-41)

Jesus spoke just a few words…and the violent, furious storm…immediately stopped. No more wind. No more crashing waves. No more water filling the boat. Just complete calm. **Jesus' words have authority.** He ordered the sea to be still, and it obeyed. **Jesus controls the wind and the waves.** He has authority over storms and weather. The disciples had already seen Jesus' authority over sickness, death, and demons. Did they still not understand that **Jesus is God almighty?** They wondered who He could be that the wind and sea obeyed Him. Why were they so afraid? Did they not have faith in Jesus?

When they got to the other side of the sea, as soon as Jesus got out of the boat, a man was there. This was no ordinary man. He lived in the hills "among the tombs." These caves were used to bury dead people, and sometimes they were homes for outcasts—those who could not live among other people. This man had evil spirits or demons living within him. The demons in him were so strong that he would act ferociously. People had tried to chain his feet and body to keep him still, but he easily broke the chains. So now he lived among the tombs in the hills "crying out and cutting himself with stones."

He had seen Jesus from far away and ran. But he didn't run away. He ran and fell down in front of Jesus. Jesus sternly commanded, *"Come out of the man, you unclean spirit!"* But the demonized man cried out, *"What have you to do with me, Jesus, Son of the Most High God? I adjure you by God, do not torment me."* Most of the people in this area were not Jews. They were Gentiles who often referred to the God of Israel as the Most High God. They did not believe that Yahweh is the only God but rather the most powerful of the gods. Even though the Jews Jesus preached to were not sure who Jesus was, the demons knew that Jesus is the Son of the God of Israel!

Jesus asked the demon his name and he answered, *"My name is Legion, for we are many."* This poor man did not have just one evil spirit but many evil spirits tormenting him. The demons knew they had to obey Jesus because **Jesus has authority over evil spirits.** They begged him not to send them out of the country but instead into a herd of pigs eating on the side of the hill. To the Jews, pigs were "unclean"

animals that they could not eat. But the Gentiles raised pigs, and Jesus gave the demons permission to enter the pigs. *Do you know what happened next?*

The demons had to follow Jesus' command. The evil spirits came out of the man and went into the herd of 2,000 pigs. Of course, this caused the pigs to go wild, and they "rushed down the steep bank into the sea and were drowned in the sea." *Can you imagine how much the man must have been tormented by these evil spirits?*

The men who were caring for the pigs ran away in terror! What a terribly frightening thing they had seen! On their way to the city, they told others what had happened. Nothing like this had ever happened before! How could this be? The people came out to the hillside to check it out…and there was the demon-possessed man, calmly sitting there, in his right mind—perfectly fine. Once again, the people heard the story of what had happened.

The people were so scared that they asked Jesus to leave. What else might happen with Jesus around? But the man who had been delivered from the demons wanted to be with Jesus. It was like he had had an evil storm inside of him and Jesus had made it still—Jesus had stopped the torment and fear and confusion and destruction that had swirled around inside him. The man had lived in a place of "unclean" Gentiles and "unclean" animals, among "unclean" dead bodies, with "unclean" spirits… and Jesus had made him clean and whole!

When Jesus got in the boat to leave, the man wanted to go with him. But Jesus told him to stay and gave him an important work to do. *"Go home to your friends and tell them how much the Lord has done for you, and how he has had mercy on you." And he went away and began to proclaim in the Decapolis how much Jesus had done for him, and everyone marveled.* So the Gentiles in the Decapolis—ten Gentile cities—heard of the amazing miracle of Jesus and the mercy Jesus has on hurting, sinful people.

You too have seen the works of God—in the Bible, in the world, in your church or community, and in your life. God has proclaimed who He is through His daily work in this world. Every day when the sun comes up, God is saying, "I am here keeping the world going." Every summer that turns into fall that turns into winter that turns into spring and starts over again is God saying, "I never change." Every storm, tornado, hurricane, or earthquake shows His power, and every breath of air shows His care.

Do you believe in Jesus, the Son of God and trust Him fully? The disciples had been with Jesus, yet Jesus knew they did not fully trust Him when He said, "Why are you so afraid? Have you still no faith?" *The people seeing the man with the evil spirit released from his torment and the drowned pigs were afraid and asked Jesus to leave. How will you respond to Jesus? Do you want Jesus to go away and leave you alone? Or do you want to have a relationship with Jesus? Will you trust Him even when life seems difficult or scary? Will you believe and tell others the amazing mercy of God, who makes sinners clean and whole?*

Draw near to God, and he will draw near to you. (James 4:8a)

THAT YOU MAY BELIEVE

What does this chapter tell us about God?

Talk about and apply the **biblical truths** in **bold** text. Make them personal and apply them to what is happening in your family, church, community, or the world today.

What are some mercies God has shown to your family? What is the greatest mercy we can receive from God? How can you "draw near to God"?

Talk About: *Draw near to God, and he will draw near to you. (James 4:8a)*

Why did Jesus cross the lake on the boat—was He going somewhere? What purposes of God were accomplished in these events?

Pray: Praise God for His absolute authority over all things. Thank Him for His mercy to suffering sinners. Ask God to give you boldness in telling others about Him.

Think About: *Since God is in charge of all things, why should I worry or be afraid?*

CHAPTER 110
DO NOT FEAR, ONLY BELIEVE

People Respond to Jesus' Miracles in Faith, Unbelief, or Confusion—Mark 5:21-6:29

"Do not fear, only believe." (Mark 5:36b)

What do you think was waiting for Jesus when he got back to the other side of the sea? A crowd of people were waiting for Jesus. One man there was Jairus, a ruler of the synagogue. He made his way through the crowd and fell at Jesus' feet. Jairus's daughter was at the point of death, and Jairus came to desperately plead with Jesus to heal his daughter—*"Come and lay your hands on her, so that she may be made well and live."* So Jesus, who is full of compassion, went with Jairus, and a big crowd of people followed them.

In the crowd was a woman who had suffered for twelve years with a bleeding disease. She had gone to many doctors and spent all her money, but it didn't help. Instead of getting better, she got worse! But she had heard of Jesus, and she had hope—*"If I touch even his garments, I will be made well."* Coming up behind Jesus, she reached out...and touched his robe. *Immediately* the blood dried up and she was healed! *Immediately!* What amazing power Jesus has!

Jesus stopped and turned around. He knew that power had gone from Him, and He said, *"Who touched my garments?"* The disciples thought that surely Jesus must be joking! Who touched Jesus' robe? There was a huge crowd around Him! Probably lots of people touched His arm, His hands, His leg, His robe...But Jesus knew, and so did the woman, that this was a special touch. She came "in fear and trembling and fell down before him" and told Jesus what had happened. But Jesus wasn't upset; He was pleased. Jesus looked at her and said, *"Daughter, your faith has made you well; go in peace, and be healed of your disease."* *Was it touching the robe of Jesus that made her well?* It was the healing power of Jesus given to her because of her faith in Him. She touched his garment because she had faith that Jesus had the power to heal her. **Jesus loves it when people have faith in Him.**

While Jesus was speaking to the woman, someone brought Jairus the news that his daughter had died. There was no need to bother Jesus now. It was too late. But Jesus heard this and said to Jairus, *"Do not fear, only believe."* Then Jesus told the crowd to stay behind, and He went with Peter, James, and John to Jairus's house. *What do you think Jesus saw there?*

Jesus saw people weeping and wailing loudly. *And when he had entered, he said to them, "Why are you making a commotion and weeping? The child is not dead but sleeping."* *Did the people get excited and praise God?* No, they laughed at Jesus in a mocking way. Sleeping? She wasn't sleeping; she was dead! They did not believe Jesus but ridiculed Him instead.

Jesus sent these unbelieving mockers outside. Along with the parents and the three disciples, Jesus went to the little girl. Jesus took her by the hand and said, *"Little girl, I say to you, arise."* *Immediately* the girl got up and walked around! The parents and the disciples were amazed! Once again, Jesus had shown His power over death—something that only God can do.

Jesus' message—"Do not fear, only believe;" have faith—was strengthened by the many signs and wonders He did. Only God could do the things Jesus did. Who else could do these mighty works? Who else could have such wisdom? **Jesus is God.** But many people did not believe in Him.

Then Jesus sent out His disciples in pairs. But first, He gave them authority over evil spirits. He sent them out to preach—to urge others to repent and to tell them about the glorious Kingdom of God. Along with their teaching, they cast out many demons and healed many people through the authority of Jesus. By now many people were talking about the mighty miracles of Jesus. Who was this Jesus who was doing these miracles? Some people thought that John the Baptist had been raised from the dead. Some thought He was Elijah. Others thought Jesus was a prophet like the Old Testament prophets.

Even King Herod heard about the miracles of Jesus and was sure that Jesus was John the Baptist who had come back from the dead. *Do you remember how John died?* Herod's unlawful wife, Herodias, had hated John and wanted him put to death. But Herod "feared John, knowing that he was a righteous and holy man" and so, Herod kept John safe in prison and was even interested in John's teaching.

But Herodias finally had an opportunity to get revenge on John. Herod gave a banquet and invited many important men. Herodias' daughter danced at the banquet, and this pleased Herod greatly. He was so pleased that he promised her whatever she wanted—even half of his kingdom! *What would you want if you were made an offer like that?*

Herodias' daughter chose a very strange reward. She talked to her mother for advice, and her mother asked her to have John the Baptist beheaded! So the girl went back to Herod and made this evil request. Because Herod had promised in front of all these important men, he felt he had to keep his promise. So he had John killed, and John's disciples took his body and put it in a tomb. Now Herod wondered if this Jesus was John the Baptist come back to life.

But Jesus was not John the Baptist raised from the dead. **Jesus is the Son of God who performed miracles because He is God. Jesus has all power and authority.**

John was a faithful messenger who boldly spoke the message of repentance and faith. He had faithfully prepared the way for Jesus and had even died for his faithfulness. This is what Jesus said about John the Baptist:

"Truly, I say to you, among those born of women there has arisen no one greater than

John the Baptist. Yet the one who is least in the kingdom of heaven is greater than he." (Matthew 11:11)

It was a great honor for John the Baptist to be the messenger announcing that Jesus is the Savior, the Lamb of God. But it is an even greater honor for John and anyone who truly believes in Jesus to be a part of God's family and live forever with Him in His Kingdom. John announced the coming Kingdom of God, but what a joy and honor and blessing it will be to *live* in God's Kingdom! **Someday Jesus will reign in a new Kingdom**—a Kingdom without sin and sickness, evil, and death. All those who are trusting in Jesus as their Savior will reign with Him! And that will be greater than anything that we can ever experience on earth.

Some of the people who met Jesus did not believe that He is the Son of God, and they rejected Him. Others were confused. Was Jesus a prophet, a good teacher, a miracle worker? They really weren't sure who Jesus is. But some BELIEVED! They had faith that Jesus is the Son of God, the Savior. What group are you in?

Do you want to trust in Jesus and live forever in His new Kingdom? "Do not fear, only believe." *Believe that Jesus is the Son of God, the Savior of the world. Believe that He can fully pay for your sins and give you His righteousness. Believe that He is coming again to bring those who are trusting in Him into His wonderful new Kingdom!*

> "Not everyone who says to me, 'Lord, Lord,' will enter the kingdom of heaven, but the one who does the will of my Father who is in heaven." (Matthew 7:21)

THAT YOU MAY BELIEVE

What does this chapter tell us about God?

Talk about and apply the **biblical truths** in **bold** text. Make them personal and apply them to what is happening in your family, church, community, or the world today.

Jesus was delayed in going to help Jairus's daughter when the sick woman touched His garment. How was this God's good plan?

Talk About: *"Not everyone who says to me, 'Lord, Lord,' will enter the kingdom of heaven, but the one who does the will of my Father who is in heaven." (Matthew 7:21)*

Is Matthew 7:21 a scary verse to you? Why or why not? What is "the will" of God? (You may want to look back at Chapter 105.) *What is the Kingdom of God like?*

Pray: Thank God for His coming Kingdom. Praise Him for having power over all things. Ask Him to give you a strong faith in Him.

Think About: *Do I have the kind of faith the woman with the bleeding disease had? How is this seen in my life?*

CHAPTER 111
JESUS IS THE BREAD OF LIFE THAT SATISFIES FOREVER

Jesus, the Bread of Life, Feeds Five Thousand— John 6; Matthew 14:13-21

…"This is the work of God, that you believe in him whom he has sent." (John 6:29)

When Jesus heard of the death of John the Baptist, He went to a "desolate place" to be alone. Surely, He mourned the loss of His cousin and the brokenness of this world caused by sin. It would be good to be alone. It would be good to pour out His heart to His Father. However, a large crowd followed Him…mostly because they saw His healing miracles. But Jesus didn't tell them to leave Him alone. Instead, Jesus saw their brokenness. He had compassion on them and healed the sick.

Evening came and people were hungry. So the disciples asked Jesus to send the crowd away to get their own food. *Do you know how Jesus answered them?* Jesus told them to give the people food.

This was an impossible situation. The disciples didn't have enough money to buy food for such a large crowd—a crowd of 5,000 men, plus women and children! It would take all the money earned in eight months to feed the crowd! Andrew told Jesus, *"There is a boy here who has five barley loaves and two fish, but what are they for so many?"* Indeed, what are five loaves and two fish with so many people to feed? But it wasn't just five loaves and two fish. It was five loaves and two fish in the hands of Jesus.

Jesus told the disciples to tell the people to sit down. Then He took the loaves and fish, looked up to heaven, and thanked His Father for them. Then Jesus, the Son of God, provided food for all the people! The disciples started passing out the bread and fish...and bread and fish... and bread and fish...and the food never ran out! Everyone ate as much as he wanted. Then Jesus told the disciples to pick up the leftover food. The leftovers alone filled twelves baskets! Jesus had not only provided enough for the people; He provided *more* than enough! **Jesus fully satisfies. He is more than enough.**

When the people saw the miraculous multiplication of food, they said, *"This is indeed the Prophet who is to come into the world!"* Jesus knew what was in their minds and hearts. They wanted to make Him the king who would free them from the rule of the Romans. But Jesus didn't come to be an earthly king with an earthly kingdom. So Jesus told His disciples to get into a boat and cross the Sea of Galilee, and He went up into the hills to pray by Himself.

When Jesus finished praying, the disciples were in the boat halfway across the lake. Jesus could see that the wind was pushing against them and they were having a hard time crossing the lake. Jesus, the Maker of the sea and wind and waves, walked across on the water to meet them. *But when the disciples saw him walking on the sea, they were terrified, and said, "It is a ghost!" and they cried out in fear. But immediately Jesus spoke to them, saying, "Take heart; it is I. Do not be afraid."*

"It is I" is actually "I Am" in the original language of the Bible. *Where have we seen that before?* It is the name God told to Moses as His personal name. When Jesus said, "I Am," He was not just letting the disciples know that it was Him on the water; He was letting them know that He is God.

> *And Peter answered him, "Lord, if it is you, command me to come to you on the water." He said, "Come." So Peter got out of the boat and walked on the water and came to Jesus. But when he saw the wind, he was afraid, and beginning to sink he cried out, "Lord, save me." Jesus immediately reached out his hand and took hold of him, saying to him, "O you of little faith, why did you doubt?" And when they got into the boat, the wind ceased. And those in the boat worshiped him, saying, "Truly you are the Son of God." (Matthew 14:28-33)*

Jesus truly is the Son of God. And when He got in the boat, "immediately the boat was at the land to which they were going." However, the crowd was on the other side of the sea. So when they realized that Jesus had left, they hurried to find Him. When they found Jesus, He had a serious word for them:

> *Jesus answered them, "Truly, truly, I say to you, you are seeking me, not because you saw signs, but because you ate your fill of the loaves.* **Do not work for the food that perishes, but for the food that endures to eternal life,** *which the Son of Man will give to you. For on him God the Father has set his seal." (John 6:26-27)*

"Truly, truly"—"I tell you the truth." Jesus spoke very honestly to the people. They needed to hear their true spiritual condition. They loved the miracles of Jesus—the healings, deliverance from demons, the loaves and fishes—but they missed the "signs." The miracles were like lighted signs saying, **"JESUS IS THE MESSIAH. JESUS IS GOD. JESUS IS THE GREAT TREASURE WHO SATISFIES EVERY LONGING."** They loved the miracles...but not the Miracle-Maker. They marveled at Jesus's miracles...but they did not worship Him. They wanted the physical food—the bread and fish. But they didn't want the "spiritual food"—Jesus the Savior who could save them from the wrath of God against sin and give them eternal life. They wanted an earthly king to deliver them from Roman rule; but they had no desire for a heavenly king, the King Eternal, to deliver them from their hearts of stone. So Jesus pleaded with them not to *work for food that perishes*—not to desire and strive for the earthly things that don't last. Instead, they should work for spiritual blessing that leads to eternal life.

The people answered Jesus, *"What must we do, to be doing the works of God?"* They didn't understand that they could not be saved by their good works. They could not inherit heaven by being "good enough." *Jesus answered them, "This is the work of God, that you believe in him whom he has sent."* **Salvation comes through faith in Christ alone.** Man cannot save himself. Jesus' answer was simply, "Trust Me." **God wants people to believe in His Son whom He sent to pay for man's sin.**

The people had seen Jesus heal the sick and multiply loaves and fishes, but they still asked for another sign so they could believe in Him! They still thought of Jesus as another prophet, like Moses, who gave them manna from heaven. But Jesus corrected them—*God* had given them manna, not Moses, and now God was giving "the true bread from heaven."

> Jesus said to them, *"I am the bread of life; whoever comes to me shall not hunger, and whoever believes in me shall never thirst. But I said to you that you have seen me and yet do not believe. All that the Father gives me will come to me, and whoever comes to me I will never cast out."* (John 6:35-37)

Why did Jesus call Himself "the bread of life"? Jesus is God, "I Am," the One who gives joy-filled life and eternal life. Believing in Jesus will satisfy a person's hunger and thirst to be made righteous. But the people just couldn't and didn't want to understand Jesus. They were talking about physical things while Jesus was talking about spiritual things. Jesus reminded them that their ancestors had eaten manna in the wilderness, and they had died. But Jesus is the living bread, and whoever eats the living bread will live forever. The "bread" that Jesus was offering was His very life. Jesus would give His life so that man could live forever.

Sadly, the people just got angry and began to grumble. Many of the people who were following Jesus didn't like what Jesus was saying. They were offended that they could not come to God by their own efforts, by their own good works. They didn't like Jesus' claim that *"no one can come to me unless it is granted him by the Father."* Jesus was saying that they were spiritually blind and unable to see that He was the way to salvation. So they indignantly walked away. They no longer wanted to follow Jesus.

Jesus turned to His twelve disciples and said, *"Do you want to go away as well?" Simon Peter answered him, "Lord, to whom shall we go? You have the words of eternal life, and we have believed, and have come to know, that you are the Holy One of God."*

There are two kinds of people in the world. Those who simply want physical bread—all that this world has to offer; and those who want spiritual bread—all that God has to offer. Those who believe in Jesus, and those who don't. Which kind are you?

> **Jesus said to them, "I am the bread of life; whoever comes to me shall not hunger, and whoever believes in me shall never thirst." (John 6:35)**
>
> **"All that the Father gives me will come to me, and whoever comes to me I will never cast out." (John 6:37)**

THAT YOU MAY BELIEVE

What does this chapter tell us about God?

Talk about and apply the **biblical truths** in **bold** text. Make them personal and apply them to what is happening in your family, church, community, or the world today.

Our sinful hearts naturally love the things that Jesus can give us and love this world instead of long for Jesus Himself and spiritual things. How can you tell if you love Jesus Himself and not just the good things God gives you?

Talk About: *Jesus said to them, "I am the bread of life; whoever comes to me shall not hunger, and whoever believes in me shall never thirst." (John 6:35)*

What is Jesus promising in John 6:37? What does this tell you about Jesus?

Pray: Praise God for giving life. Thank Him for sending Jesus to receive the punishment sinners deserve. Thank God for the promise of eternal life with Him through faith in Jesus. Ask God to give you a hunger for spiritual things and to draw you to Himself.

Think About: *What is my relationship with God?*

CHAPTER 112

JESUS IS GOD'S SON WHO CAME TO DIE AND BUILD HIS CHURCH

Jesus Foretells His Death and Describes a True Disciple; Jesus' Transfiguration—Matthew 16:13-17:13; Luke 9:28-36

..."If anyone would come after me, let him deny himself and take up his cross and follow me. For whoever would save his life will lose it, but whoever loses his life for my sake will find it." (Matthew 16:24-25)

"Who do you think he is?" "I think he is a prophet." "No, he must be John the Baptist come back to life." The whispered conversations and the energetic debates continued. The crowd was surely confused. The people saw the miracles that Jesus did. They knew He wasn't an ordinary person. But who was He?

Jesus asked His disciples about this, *"Who do people say that the Son of Man is?"* They had heard different answers—John the Baptist, Elijah, Jeremiah, one of the other prophets. But what Jesus really wanted the disciples to confess was what *they* thought about Him. Did the disciples really know who Jesus is and why He came to earth?

He said to them, "But who do you say that I am?" Simon Peter replied, **"You are the Christ, the Son of the living God."** *And Jesus answered him, "Blessed are you, Simon Bar-Jonah! For flesh and blood has not revealed this to you, but my Father who is in heaven." (Matthew 16:15-17)*

Peter was convinced that Jesus was the Christ—the "anointed One," the Messiah who would save His people. **Only God can show a person who Jesus truly is** with such a strong belief that he is convinced of the truth. Peter's answer gave Jesus great joy! *"And I tell you, you are Peter, and on this rock I will build my church, and the gates of hell shall not prevail against it."* Simon Peter was chosen by God to bring God's message of salvation through faith in Christ. God had a special work for Simon Peter, and Jesus now told Peter that He was gathering a people for God—a new Israel. He was gathering a people with new hearts of faith, and His disciples were part of that great work.

After this, Jesus started to prepare His disciples for what was ahead. He told them that He had to go to Jerusalem. The religious leaders there would cause much suffering for Jesus. In fact, they would put Him to death. But three days later, He would rise from the dead.

What? This couldn't be! Wasn't the Messiah going to deliver the Jews from foreign rule? Wouldn't He defeat the Romans and make Israel its own nation again? Peter decided he needed to correct Jesus. So he went to Jesus privately and scolded Him saying, *"Far be it from you, Lord! This shall never happen to you."* It seems like Peter was trying to protect or encourage Jesus. Surely the Messiah wouldn't die! But Peter still did not really understand why Jesus had come to earth.

Jesus is the Son of God, and He came to do what only God can do. Jesus didn't come just to heal the bodies of sick people. **Jesus came to heal people's souls and break the power of sin. Jesus came to obey His Father's will perfectly.** Anything that would tempt Jesus away from dying on the cross was a temptation from Satan. Jesus *turned and said to Peter, "Get behind me, Satan! You are a hindrance to me. For you are not setting your mind on the things of God, but on the things of man."*

His disciples had so much to learn about what it means to be a true disciple—what it means to be a follower of Christ. It is not about worldly goals or being comfortable. It is a life of obedience and willingness to do what God has planned, following wherever He leads. *And calling the crowd to him with his disciples, he said to them:*

"If anyone would come after me, let him deny himself and take up his cross and follow me. For whoever would save his life

*will lose it, but whoever loses his life for my sake will find it. For what will it profit a man if he gains the whole world and forfeits his soul? Or what shall a man give in return for his soul?"..."For whoever is ashamed of me and of my words in this adulterous and sinful generation, of him will the Son of Man also be ashamed when he comes in the glory of his Father with the holy angels."...***"For the Son of Man is going to come with his angels in the glory of his Father, and then he will repay each person according to what he has done."** *(Mark 8:34-35; Matthew 16:24-26; Mark 8:38; Matthew 16:27)*

Jesus would build the true Church of God through His disciples. His followers would be more concerned about God and His Kingdom than about their own interests. A true disciple of Jesus is committed to following Jesus and standing on the truth of God's Word, even if it brings suffering. And he continues to follow Jesus his whole life without turning away. Jesus spoke about a wonderful promise He gives to true Christians who follow Him faithfully—a promise for those who are not ashamed to be called a Christian and stand up for what God says is right. They will receive a reward from Jesus when He returns.

But this did not at all fit with what the Jews thought about the Messiah. All this talk about Jesus being put to death must have shaken the disciples' weak faith. This talk about taking up their cross and losing their life didn't fit with defeating the Romans' rule. Wasn't the Messiah going to restore Israel? Jesus was the Son of God…wasn't He?

Jesus knew the disciples were confused. He knew they needed to be reassured about who He is so they would have the faith to carry them through the coming days. So Jesus brought Peter, James, and John up to a high mountain to pray. *And as he was praying, the appearance of his face was altered [changed], and his clothing became dazzling white…he was transfigured before them, and his face shone like the sun, and his clothes became white as light…And behold, two men were talking with him, Moses and Elijah, who appeared in glory and spoke of his departure, which he was about to accomplish at Jerusalem.*

This must have been a wonderful, amazing, and yet terrifying sight for the disciples to watch! The radiant light and dazzling white must have been astounding! Jesus' work on earth was coming to an end, and now these three disciples saw a little glimpse of Jesus in His glory. *Can you imagine what Peter, James, and John must have thought of all this?*

Peter, always the one to jump in first, said he would make three tents—one for Jesus, one for Moses, and one for Elijah. We don't really know what Peter was thinking, but as he was talking, *a bright cloud came and overshadowed them… and a voice came out of the cloud saying, "This is my Son, my Chosen*

One; listen to him." God Himself spoke and proved that Jesus is His Son—just as He did when Jesus was baptized by John the Baptist.

What do you think the disciples did when they heard the voice of God? They fell on their faces and were terrified. But Jesus went over and gently touched them. He told them to get up and to not be afraid. When the disciples opened their eyes, only Jesus was there. Elijah and Moses were gone.[16] On the way down the mountain, Jesus told the disciples not to tell anyone about what happened "until the Son of Man is raised from the dead." What could this mean? The disciples were confused. They still did not really understand what would happen to Jesus in Jerusalem. But they had the witness of Elijah, Moses, and God Himself to prove that **Jesus is the Son of God.**

Do you truly believe that Jesus is God's Son who came to save sinners? Are you willing to "deny yourself" and follow Jesus your whole life? Is Jesus your greatest treasure?

> Indeed, I count everything as loss because of the surpassing worth of knowing Christ Jesus my Lord. For his sake I have suffered the loss of all things and count them as rubbish, in order that I may gain Christ and be found in him, not having a righteousness of my own that comes from the law, but that which comes through faith in Christ, the righteousness from God that depends on faith– (Philippians 3:8-9)

THAT YOU MAY BELIEVE

What does this chapter tell us about God?

Talk about and apply the **biblical truths** in **bold** text. Make them personal and apply them to what is happening in your family, church, community, or the world today.

How can you know that Jesus truly is the Son of God?

Talk About: *Indeed, I count everything as loss because of the surpassing worth of knowing Christ Jesus my Lord. For his sake I have suffered the loss of all things and count them as rubbish, in order that I may gain Christ and be found in him, not having a righteousness of my own that comes from the law, but that which comes through faith in Christ, the righteousness from God that depends on faith– (Philippians 3:8-9)*

What does it mean to be "ashamed" of Jesus and His words? Give some practical examples.

Pray: Praise God for His willingness to give up His Son and send Him to earth. Ask God to give you the desire to deny yourself, take up your cross, and follow Jesus. Ask Him to make you a faithful follower of Jesus.

Think About: *What am I willing to give up for the Kingdom of God?*

---

16 Although Moses was denied entrance into the Promised Land because of his disobedience, here was Moses standing with the transfigured Jesus in the land. God gave Moses a greater experience of being in the Promised Land with the Savior! What an amazing picture of God's grace and mercy. But even greater, Moses had the Promised Land of heaven!

CHAPTER 113
KINGDOM GREATNESS

Jesus Teaches Humility through Children and Stories of the Pharisee and the Tax Collector, and the Good Samaritan— Mark 9:33-37; Matthew 18:1-6; Luke 18:9-14; Luke 10:25-37

"For he who is least among you all is the one who is great." (Luke 9:48b)

Do you and your friends agree on who is the greatest baseball player, the best sports team, or the finest singer? Maybe you have even argued about this. *But have you ever wondered who is the greatest in the Kingdom of heaven?* Well, Jesus' disciples did. In fact, they were arguing among themselves about which of them was the greatest. Jesus knew about this argument, and He said something very unusual about being great in God's Kingdom. *"If anyone would be first, he must be last of all and servant of all."* Being "last" and the "servant of all" doesn't sound like greatness, does it? But it is, and the disciples needed to change the way they thought about greatness. Kingdom greatness is not like earthly greatness. **Kingdom values— what is important to God—are very different from what is important in the world.** So Jesus gave the disciples an example to help them understand true greatness. He took a child in His arms and said, *"Truly, I say to you, unless you turn and become like children, you will never enter the kingdom of heaven. Whoever humbles himself like this child is the greatest in the kingdom of heaven."*

119

Jesus used children as an example of weakness and dependence. Children know they must depend on others for food, clothing, protection, and other things. True greatness is being humble like a child and depending on God. In Jesus' day, children had a lowly position—like a servant would have. True childlike humility means not being concerned about having power or an important position.

Jesus once told a story to explain true humility. It was about two men who went to the temple to pray. One was a Pharisee—an important religious ruler. The other was a tax collector—a person despised by the Jews.

"The Pharisee, standing by himself, prayed thus: 'God, I thank you that I am not like other men, extortioners, unjust, adulterers, or even like this tax collector. I fast twice a week; I give tithes of all that I get.' But the tax collector, standing far off, would not even lift up his eyes to heaven, but beat his breast, saying, 'God, be merciful to me, a sinner!'" (Luke 18:11-13)

The proud Pharisee thought he was great and important because of the things he did or didn't do. He was depending on his "good behavior" or good works to be acceptable to God. He thought God must be quite impressed with him! But the tax collector was very different. He recognized that he had a sinful heart and needed God's mercy. He knew he had no righteousness of his own. He was humble and admitted his need for God and for forgiveness. He had true humility, and his humble, repentant heart made him great in God's eyes. In God's Kingdom, the humble tax collector will someday be exalted—He will be considered righteous by God.

But let's go back to something else Jesus taught His disciples about Kingdom greatness. Holding the child in his lap, Jesus continued, *"Whoever receives one such child in my name receives me, and whoever receives me, receives not me but him who sent me."* Do you know what "to receive one such child" means? It means to be welcoming and to show kindness. Humble people care about other people; they serve them or help them. This is being a "servant of all." When you show kindness to someone because of your love for Jesus, you are actually showing kindness to Jesus.

Do you know how Jesus described true kindness? He used a parable to explain it. You have surely heard the story before. It is a great story with a lot to teach us. Jesus told this story after a man asked Jesus how he could have eternal life. Jesus answered by asking him what God's Law says. The man was a lawyer. So he knew the Law and rightly answered, *"You shall love the Lord your God with all your heart and with all your soul and with all your strength and with all your mind, and your neighbor as yourself."* This is the Great Commandment—love God and love others. It is easy to remember…but hard to do, especially without a humble heart.

Jesus told the man that he was correct, and if he would do this and keep doing it, he would live—meaning he would have eternal life. But then the lawyer had a little problem because he knew he didn't love his neighbor like he loved himself—at least not all of them. There are some people in the world who can be very hard to love. Certainly, he thought, not all of them deserve to be loved! So he asked Jesus, *"And who is my neighbor?"*

That's when Jesus told the story. It is called the Parable of the Good Samaritan. Jesus started His story, *"A man was going down from Jerusalem to Jericho, and he fell among robbers, who stripped him and beat him and departed, leaving him half dead."*

Then Jesus talked about three men who walked down the road and saw the poor broken, beaten man…and what they did. The first man was a priest—a religious person. He had an important position. Surely, he would help the man. But no! Instead, he crossed to the other side of the road and walked by. He ignored the man. Then along came another man. He was a Levite and probably helped in the temple but was not a priest. Maybe he would help the bruised, beaten man. But he did the same thing as the priest. He walked by on the other side. Neither one had care or concern for the wounded man.

The next person was a Samaritan. *Do you remember who the Samaritans were?* The Jews would not consider them "neighbors." They hated the Samaritans because they were not "pure Jews." So why should a hated Samaritan help a Jew? It would seem likely that the Samaritan would walk by the man on the road.

But when the Samaritan saw the injured man, he had compassion on him. He cared for his wounds, pouring oil and wine on them. He kindly bandaged the man's injuries. Then the Samaritan carefully put the man on his own animal while he walked until they got to an inn. He stayed that day and cared for the man. But his kindness did not end there. The next day the Samaritan gave the owner of the inn some money and asked him to take care of the injured man. He would be coming back through after his trip. If it cost more money than he had given the innkeeper, the Samaritan would gladly pay him the rest of the money.

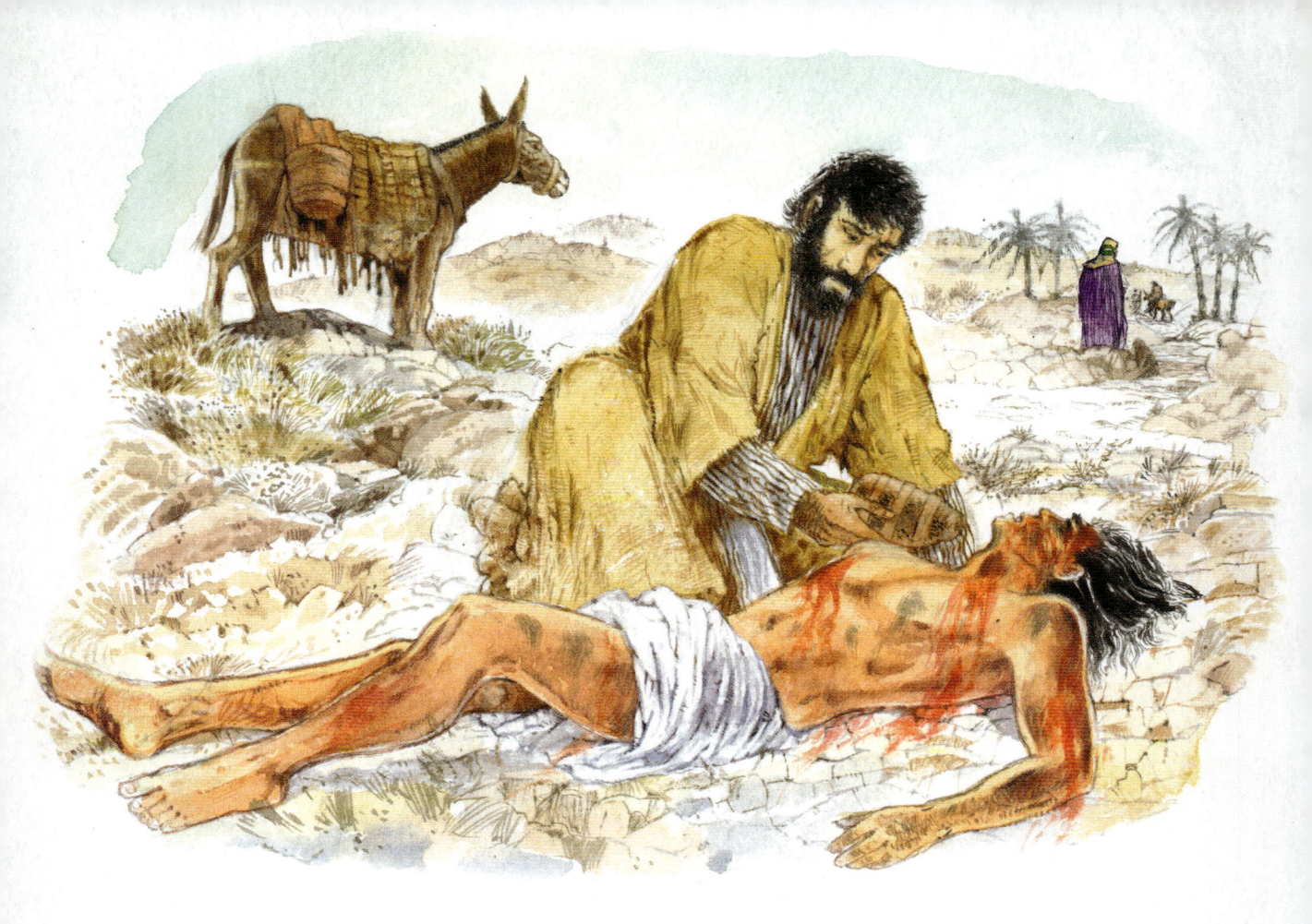

Jesus made His point when He asked, *"Which of these three, do you think proved to be a neighbor to the man who fell among the robbers?"* The lawyer naturally had to say, *"The one who showed him mercy." And Jesus said to him, "You go and do likewise."* The lawyer had wanted to find out what people he needed to consider as his neighbor—what people met the standard, who were qualified or deserved to be a neighbor to him. But Jesus was more concerned about being a loving neighbor.

A humble person does not worry if a person is "worthy" to be treated kindly. A humble person treats all people kindly. The only way a person can be like this in any way is to have the heart of Jesus—to have a changed heart. **To receive others in Jesus' name, a person must first receive Jesus as his Savior—who will give him a new heart.** Jesus will take out the heart of stone; the heart that thinks mostly about self—about "who do I have to be a neighbor to?" Jesus will replace the heart of stone with a heart of flesh—a humble heart that has compassion and *wants to be* a good neighbor.

Do you have a humble heart—one that recognizes that you are a sinner in need of God's mercy; one that has compassion on others? Have you received Jesus as your Savior and been given a new heart? What must you do to inherit eternal life?

But whoever would be great among you must be your servant, and whoever would be first among you must be your slave, even as the Son of Man came not to be served but to serve, and to give his life as a ransom for many. (Matthew 20:26b-28)

Do nothing from rivalry or conceit, but in humility count others more significant than yourselves. Let each of you look not only to his own interests, but also to the interests of others. (Philippians 2:3-4)

THAT YOU MAY BELIEVE

What does this chapter tell us about God?

Talk about and apply the **biblical truths** in **bold** text. Make them personal and apply them to what is happening in your family, church, community, or the world today.

What other titles could you give the Parable of the Good Samaritan? Can you tell a modern-day Good Samaritan story (one that could happen in your everyday life)?

Talk About: *Do nothing from rivalry or conceit, but in humility count others more significant than yourselves. Let each of you look not only to his own interests, but also to the interests of others. (Philippians 2:3-4)*

How is God's idea of greatness very different from the world's? How did Jesus, who was the greatest of all, show humility?

Pray: Thank God that His ways are higher (better) than our ways. Ask Him to give you a humble, caring heart. Confess your pride and lack of compassion. (Be specific.)

Think About: *Am I humble? Or do I see myself as better than others? Am I a good neighbor?*

CHAPTER 114

RECEIVING MERCY AND SHOWING MERCY

Parable of the Unforgiving Servant; Jesus' Teaching on Forgiveness—Matthew 18:15-35; Luke 17:11-19

Be kind to one another, tenderhearted, forgiving one another, as God in Christ forgave you. (Ephesians 4:32)

If you could ask Jesus a question, what would you ask Him? Well, Peter had a question for Jesus...and Jesus had a very strange answer for him.

The Jewish rabbis (teachers) taught that a person must forgive another person three times. But Peter had been around Jesus long enough to know that "God's ways are higher" or better than our ways. So he figured that maybe Jesus would think that three times wasn't enough. So he asked Jesus, *"Lord, how often will my brother sin against me, and I forgive him? As many as seven times?"* Peter was being generous. Seven times is more than twice as much as three times. But Jesus' answer must have shocked Peter. *Jesus said to him, "I do not say to you seven times, but seventy times seven."*

Seventy times seven! *How many times is that?* 70 x 7= 490. Four hundred and ninety times! That's a lot of forgiveness! But Jesus wasn't saying exactly 490 times...He was showing that **our forgiveness should not be limited**. In other words, we shouldn't count how many times we forgive someone; we should just forgive.

To show what He meant, Jesus told Peter a parable—a story with a special hidden meaning. The parable was about two servants who owed the king some money. The day came when the king decided it was time to collect his money. The first man who was brought to the king owed him 10,000 talents or coins. *How long do you think it took an ordinary person to earn a talent?* About fifteen years! And this man owed 10,000 talents! How long would it take to pay his debt? Let's see...10,000 talents multiplied by fifteen years...This was an enormous amount of money! More than he could ever earn in his lifetime. Or in hundreds of lifetimes! So his master, the king, ordered that he be sold...along with his wife and children...In fact, everything he had should be sold to pay his debt. *Do you know what the servant did?*

The man fell on his knees and begged his master to be patient and give him more time to pay what he owed. The king had compassion on him and let him go. Not only that, but he "forgave the debt"—which means that he erased it. The man didn't have to pay the king anything! The king showed amazing mercy to the man.

But…here is where the story gets really interesting… When the man left, he went and found a servant who owed him 100 denarii—which was only about three month's worth of earnings. *Do you know what the first man did?* He grabbed the other man and started choking him, telling him to pay him his money! Well, the second man didn't have the money. So *he* fell down and begged the man to give him more time to pay the debt. But the first man refused. He did not have compassion on the man who owed him money. He had no mercy, and he put the man in jail until his debt was paid.

The rest of the king's servants were very upset when they learned what had happened. They went to their master and told him about it. *Do you know what happened then?*

> "Then his master summoned him and said to him, 'You wicked servant! I forgave you all that debt because you pleaded with me. And should not you have

125

had mercy on your fellow servant, as I had mercy on you?' And in anger his master delivered him to the jailers, until he should pay all his debt." (Matthew 18:32-34)

Then Jesus said something very frightening. You see, Jesus wasn't just telling a story, He was teaching an important spiritual truth.

"So also my heavenly Father will do to every one of you, if you do not forgive your brother from your heart." (Matthew 18:35)

Why couldn't the first servant forgive the man who owed him money? He couldn't forgive the small debt owed him because he was not grateful for the mercy shown to him. He really did not have a heart understanding of how much he had been forgiven—perhaps he even thought he deserved to be forgiven. But his debt was huge, and the mercy shown to him should have resulted in overflowing mercy to others.

Jesus' story shows how serious His warning is. **Sinners who have been forgiven by God have been forgiven a debt they could never repay—ever.** But God is merciful to forgive huge mountains of sins against Him. A person who does not forgive others, doesn't really see the seriousness of his sin and is very ungrateful for mercy. He is not a true follower of Jesus, and God will not forgive him. **Those who are grateful for mercy, eagerly show mercy to others.** *Are you grateful for God's mercy—His mercy toward sinners in forgiving sin and His mercies that "are new every morning"?*

When Jesus was on earth, He was a living example of mercy. One time, Jesus entered a village and ten lepers saw Him and called to him from a distance. *"Jesus, Master, have mercy on us."* How did Jesus respond to them?

Jesus responded with mercy. He told them to go show themselves to the priests. Only the priests could determine that a leper no longer had leprosy. As they were going to see the priests...they...were...healed!

Then one of them, when he saw that he was healed, turned back, praising God with a loud voice; and he fell on his face at Jesus' feet, giving him thanks. Now he was a Samaritan. (Luke 17:15-16)

This was a man who truly understood that he had been given undeserved mercy. He was so grateful that he turned right around and bowed at Jesus' feet with sincere words of thanks. But what had happened to the other men?

Then Jesus answered, "Were not ten cleansed? Where are the nine? Was no one found to return and give praise to God except this foreigner?" And he said to him, "Rise and go your way; your faith has made you well." (Luke 17:17-19)

How easy it is to forget the mercy of God. How easy it is to feel that mercy is deserved and fail to thank God every single day for His goodness to us. **When we truly understand God's mercy toward us, we have grateful and forgiving hearts.**

Are you truly grateful to God? Do you thank God for His mercy toward you? Do you forgive others easily, knowing you have been forgiven much? How do you respond when others wrong you? Do you hold a grudge, or are you quick to forgive? Does it scare you that if you do not forgive others God will not forgive you?

> Put on then, as God's chosen ones, holy and beloved, compassionate hearts, kindness, humility, meekness, and patience, bearing with one another and, if one has a complaint against another, forgiving each other; as the Lord has forgiven you, so you also must forgive. (Colossians 3:12-13)

THAT YOU MAY BELIEVE

What does this chapter tell us about God?

Talk about and apply the **biblical truths** in **bold** text. Make them personal and apply them to what is happening in your family, church, community, or the world today.

Make a list of mercies God has shown you today or this week. Are any of these deserved?

Why does Luke tell us that leper who came back to see Jesus was a Samaritan?

Talk About: *Put on then, as God's chosen ones, holy and beloved, compassionate hearts, kindness, humility, meekness, and patience, bearing with one another and, if one has a complaint against another, forgiving each other; as the Lord has forgiven you, so you also must forgive. (Colossians 3:12-13)*

Can you "put on" true compassion, kindness, humility, meekness, and patience without the work of the Holy Spirit in your heart? Explain.

Pray: Praise God for being a merciful God. Thank Him for the mercies He has shown you. Confess any ingratitude, unforgiveness, or pride (feeling you deserve God's mercy). Ask God to give you a truly grateful heart.

Think About: *Does my life show that I am grateful for God's mercy? Is there anyone I must forgive?*

CHAPTER 115

JESUS WELCOMES PEOPLE INTO HIS KINGDOM

Jesus Welcomes Children; the Parables of the Lost Sheep, Lost Coin, and Prodigal Son—Mark 10:13-16; Luke 15

"Just so, I tell you, there is joy before the angels of God over one sinner who repents." (Luke 15:10)

Many people came to Jesus. Some came to hear His teaching. Some came for healing. Some came just because they were curious. Others came to find fault with Jesus. Even parents came bringing their children so that Jesus could pray for them. When the disciples saw the parents bringing their children, the disciples scolded them. Perhaps they thought Jesus was too important to bother with children.

But when Jesus saw it, he was indignant and said to them, "Let the children come to me; do not hinder them, for to such belongs the kingdom of God. Truly, I say to you, whoever does not receive the kingdom of God like a child shall not enter it." And he took them in his arms and blessed them, laying his hands on them. (Mark 10:14-16)

Jesus welcomed all kinds of people—lepers, Samaritans, paralyzed and blind people, even tax collectors. However, the Pharisees and scribes complained and grumbled about Jesus. They really did *not* like the way He welcomed all kinds of people. They criticized Jesus saying, *"This man receives sinners and eats with them."* This was totally against all their rules about befriending and eating with "unclean" people. They just couldn't understand Jesus at all! So Jesus told them a few parables to show the heart of God.

The Parable of the Lost Sheep

"What man of you, having a hundred sheep, if he has lost one of them, does not leave the ninety-nine in the open country, and go after the one that is lost, until he finds it? And when he has found it, he lays it on his shoulders, rejoicing. And when he comes home, he calls together his friends and his neighbors, saying to them, 'Rejoice with me, for I have found my sheep that was lost.'" (Luke 15:4-6)

The Parable of the Lost Coin

"Or what woman, having ten silver coins, if she loses one coin, does not light a lamp and sweep the house and seek diligently until she finds it? And when she has found it, she calls together her friends and neighbors, saying, 'Rejoice with me, for I have found the coin that I had lost.' Just so, I tell you, there is joy before the angels of God over one sinner who repents." (Luke 15:8-10)

The Prodigal Son

Jesus also told a story about a man who had two sons. The younger son wanted to leave home and be on his own. So he asked his father to give him the money that his father had stored up for his inheritance. A few days later, the son took all his things and traveled far away. He foolishly wasted all his money there on "wild living," doing all kinds of wrong things. Then after all his money was gone, there was a famine. He had no money and no food. So he had to get a job. *Do you know what kind of job he got?*

His job was to feed a man's pigs. He was so hungry himself that he actually wanted to eat the pigs' food! But no one gave him anything. He was all alone and very hungry. Finally, he realized that his father's servants had plenty of food to eat, but he was starving! So he decided to go home thinking, *"I will arise and go to my father, and I will say to him, 'Father, I have sinned against heaven and before you. I am no longer worthy to be called your son. Treat me as one of your hired servants.'"*

So he started on his way home. Before he even got home, "while he was still a long way off" his father saw him. (I wonder if the father had been looking for him...wondering if he would come home...hoping he would come

130

home.) *Do you know what the father did when he saw his son?* He *"felt compassion, and ran and embraced him and kissed him."* How he had missed his son. How much he loved his son. He was so glad his son was back!

"And the son said to him, 'Father, I have sinned against heaven and before you. I am no longer worthy to be called your son.'" The son was humble and repentant. He knew he had sinned and hurt his father. He knew he did not deserve any mercy.

> *"But the father said to his servants, 'Bring quickly the best robe, and put it on him, and put a ring on his hand, and shoes on his feet. And bring the fattened calf and kill it, and let us eat and celebrate. For this my son was dead, and is alive again; he was lost, and is found.' And they began to celebrate." (Luke 15:22-24)*

His father welcomed him back…not as a servant but as his son! He fully forgave his son and celebrated his return! What a happy, joyful day this was!

However, when the older brother came in from the field and heard the music and dancing, he wondered what was going on. After finding out from one of the servants that his brother was back and his father was celebrating, he was not happy at all. He was angry and jealous. In fact, he was so mad, he wouldn't even go in the house! He was not going to celebrate his brother's return.

His father came out to him and asked him to come in and celebrate. But instead of coming in, the older son complained. *"Look, these many years I have served you, and I never disobeyed your command, yet you never gave me a young goat, that I might celebrate with my friends. But when this son of yours came, who has devoured your property…you killed the fattened calf for him!"* He knew his rebellious younger brother had lived a sinful life while he faithfully served his father as a good son. It didn't seem fair that his father would have a party for his brother!

But his father said to him, *"Son, you are always with me, and all that is mine is yours. It was fitting to celebrate and be glad, for this your brother was dead, and is alive; he was lost, and is found."*

Why did Jesus tell these stories? He had been criticized by the Pharisees for being a friend of sinners. Yet sinful people were coming to Jesus to repent. God always rejoices when people humbly repent and come to Him. What a wonderful thing to celebrate! God welcomes repentant sinners with great joy!

But the Pharisees and other religious leaders were like the older brother. They were prideful and resented Jesus' attention to sinners. They didn't want to welcome sinners, and they refused to accept Jesus' offer to repent and be saved. **Jesus' invitation to come into His Father's eternal Kingdom was an offer for everyone**. The Pharisees, however, were trusting in their works—what they did for God. But their works were not done out of love for God or trust in His grace.

God called Abraham and his descendants to be a blessing to all nations. The Jews should have rejoiced that God was inviting all peoples to enter His Kingdom. They should have rejoiced that **God welcomes repentant sinners**. But many of them didn't. How sad it is that they did not reflect the Father's heart.

You, too, can be proud of your "faithfulness." That you "have been good." But that is not a true relationship with God. A true relationship with God begins with understanding that you need God—that you "have sinned and are not worthy to be called His son." Jesus welcomes anyone who comes to Him in repentance and faith. Have you come to Him to be saved?

"For the Son of Man came to seek and to save the lost." (Luke 19:10)

But God, being rich in mercy, because of the great love with which he loved us, even when we were dead in our trespasses, made us alive together with Christ—by grace you have been saved— (Ephesians 2:4-5)

THAT YOU MAY BELIEVE

What does this chapter tell us about God?

Talk about and apply the **biblical truths** in **bold** text. Make them personal and apply them to what is happening in your family, church, community, or the world today.

What do these parables tell you about God's heart for people? Why would "A Faithful Father" be a fitting title for the Parable of the Prodigal Son?

Talk About: *But God, being rich in mercy, because of the great love with which he loved us, even when we were dead in our trespasses, made us alive together with Christ—by grace you have been saved— (Ephesians 2:4-5)*

What does it mean not to trust in your good works but to trust in the work of Jesus on the cross? Does this mean it is not right to be good?

Pray: Praise God for being a faithful Father. Thank Him for welcoming sinners. Confess your pride in "being good." Ask Jesus to give you a heart that trusts in Him alone.

Think About: *Am I like the older brother in the Parable of the Prodigal Son?*

CHAPTER 116

JESUS AND TWO KINDS OF BLINDNESS

Rich Young Ruler; Bartimaeus; Zacchaeus—
Mark 10:17-31; Luke 18:35-19:10

"No one can serve two masters, for either he will hate the one and love the other, or he will be devoted to the one and despise the other. You cannot serve God and money." (Matthew 6:24)

Do you remember that Jesus was on His way to Jerusalem? Well, on the way, God had some other work for Jesus to do. He had three men for Jesus to meet.

A rich young man came up to Jesus to ask Him a question. *Do you know what he called Jesus?* Good Teacher. *"Good Teacher, what must I do to inherit eternal life?"* He wanted to know what he had to do to go to heaven. But there were some things wrong with his thinking. So Jesus needed to correct his thinking. *"Why do you call me good? No one is good except God alone."* Jesus said that only God is *truly* good. Did the young man believe that Jesus is God? No. He simply said words without thinking about them. He didn't understand that to be *truly* "good," a person has to be without sin and keep God's Law perfectly.

Then Jesus reminded the rich young man about the Ten Commandments. *Can you tell me some of the commandments?* Some of them are do not murder, do not steal, do not tell lies about others, and honor your father and your mother.

Do you know what that foolish young man said to Jesus? "Teacher, I have obeyed all the commandments, ever since I was little." *Do you think he really kept all the commandments all his life?* No, he really didn't think rightly about his own life. He was blind to his own sin. His eyes worked fine, but he was *spiritually blind*. He did not see when he disobeyed God's Law in his heart. He thought he was truly good, even though Jesus had told him that *only God* is truly good.

Jesus is God. And **God knows everything.** Jesus knew all about this young man's heart and what he loved most of all. He knew how the young man broke the commandments. Jesus loved the rich young man and knew he needed to see the truth about his heart and about his sin. And Jesus truly is a good teacher. So Jesus said to the young man, *"You lack one thing: go, sell all that you have and give to the poor, and you will have treasure in heaven; and come, follow me."* Jesus was sad because He knew that the young man did not love God most of all. God was not his treasure. Money was his treasure. His love for money was greater than his love for God. The young man thought he was good and that he kept all the commandments, but Jesus showed him that he was breaking the very first commandment (and many others, too). *Do you remember the first commandment?* It says, *"You shall have no other gods before me."* Do you know what the young man did next?

He went away sad. He did not want to give up all his money and things. He could not make himself love God most of all. He could not *do* what was needed to have eternal life.

Jesus looked at His disciples and said, *"How difficult it will be for those who have wealth to enter the kingdom of God!...It is easier for a camel to go through the eye of a needle than for a rich person to enter the kingdom of God"*! Easier for a camel to go through the eye of a needle? *Do you think a camel could go through the hole of a sewing needle?*

The disciples were surprised by what Jesus said, and they asked Jesus, *"Then who can be saved?"* How could anyone get to heaven? Just as it is impossible for a camel to go through the hole of a needle, it is impossible for anyone to get to heaven by himself.

But Jesus had good news for this most awful problem. *"With man it is impossible, but not with God. For all things are possible with God."* Man cannot *do* anything to get to heaven. He cannot keep the commandments perfectly—obeying all of them all the time. He cannot even obey the first commandment to love God most of all. It is impossible for man. But **God has made a way for sinners to have eternal life**. And it is not by anything man can do, but by what God does. God can change the heart of any sinful man. God can make a man treasure Him most of all. God can help a man trust in Him instead of in money. God can give a man faith to believe that Jesus is the Son of God and not just a good teacher. God can make a *blind* man see his sin and know that he is *not* truly good.

And God can give sinful men real treasure in heaven. Jesus told the disciples that whoever leaves a house or family to follow Him will have a great treasure in heaven—a treasure that is ten times more than he had before!

On the way to Jerusalem, Jesus met another blind man and another rich man. This blind man was *physically blind*—he could not see. The blind man was named Bartimaeus. He was sitting by the side of the road yelling to Jesus, *"Son of David, have mercy on me."* Do you remember why Jesus is called Son of David? The man called Jesus this because Jesus was born into David's family. Bartimaeus knew that Jesus is the Messiah, the Son of David, the Son of God. There was a crowd around Jesus—everyone was trying to get Jesus' attention. All Bartimaeus could do was to try to yell above the noise of the crowd. The people in front of Bartimaeus told him to be quiet. *But he cried out all the more...And Jesus stopped and commanded him to be brought to him.* Jesus paid attention to Bartimaeus. He didn't tell him to be quiet. Instead, Jesus asked Bartimaeus what he wanted Jesus to do for him. Bartimaeus wanted to see, and Jesus said to him, *"Recover your sight; your faith has made you well." And immediately he recovered his sight and followed him, glorifying God.* Bartimaeus may have had blind eyes, but He was not *spiritually blind* like the rich young ruler. He saw and had faith in who Jesus truly is.

The other rich man Jesus met was named Zacchaeus. He was in a crowd of people waiting for Jesus to walk by, and he was a tax collector. *Do you remember what a tax collector was, and why many of them were rich?* A tax collector collected taxes for the government. They were usually rich because they told the people that they had to pay more money than they really had to pay. Then they took the extra money and kept it for themselves.

This tax collector was shorter than most men, and he had a hard time seeing over the crowd of people. So Zacchaeus ran ahead of the crowd and ahead of Jesus and climbed up into a tree so that he could see Jesus when Jesus passed by. But Jesus didn't pass by. He stopped. And He looked up into the tree. And Jesus called Zacchaeus by name. *"Zacchaeus, hurry and come down, for I must stay at your house today."* Jesus did not turn away from tax collectors like other people did. Jesus wanted to visit with Zacchaeus! The crowd grumbled against Jesus because Jesus wanted to go to the house of a sinner. They were blind to their own sin, just like the rich young man was blind to his own sin. They were all sinners, not just Zacchaeus!

Zacchaeus did not go away sad like the rich young ruler had. He hurried down the tree and joyfully greeted Jesus! He told Jesus, "Half of what I have, I want to give to poor people. And anyone I took too much money from, I want to give him back four times as much money as I took." Zacchaeus was not blind to his sin—he saw his sin and wanted to turn away from it! He repented of his sin.

God had given Zacchaeus faith in Jesus. And Jesus gave Zacchaeus a heart to love Him more than money. What was impossible for Zacchaeus to do, God did for him! And Jesus said, *"Today salvation has come to this house."* Zacchaeus was a true son of Abraham by faith. Zacchaeus was saved from his sins. His heart was changed because Jesus, the Son of Man, the Son of David, the Son of God, the Messiah, came to seek and to save the lost. **Jesus came to save lost sinners** like Zacchaeus.

Do you see your sin? Do you love God more than anything else?

> ..."With man it is impossible, but not with God. For all
> things are possible with God." (Mark 10:27b)

THAT YOU MAY BELIEVE

What does this chapter tell us about God?

Talk about and apply the **biblical truths** in **bold** text. Make them personal and apply them to what is happening in your family, church, community, or the world today.

Share with your child how God opened your eyes to your sin and your need of Him.

Talk About: *"No one can serve two masters, for either he will hate the one and love the other, or he will be devoted to the one and despise the other. You cannot serve God and money." (Matthew 6:24)*

Explain the two kinds of blindness.

Pray: *Who are some lost people you know?* Thank Jesus that He came to save sinners. Ask Him to save the lost people.

Think About: *Everyone is either storing up treasures on earth or treasures in heaven. Identify some treasure you can store up in heaven. Identify some treasure you can store up on earth. Where are you storing up treasures?*

Memorize: Matthew 6:24a

CHAPTER 117
DO YOU BELIEVE IN THE SON OF MAN?

Jesus Gives a Blind Man Physical and Spiritual Sight—John 9

"...One thing I do know, that though I was blind, now I see." (John 9:25b)

Sickness is a consequence of the Fall, of Adam's and Eve's sin. *But does that mean that every sickness is because of someone's sin?* Jesus' disciples must have thought so because when they saw a man who had been blind since birth, they asked Jesus who had sinned. Had the man or his parents sinned and caused his blindness?

> *Jesus answered, "It was not that this man sinned, or his parents, but that the works of God might be displayed in him. We must work the works of him who sent me while it is day; night is coming, when no one can work. As long as I am in the world,* **I am the light of the world.***" (John 9:3-5)*

Jesus was not like the Pharisee or the Levite in the story of the Good Samaritan, who passed by someone with a problem. He came to bring light into a world dark with sin and sickness and evil. And He would bring light to this blind man! So Jesus spit on the ground and mixed in dirt to make mud. This seems like a strange thing to do. Then Jesus put the mud on the man's eyes and told him to wash in the Pool of Siloam. The blind man obeyed Jesus. He went to wash his eyes...*and came back seeing!* Jesus, the light of the world, gave sight to blind eyes!

But now people were confused. Was this the same blind beggar, or was this someone else? Some people thought it was the blind man; others thought it couldn't be. It must be someone who looked like him. But the man whom Jesus had healed told them he was the man who had been blind. If this was true, how could he see now? The man told them what Jesus did and how his eyes were healed.

Since the people couldn't find Jesus, they brought the man to the Pharisees. Naturally, the Pharisees wanted to know how the man had been healed. Once again, the man explained what Jesus had done. Then an argument broke out among the Pharisees! Since Jesus had healed the man on the Sabbath, some said that Jesus could not have been sent from God. But others didn't think it was possible that a sinner could do the signs Jesus did. What about the man who had been blind...what did he think? He replied that Jesus was a prophet.

But the Jews still did not believe that Jesus had healed this man. They went and asked the parents if this man was really their son who had been blind. Yes, he was their son. Then the people wanted to know how he could now see. The Jews had decided earlier that anyone who believed that Jesus was the Messiah would not be allowed to go to the synagogue. So the parents were afraid to tell the people that Jesus had healed him. *His parents answered, "We know that this is our son and that he was born blind. But how he now sees we do not know, nor do we know who opened his eyes. Ask him; he is of age. He will speak for himself."*

So, for the second time, they called the man who had been blind and questioned him about Jesus. *He answered, "Whether he is a sinner I do not know. One thing I do know, that though I was blind, now I see." They said to him, "What did he do to you? How did he open your eyes?" He answered them, "I have told you already, and you would not listen. Why do you want to hear it again? Do you also want to become his disciples?"*

This made the religious leaders really mad…and insulted. How could he think that they might want to be a disciple of Jesus! They stubbornly refused to believe that Jesus came from God and healed the man. They mocked the man saying he was a disciple of Jesus while arrogantly proclaiming that they were disciples of Moses. They also mocked Jesus by saying that God spoke to Moses, "but as for this man, we do not know where he comes from."

> *The man answered, "Why, this is an amazing thing! You do not know where he comes from, and yet he opened my eyes. We know that God does not listen to sinners, but if anyone is a worshiper of God and does his will, God listens to him. Never since the world began has it been heard that anyone opened the eyes of a man born blind. If this man were not from God, he could do nothing." (John 9:30-33)*

Yet the leaders still stubbornly refused to believe. Who was this blind man to teach them something? They were sure he was born in sin. With that, they cast him out of the synagogue.

Jesus heard what happened and went and found the man. The man may have been thrown out of the synagogue by the Jewish leaders, but he was welcomed by Jesus. Jesus asked the man if he now believed.

..."Do you believe in the Son of Man?" He answered, "And who is he, sir, that I may believe in him?" Jesus said to him, "You have seen him, and it is he who is speaking to you." He said, **"Lord, I believe," and he worshiped him.** *(John 9:35b-38)*

Jesus made a blind man see and gave him faith. He had been physically and spiritually blind, but Jesus gave Him both physical sight and spiritual sight. The Pharisees could see the works of Jesus—the amazing miracles He did—but they refused to believe the truth. Their pride and unwillingness to believe in Jesus made them guilty before God.

This story from the Bible shows us two different ways to respond to Jesus. One way is to stubbornly deny that you need Jesus and trust in your own wisdom and goodness. The other way is to admit that you are helpless to save yourself or to live a godly life and daily trust in Jesus. No one can make that choice for you. Will you put your trust in Jesus and receive spiritual sight?

But to all who did receive him, who believed in his name, he gave the right to become children of God, who were born, not of blood nor of the will of the flesh nor of the will of man, but of God. (John 1:12-13)

THAT YOU MAY BELIEVE

What does this chapter tell us about God?

Talk about and apply the **biblical truths** in **bold** text. Make them personal and apply them to what is happening in your family, church, community, or the world today.

How were "the works of God" displayed through the blind man?

Talk About: *But to all who did receive him, who believed in his name, he gave the right to become children of God, who were born, not of blood nor of the will of the flesh nor of the will of man, but of God. (John 1:12-13)*

Why do people refuse to admit they need Jesus?

Pray: Thank God that He opens spiritually blind eyes. Ask Him to give you spiritual sight. Pray for those who you know are resisting faith in Jesus.

Think About: *What are some practical ways I can trust Jesus daily?*

I AM

God said to Moses, "I AM WHO I AM." And he said, "Say this to the people of Israel, 'I AM has sent me to you.'" (Exodus 3:14)

God revealed Himself to Moses as I AM or Yahweh—the eternal, unchanging, self-existent, sovereign, almighty God. Yahweh sent Moses to tell the people He would set them free from slavery in Egypt. At Mount Sinai, God made a covenant with Israel.

Now therefore, if you will indeed obey my voice and keep my covenant, you shall be my treasured possession among all peoples, for all the earth is mine; and you shall be to me a kingdom of priests and a holy nation. (Exodus 19:5-6a)

But the people of Israel could never keep their covenant with God. They broke His Law, worshiped other gods, and turned away from Yahweh. Then they refused to listen to the prophets and repent.

But when the fullness of time had come, God sent forth his Son, born of woman, born under the law, to redeem those who were under the law, so that we might receive adoption as sons. (Galatians 4:4-5)

Jesus, the Son of God, came to establish a new covenant, a covenant of faith, not of law-keeping—to free from the curse of sin anyone who would believe in Him and give that person eternal life. Jesus is the LORD, God who came in human flesh.

Jesus said to them,

"I am the bread of life; whoever comes to me shall not hunger, and whoever believes in me shall never thirst." (John 6:35)

…"I am the light of the world. Whoever follows me will not walk in darkness, but will have the light of life." (John 8:12)

"I am the door. If anyone enters by me, he will be saved and will go in and out and find pasture." (John 10:9)

"I am the good shepherd. The good shepherd lays down his life for the sheep." (John 10:11)

…"I am the resurrection and the life. Whoever believes in me, though he die, yet shall he live," (John 11:25)

…"I am the way, and the truth, and the life. No one comes to the Father except through me." (John 14:6)

"I am the true vine, and my Father is the vinedresser…I am the vine; you are the branches. Whoever abides in me and I in him, he it is that bears much fruit, for apart from me you can do nothing." (John 15:1, 5)

Some people, like the man born blind, responded in faith—*"Lord, I believe"*—and worshiped Jesus. But others responded very differently to Jesus' claim, *"I and the Father are one." (John 10:30)*

The Jews picked up stones again to stone him. Jesus answered them, "I have shown you many good works from the Father; for which of them are you going to stone me?" The Jews answered him, "It is not for a good work that we are going to stone you but for blasphemy, because you, being a man, make yourself God." (John 10:31-33)

What is your response to Jesus?

CHAPTER 118

JESUS IS GLORIFIED IN BRINGING A DEAD MAN TO LIFE

Jesus Visits with Mary and Martha; Jesus Raises Lazarus from the Dead—Luke 10:38-42; John 11:1-45

..."Did I not tell you that if you believed you would see the glory of God?" (John 11:40)

Once, when Jesus entered a village, a woman named Martha invited Jesus to her home. While Jesus visited, Martha scurried around preparing a meal and serving it. But her sister, Mary, wasn't helping her. Instead, Mary was listening to Jesus' teaching. This irritated Martha, and she said to Jesus, *"Lord, do you not care that my sister has left me to serve alone? Tell her then to help me."* Do you know what Jesus said?

> *But the Lord answered her, "Martha, Martha, you are anxious and troubled about many things, but one thing is necessary. Mary has chosen the good portion, which will not be taken away from her." (Luke 10:41-42)*

Martha was busy getting food ready, but Mary wanted "spiritual food." Mary had made the right choice. She chose to "feed" her soul, and that would last forever. **Spiritual food is more important than physical food.** Mary, Martha, and their brother, named Lazarus, received spiritual food from Jesus. They believed in Jesus, God's Son, and became good friends with Jesus.

Later we are told in the Bible that Lazarus became very sick. The sisters sent a message to Jesus telling Him, *"Lord, he whom you love is ill."* This really wasn't news to Jesus because He knew that God had a great purpose in Lazarus' illness. So Jesus said, *"This illness does not lead to death. It is for the glory of God, so that the Son of God may be glorified through it."* What could Jesus mean? How would Jesus be glorified by His friend's illness? Jesus often said strange things that people just did not understand.

Do you know what Jesus did? Did he rush to Lazarus' house? The Bible tells us, *Now Jesus loved Martha and her sister and Lazarus. So when he heard that Lazarus was ill,…he stayed two days longer in the place where he was.*

What? He *stayed*? He didn't rush to get to them? This sounds like a mistake! But it was no mistake. **Jesus always knows what He is doing and always does the right thing.** After the two days, Jesus told the disciples they would go to Judea, the area where Lazarus lived. Judea? Okay, now this didn't seem like such a good idea to the disciples because the Jews there had recently tried to stone Jesus. Why would Jesus go back there?

Jesus explained, *"Our friend Lazarus has fallen asleep, but I go to awaken him."* Really? If Lazarus was sleeping, he would just wake up. The disciples didn't understand until Jesus explained things clearly to them, *"Lazarus has died, and for your sake I am glad that I was not there, so that you may believe. But let us go to him."* So, let's figure this out. Lazarus was sick and Jesus waited until he died, even though Jesus said, "This illness does not lead to death." Did Jesus make a mistake? And now that Lazarus was dead, Jesus was going to go where people wanted to kill Him. And Jesus was glad about this plan. This sure didn't make sense to the disciples. What did they need to believe? And why was it so important? Thomas didn't think this was a good plan, and he said to the other disciples, *"Let us also go, that we may die with him."* Even though Thomas didn't like Jesus' plan, he was willing to go with Jesus.

When they got near Bethany in Judea, Jesus was given the news that Lazarus had already died. In fact, he had been in the tomb for four days. Martha heard that Jesus was coming.

This time she rushed to find Jesus. Jesus, their close, special friend, would understand their grief and comfort them.

> *Martha said to Jesus, "Lord, if you had been here, my brother would not have died. But even now I know that whatever you ask from God, God will give you." Jesus said to her, "Your brother will rise again." Martha said to him, "I know that he will rise again in the resurrection on the last day." Jesus said to her,* **"I am the resurrection and the life. Whoever believes in me, though he die, yet shall he live, and everyone who lives and believes in me shall never die.** *Do you believe this?" She said to him, "Yes, Lord; I believe that you are the Christ, the Son of God, who is coming into the world." (John 11:21-27)*

Then Martha went to get her sister, Mary—*"The Teacher is here and is calling for you."* Mary ran quickly to find Jesus. When she got to Jesus, she fell down at His feet. She had the same faith as her sister. *"Lord, if you had been here, my brother would not have died."* Both Mary and Martha believed that Jesus would have made their brother well.

When Jesus saw her weeping, and the Jews who had come with her also weeping, he was deeply moved in his spirit and greatly troubled. And he said, "Where have you laid him?" Jesus wept as they took him to the tomb. The consequences of sin were so ugly and awful. **Death was a curse on God's good creation**. Jesus would let the light of life shine in the darkness. Some of the Jews were touched at how much Jesus loved others. But others were questioning and full of doubt—*"Could not he who opened the eyes of the blind man also have kept this man from dying?"*

Jesus was very troubled as He got to the tomb. He had come to bring the restoration of His Father's Kingdom. Sin, death, grief, jealousy, doubt, hatred—none of these things had been part of God's original creation. Jesus looked at the cave and the stone that covered the opening and told the people to move the stone. Martha was concerned. Lazarus had been dead for four days. By now there would be a terrible smell. But Jesus said to her, *"Did I not tell you that if you believed you would see the glory of God?"*

So they took away the stone. And Jesus lifted up his eyes and said, "Father, I thank you that you have heard me. I knew that you always hear me, but I said this on account of the people standing around, that they may believe that you sent me." When he had said these things, he cried out with a loud voice, "Lazarus, come out." The man who had died came out, his hands and feet bound with linen strips, and his face wrapped with a cloth. Jesus said to them, "Unbind him, and let him go." (John 11:41-44)

Jesus gives life! The Jews had just seen a man who had been dead for four days be given life again! This was something only God could do! Jesus was right—the illness did not lead to Lazarus' death but to life again! Raising Lazarus was a way of showing that Jesus is God! Jesus was glorified—His greatness was worthy of praise! Many of the Jews who saw this work of God believed in Jesus, God's Son. But others...

We will find out what others thought. But what is most important for you is what you believe... what you truly believe, not what you have been told. Do you believe that Jesus actually lived and brought a dead man back to life? What would you say to someone who would say that this is a made-up story?

> **In him was life, and the life was the light of men. The light shines in the darkness, and the darkness has not overcome it. (John 1:4-5)**

> **..."I am the resurrection and the life. Whoever believes in me, though he die, yet shall he live, and everyone who lives and believes in me shall never die. Do you believe this?" (John 11:25-26)**

THAT YOU MAY BELIEVE

What does this chapter tell us about God?

Talk about and apply the **biblical truths** in **bold** text. Make them personal and apply them to what is happening in your family, church, community, or the world today.

Why did Jesus wait two days before He went to see Lazarus? What did the disciples need to believe?

Explain John 1:4-5. When have you seen the light overcome the darkness? Give some examples.

Talk About: *..."I am the resurrection and the life. Whoever believes in me, though he die, yet shall he live, and everyone who lives and believes in me shall never die. Do you believe this?" (John 11:25-26)*

How could Jesus bring a person back to life? Most people will think you are crazy to believe this. What do you know for sure that makes this not only believable but true?

Pray: Thank God for His Word that shows us the truth. Ask Him to help you to truly and fully believe His Word.

Think About: *Why is the question of whether I believe for myself so important?*

CHAPTER 119
HARDENED HEARTS

Jewish Leaders Plan to Kill Jesus; the Rich Man and Lazarus— John 11:45-57; Luke 16:19-31

"Nor do you understand that it is better for you that one man should die for the people, not that the whole nation should perish." (John 11:50)

Two people can see the same thing...and think very differently about it. You might see a painting and think it is beautiful. But someone else might think it is really ugly. One person may watch a football game and get excited and love watching it. Another person may see a football game and be really bored.

The Jews who saw Jesus raise Lazarus from the dead did not all react the same way. We already know that some believed in Jesus. The resurrection (raising from the dead) of Lazarus proved to them that Jesus is God. But others went to the Pharisees and reported what happened. They didn't go with excitement, rejoicing in the sign they had seen. They went to "tattle" on Jesus. Some may have been confused, and some may have had hard hearts. But they did not have faith in Jesus. Their reaction showed what was in their hearts.

So the chief priests and the Pharisees gathered the council and said, "What are we to do? For this man performs many signs. If we let him go on like this, everyone will believe in him, and the Romans will come and take away both our place and our nation." (John 11:47-48)

What was in their hearts? They were envious of Jesus' power and authority. Jesus' growing popularity made them nervous. They were losing their control over the people. What if so many people followed Jesus that the Romans got nervous that there might be a revolt? Would Rome send a large army to take away the little freedom they had or destroy their temple? The religious leaders really did not understand that Jesus did not come to gain earthly power. Jesus' Kingdom is a spiritual Kingdom. But the religious leaders were hardened to the truth of who Jesus is. Nothing they had done so far had stopped Jesus. They needed to do something more drastic. What would they decide in this special meeting of the ruling Jewish leaders?

Caiaphas, the high priest, had the answer and told the others, *"You know nothing at all. Nor do you understand that it is better for you that one man should die for the people, not that the whole nation should perish."* So that was it. Jesus must die. *So from that day on, they made plans to put him to death.*

But Jesus knew it was not yet time for Him to die, so he *no longer walked openly among the Jews.* He and His disciples went to an area near the wilderness and stayed there.

When it came close to the time of the Passover, many Jews traveled to Jerusalem. There they looked for Jesus. They wondered if Jesus would come to Jerusalem. Maybe He wouldn't come this year. *Now the chief priests and the Pharisees had given orders that if anyone knew where he was, he should let them know, so that they might arrest him.* They were determined to carry out their plan to kill Jesus.

Why was there such anger toward Jesus? Why did the Jews want to kill their own Messiah? Why couldn't they all just believe in Jesus? Jesus had taught with great knowledge and understanding. He had shown them many signs—things that only God can do, yet they still did not believe in Him. Was there something more that might convince them?

Jesus had told a parable earlier that shows how blind to spiritual truth men are without the work of the Holy Spirit opening their eyes. The story is about a rich man and a poor man who was named Lazarus. The rich man had expensive clothes and plenty of delicious food. Lazarus lay at the gate of the rich man's house, probably because

149

he couldn't walk. He was covered with sores and would have been happy just to have a few crumbs of leftovers. But the rich man didn't even give him that. Poor Lazarus was even tormented by roaming dogs who often bothered him by licking his sores.

Well, Lazarus died and went to heaven. The rich man also died. But he didn't go to heaven; he went to hell where he was in terrible torment! However, he "lifted up his eyes," and far away he could see Abraham and Lazarus together. The rich man who had shown no mercy called out to Abraham, *"have mercy on me, and send Lazarus to dip the end of his finger in water and cool my tongue, for I am in anguish in this flame."* But Abraham reminded the rich man of all the good things he had on earth while Lazarus had none of these things. Now things were the opposite. Lazarus was comforted by God, and the rich man was tormented.

Besides, it was impossible to cross between heaven and hell. Jesus said in the story that there was a great canyon or wide gap between them. So the rich man begged Abraham to send Lazarus to warn his five brothers about the torments of hell. Maybe they could escape such suffering! But Abraham reminded the rich man that his brothers had the teachings of Moses and the prophets. These brothers had not responded to their teaching or repented. The rich man argued that if someone would go from the dead to warn them, they would repent. But Abraham knew better—*"If they do not hear Moses and the Prophets, neither will they be convinced if someone should rise from the dead."*

Why do you think Jesus told this story? It was a picture of the unbelieving Jews. They had all the teaching they needed to believe in Jesus, but they would not repent. They would not believe even if someone came from the dead to warn them.

Knowing the truth without accepting it in the heart does not change sinful hearts. The religious leaders knew the teachings of Moses and the prophets, but they did not believe that Jesus was the fulfillment of the Old Testament promises. Now they had seen Jesus raise someone from the dead. They saw Lazarus alive again. And still many of them refused to believe that Jesus is God's Son. Their unbelief did not come from lack of evidence. They had seen enough miracles to show them that Jesus is God. Their hearts were hardened, and their eyes were blind. **Only God can open blind eyes and soften hard hearts.**

We are all like these hardened, blind Jews unless the Holy Spirit works in our hearts. Unless God's Spirit opens our blind eyes, we cannot see who Jesus is. We cannot believe the truth of who Jesus is and what He has done for us. God has given you His Word so that you might know who He is and have a personal relationship with Him. Will you open His Word and look for Him there?

..."Today, if you hear his voice, do not harden your hearts." (Hebrews 4:7b)

"For God so loved the world, that he gave his only Son, that whoever believes in him should not perish but have eternal life. For God did not send his Son into the world to condemn the world, but in order that the world might be saved through him." (John 3:16-17)

THAT YOU MAY BELIEVE

What does this chapter tell us about God?

Talk about and apply the **biblical truths** in **bold** text. Make them personal and apply them to what is happening in your family, church, community, or the world today.

It is easy to blame the Jewish leaders for not believing in Jesus. But all of us have an evil, unbelieving heart without the work of the Holy Spirit. Ask your mother and father or others how God brought them to saving faith.

Talk About: *"For God so loved the world, that he gave his only Son, that whoever believes in him should not perish but have eternal life. For God did not send his Son into the world to condemn the world, but in order that the world might be saved through him." (John 3:16-17)*

Why is unbelief and disinterest in spiritual things so strong? What does this tell you about the natural heart of man? How can your family share the truth of who Jesus is and what He has done?

Pray: Thank God for sending His Son to save the world. Thank God for not condemning the world. Praise Him for His mercy toward undeserving sinners. Ask God to give you a desire to read His Word. Ask Him to open your eyes and heart to spiritual truth. Confess any unbelief you have in your heart.

Think About: *Am I hardening my heart?*

Memorize: John 3:16-17

CHAPTER 120
JESUS CAME TO GLORIFY THE FATHER

Mary Anoints Jesus; Jesus Goes to Jerusalem Knowing His Destiny—Mark 14:3-9; John 12:1-19; Mark 11:1-10; Luke 19:29-44; Matthew 21:12-16

Rejoice greatly, O daughter of Zion! Shout aloud, O daughter of Jerusalem! Behold, your king is coming to you; righteous and having salvation is he, humble and mounted on a donkey, on a colt, the foal of a donkey. (Zechariah 9:9)

It was six days before the Passover. What would Jesus do? Would He safely stay away from Jerusalem, or would He go to the Passover feast there? Jesus wasn't afraid of what men might do to Him. The greatest danger is not physical danger—being hurt or killed. Jesus had taught that earlier when He said, *"And do not fear those who kill the body but cannot kill the soul. Rather fear him who can destroy both soul and body in hell."* **The greatest danger is spiritual danger.** Jesus knew He came to die. He had told His disciples about this. He would not disobey His Father. He would do what He was sent to do.

Jesus set out for Jerusalem. On the way, he stopped in Bethany where His good friends Mary, Martha, and Lazarus lived. A special dinner was prepared to honor Jesus and to thank him for raising Lazarus from the dead. It was a celebration of Jesus' powerful miracle! At the dinner, Mary took a very expensive jar of sweet-smelling oil, broke the jar, and poured the oil on Jesus' head and feet. Mary was not only pouring out perfume on Jesus, but she was also pouring out her love and respect for Him. She was full of joy and wonder at Jesus' goodness, kindness, power, and love. She was honoring God's very own Son.

Some of the disciples there scolded Mary for wasting such expensive perfume.[17] It could have been sold and the money given to the poor. Judas was one of the disciples who voiced his disapproval, but it wasn't because he cared about poor people. It was because he was in charge of the money bag, and he often stole money from it. How he would have liked the money from the expensive perfume in the money bag where he could take some of it.

> But Jesus said, "Leave her alone. Why do you trouble her? She has done a beautiful thing to me. For you always have the poor with you, and whenever you want, you can do good for them. But you will not always have me. She has done what she could; she has anointed my body beforehand for burial. And truly, I say to you, wherever the gospel is proclaimed in the whole world, what she has done will be told in memory of her." (Mark 14:6-9)

Once more, Jesus mentioned that He was going to die. He was pleased at the sacrifice Mary had made and the honor she had shown Him. **Jesus loves true worship.**

Some of the Jews found out that Jesus was in Bethany, and a large crowd gathered not only to see Jesus, but also to see Lazarus. They wanted to see the living proof of Jesus' miracle—this man who had been made alive again. This worried the chief priests since many Jews were beginning to believe in Jesus because of Lazarus. How were the chief priests going to stop the people from following Jesus? They had to get rid of the evidence of Jesus' miracle. So the chief priests made plans to kill Lazarus, too.

The next day, Jesus and His disciples started out for Jerusalem. Jesus sent two of the disciples ahead of Him *saying, "Go into the village in front of you, where on entering you will find a colt tied, on which no one has ever yet sat. Untie it and bring it here. If anyone asks you, 'Why are you untying it?' you shall say this: 'The Lord has need of it.'" So those who were sent went away and found it just as he had told them.*

How did Jesus know this? What does this tell you about Jesus? **Jesus knows everything because Jesus is God.**

The disciples brought the young donkey to Jesus and threw their cloaks on the colt for Jesus to sit on. A large crowd was gathering as Jesus rode toward Jerusalem. Some of them laid their cloaks on the road to honor him. Others took palm branches and went to meet Him, waving their branches and throwing them down on the road before Him. There was so much excitement! Jesus was riding into Jerusalem! Jesus was a hero, a miracle worker, a healer, a king! Here was the One who had raised the dead! The people were rejoicing and shouting praises to Jesus. *"Hosanna! Blessed is he who comes in the name of the Lord, even the King of Israel!" "Blessed is the coming kingdom of our father David! Hosanna in the highest!" "Blessed be the King who comes in the name of the Lord! Peace in heaven and glory in the highest!"* It was just as the prophet Zechariah had prophesied.

> *Rejoice greatly, O daughter of Zion! Shout aloud, O daughter of Jerusalem! Behold, your king is coming to you; righteous and having salvation is he, humble and mounted on a donkey, on a colt, the foal of a donkey. (Zechariah 9:9)*

What do you think the Pharisees thought of this? They were very upset—actually they were *more* than upset! They were angry, jealous, and scared! More and more people were hearing about the raising of Lazarus. The people were so excited about Jesus! Things were getting out of control! The "world has gone after him," the Pharisees told each other. *And some of the Pharisees in the crowd said to him, "Teacher, rebuke your disciples."* They wanted Jesus to tell the crowd to calm down! But Jesus answered them, *"I tell you, if these were silent, the very stones would cry out."* **Jesus is worthy to be praised!**

> *And when he drew near and saw the city, he wept over it, saying, "Would that you, even you, had known on this day the things that make for peace! But now they are hidden from your eyes. For the days will come upon you, when your enemies will set up a barricade around you and surround you and hem you in on every side and tear you down to the ground, you and your children within you. And they will not leave one stone upon another in you, because you did not know the time of your visitation." (Luke 19:41-44)*

Jesus, who was always full of compassion, wept over Jerusalem. He knew the day was coming when it would be destroyed. He also wept because He knew the hearts of men. The people marveled at Jesus' miracles...but they did not worship Him as the Son of God, the Savior of the world. Today they were rejoicing over Him, but most of them did not understand what He came to accomplish. Jesus knew that many would soon reject Him.

Jesus entered the temple—His Father's house. It was meant to be a house of prayer, but it had become a place of buying and selling. He chased out the sellers and threw down "the tables of the money-changers and the seats of those who sold pigeons."[18]

> *And the blind and the lame came to him in the temple, and he healed them. But when the chief priests and the scribes saw the wonderful things that he did, and the children crying out in the temple, "Hosanna to the Son of David!" they were indignant, and they said to him, "Do you hear what these are saying?" And Jesus said to them, "Yes; have you never read, 'Out of the mouth of infants and nursing babies you have prepared praise'?" (Matthew 21:14-16)*

So many people. So many different emotions. Some praising. Others angry. People cheering for their King. Jesus weeping over Jerusalem. How would this week end? It would end just as

God had planned. Surely, it would not be easy for Jesus, who was fully man as well as fully God, to follow the path ahead of Him.

"Now is my soul troubled. And what shall I say? 'Father, save me from this hour'? But for this purpose I have come to this hour. Father, glorify your name." Then a voice came from heaven: "I have glorified it, and I will glorify it again." (John 12:27-28)

Jesus would obediently follow God's will, knowing the agony and the joy that was ahead. He would bring glory to His Father; He would show the greatness and worth of Yahweh.

In the crowd watching the triumphal entry of Jesus into Jerusalem, there were some true believers; there were others who were just swept away by the emotions of the moment and would later reject Jesus; and there were those who hated Jesus. There were also some who wanted to believe but wouldn't admit it because they were afraid of the Pharisees, for they loved the glory that comes from man more than the glory that comes from God. *What about you? Do you truly worship Jesus? Can you boldly confess Christ no matter what others think? Do you want the praise of man, or God's praise? Do you want to glorify God in all you do? Or do you just want to follow along after others?*

"If anyone serves me, he must follow me; and where I am, there will my servant be also. If anyone serves me, the Father will honor him." (John 12:26)

THAT YOU MAY BELIEVE

What does this chapter tell us about God?

Talk about and apply the **biblical truths** in **bold** text. Make them personal and apply them to what is happening in your family, church, community, or the world today.

Was Mary foolish to "waste" the special perfume on Jesus? Why or why not? What did Jesus mean when He said, "For you always have the poor with you, but you will not always have me" (Matthew 26:11)? How did Mary show true worship and adoration for Jesus? How is this like what Jesus said in John 12:25-26?

Talk About: *So, whether you eat or drink, or whatever you do, do all to the glory of God. (1 Corinthians 10:31)*

How can you "do all to the glory of God"? Give some practical examples.

Pray: Praise Jesus for being the true King. Thank Him for His obedience to His Father. Confess any time you have been ashamed of Christ—any time you have not wanted to admit belief in God or His Word. Ask God to help you to live for His glory.

Think About: *Do I want the praise of others or God's praise? Do I want to bring glory to God in all I do?*

---

17 The perfume was worth about 300 denarii. A denarii was the amount an ordinary worker would earn in a day.

18 Scholars disagree about whether there was one incident of Jesus cleansing the temple or two. It seems reasonable that there could have been two separate accounts.

CHAPTER 121

JESUS, THE PERFECT PROPHET, WARNS THE JEWS

Jesus Teaches in the Temple; the Parable of the Tenants;
the Woes to the Scribes and Pharisees—
Luke 20:1-18; Matthew 21:33-22:14; Matthew 23:1-24:2

---

*"...'The stone that the builders rejected has become the cornerstone...'
Therefore I tell you, the kingdom of God will be taken away from you
and given to a people producing its fruits." (Matthew 21:42-43)*

The religious leaders were both angry and scared. Jesus was welcomed into Jerusalem by a large crowd, He refused to quiet the people shouting His praises, and He had the nerve to disrupt business in the temple! Even the children were praising Him and calling Him the "Son of David"! This was too much! They approached Jesus as He was preaching in the temple and indignantly asked Jesus who gave Him the authority to teach and "do these things" (like heal people and cleanse the temple). *What is the answer to that question?* Jesus was very clever. He knew the religious leaders were trying to trap Him. He told them He would answer their question if they would answer His question. *Do you know what Jesus' question was?* Jesus asked if John's baptism was from heaven—from God—or from man.

The leaders knew they were trapped. If they said it was from heaven, the people would ask why they didn't believe John. If they said it was from man, the people would stone them because they were sure John was a prophet. What could they do? They were trapped. So they just said they didn't know the answer. *And Jesus said to them, "Neither will I tell you by what authority I do these things."*

But Jesus did have some other things to say, and **Jesus spoke with the authority of God. Jesus is the Perfect Prophet**—boldly teaching and warning, speaking a word from God. Jesus began with two parables. In a way, Jesus did tell the people who gave Him the authority to do "these things." He told them in a parable about a man who planted a vineyard. The man went on a long trip to another country and rented the land to some farmers. When the fruit was ripe, the owner sent a servant to the renters or tenants to get his share of the fruit. But the farmers wouldn't give him anything. The man sent other servants. But they beat one, stoned another...every servant he sent they mistreated. Finally, the owner said, *"I will send my beloved son; perhaps they will respect him."*

But when the tenant farmers saw him, they said, *"'This is the heir. Let us kill him, so that the inheritance may be ours.' And they threw him out of the vineyard and killed him."* Then Jesus made His point, *"What then will the owner of the vineyard do to them? He will come and destroy those tenants and give the vineyard to others."* When the people heard this part of the story, they were shocked and said to Jesus, *"Surely not!"*

But he looked directly at them and said, "What then is this that is written: 'The stone that the builders rejected has become the cornerstone'? Everyone who falls on that stone will be broken to pieces, and when it falls on anyone, it will crush him." (Luke 20:17-18)

No wonder the people reacted so strongly. Jesus was telling the people a sad and serious truth. *Do you know what it was?* God had sent the prophets to warn Israel, but the Jews had not listened to them. In fact, they mistreated the prophets. Now God had sent His "beloved Son." But the Jews rejected God's Son, too…and they would kill Him. So God was gathering in Gentiles (people of other nations) and giving His covenant mercies to them—He was including them in His Kingdom, and many of the Jews would not enter the Kingdom of God. Judgment would come to those Jews who rejected Jesus.

When they heard this parable, the chief priests and Pharisees knew Jesus was talking about them. How angry and upset they must have been! They wanted to arrest this accusing Jesus! But they were afraid of what the crowd might do, for the crowd thought Jesus was a prophet.

The other parable was about a king who gave a wedding feast for his son, but those who were invited to the wedding would not come. They just ignored the invitation. So the king sent his servants back out to tell the guests that the meal had been prepared and everything was ready. But the guests still wouldn't come and even killed some of the servants. Now the king was angry! He sent his soldiers to destroy the guests, and he sent his servants out into the streets to invite as many as they could find to attend the feast.

This parable was also a warning to the Jews about rejecting God's Messiah—about not accepting God's Son. Jesus was not afraid to say the hard things that people may not like because He cared more about their hearts than about what they might do to Him. **Jesus wants people to repent and be saved.** So Jesus continued with a warning about the Pharisees and scribes (teachers of the law). Jesus used a strong word to warn them: "woe to you." If the religious leaders did not repent, they would receive God's fierce anger and judgment. *What did the Pharisees and scribes need to repent of?* Jesus said, *"They preach, but do not practice"* and, *"They do all their deeds to be seen by others."*

The Pharisees prevented others from entering the Kingdom of heaven by rejecting Jesus and encouraging others to do the same. They added many duties to the law and kept people from seeing the truth. They were *"blind guides"* deceiving others. The Pharisees kept their picky rules, but failed to practice justice, mercy and faithfulness. They were hypocrites, worrying about the cleanliness of their cups and plates, but their hearts were not clean. Their hearts were greedy. They were like "whitewashed tombs"—beautiful outside, but full of hypocrisy and wickedness inside. They even bragged that, had they lived long ago, they would not have killed the prophets. (Yet they were plotting the death of Jesus, God's own

Son!) Jesus ended with this warning, *"You serpents, you brood of vipers, how are you to escape being sentenced to hell?"*

Does this sound overly rude or harsh to you? **It is a loving thing to warn people of God's judgment.** It is loving to be more concerned about their souls than about their feelings. Also, Jesus saw that these leaders were keeping others from repenting and believing—which is a very serious thing to do. In His earlier teaching, Jesus had warned against this kind of sin. Jesus was talking about causing spiritual harm to children, but the warning is the same for others.

> *"Whoever causes one of these little ones who believe in me to sin, it would be better for him if a great millstone were hung around his neck and he were thrown into the sea." (Mark 9:42)*

Jesus spoke with force, but His heart was very tender. He knew judgment was coming to the Jews, and it made Him sad. Jerusalem would be destroyed, and the temple smashed and ruined.

> *"O Jerusalem, Jerusalem, the city that kills the prophets and stones those who are sent to it! How often would I have gathered your children together as a hen gathers her brood under her wings, and you would not! See, your house is left to you desolate"…Jesus left the temple and was going away, when his disciples came to point out to him the buildings of the temple. But he answered them, "You see all these, do you not? Truly, I say to you, there will not be left here one stone upon another that will not be thrown down." (Matthew 23:37-38; 24:1-2)*

Things did not look good for the Jews. Was there any hope that the Jews would repent? Would they just repeat the Old Testament cycle of turning away from God? Would they ever truly love God with their whole hearts?

Or would they just argue about the Law, like the scribes did when they decided to ask Jesus His opinion? The scribes were arguing about which commandment was the most important, so one of them asked Jesus.

> *Jesus answered, "The most important is, 'Hear, O Israel:* **The Lord our God, the Lord is one. And you shall love the Lord your God with all your heart and with all your soul and with all your mind and with all your strength.'** *The second is this:* **'You shall love your neighbor as yourself.'** *There is no other commandment greater than these." And the scribe said to him, "You are right, Teacher. You have truly said that he is one, and there is no other besides him. And to love him with all the heart and with all the understanding*

and with all the strength, and to love one's neighbor as oneself, is much more than all whole burnt offerings and sacrifices." And when Jesus saw that he answered wisely, he said to him, "You are not far from the kingdom of God." (Mark 12:29-34a)

Being "not far" from the Kingdom of God is still being outside God's Kingdom. Most of the scribes and Pharisees continued to miss the heart of the Law, thinking only about outward actions. They could not love God with all their hearts, souls, minds, and strength. They could not admit they needed a Savior to give them the heart to truly love God.

But not all the Jews would reject Jesus and God's offer of salvation by faith. Some of the Jews received Jesus' call to repentance and faith. God preserved a faithful remnant of believing Jews, even though most of them rejected the Savior.

Jesus' warnings are loving pleas to repent and be saved. How far are you from the Kingdom of heaven?

> **...if my people who are called by my name humble themselves, and pray and seek my face and turn from their wicked ways, then I will hear from heaven and will forgive their sin and heal their land. (2 Chronicles 7:14)**

THAT YOU MAY BELIEVE

What does this chapter tell us about God?

Talk about and apply the **biblical truths** in **bold** text. Make them personal and apply them to what is happening in your family, church, community, or the world today.

Read and discuss the Parable of the Wedding Feast in Matthew 22:1-14. How does this apply to today?

Talk About: *..."The stone that the builders rejected has become the cornerstone'? Everyone who falls on that stone will be broken to pieces, and when it falls on anyone, it will crush him." (Luke 20:17b-18)* (Be sure that your child understands that Jesus offers salvation but rejecting Jesus means judgment.)

How are we sometimes like the scribes and Pharisees? Why are these warnings for us too? Do we sometimes try to obey God with outward obedience only? What heart attitudes does God expect from us? Give some examples of how you can love your neighbor.

Pray: Thank God for His warnings of judgment. Thank Him because He desires repentance instead of judgment. Confess any hypocrisy you see in your heart. Ask God to give you a heart to love Him and your neighbor.

Think About: *Do I love God with all my heart, soul, mind, and strength and my neighbor as myself?*

CHAPTER 122
BE READY
Signs of the End of the Age—Matthew 24-25

"Therefore you also must be ready, for the Son of Man is coming at an hour you do not expect." (Matthew 24:44)

You know how the world began. *But have you ever wondered about how the world will end? What will it be like when Jesus returns?* Jesus' disciples wondered, too, and wanted to know about the signs of the end. So on the Mount of Olives outside the city of Jerusalem, Jesus spoke to His disciples privately. Though the end of the world would not come in the disciples' lifetime, Jesus knew they would face persecution and temptation. He wanted to prepare His disciples to stand strong in their faith. First, He warned them—and us—not to be deceived by false teachers. Many people will teach what is not true, which is why **we must know God's Word well**. There will also be wars, famines, and earthquakes and times of great suffering.

*"Then they will deliver you up to tribulation and put you to death, and you will be hated by all nations for my name's sake. And then many will fall away and betray one another and hate one another. And many false prophets will arise and lead many astray. And because lawlessness will be increased, the love of many will grow cold. But **the one who endures to the end will be saved**." (Matthew 24:9-13)*

Believers will be persecuted, but they must stay strong by depending on God. Immediately before Christ returns there will be the greatest "tribulation" or time of intense trouble that the world has ever seen. But God will shorten this time for the sake of true believers. This terrible, dreadful time will surely come.

"Immediately after the tribulation of those days the sun will be darkened, and the moon will not give its light, and the stars will fall from heaven, and the powers of the heavens will be shaken. Then will appear in heaven the sign of

the Son of Man, and then all the tribes of the earth will mourn, and they will see the Son of Man coming on the clouds of heaven with power and great glory. And he will send out his angels with a loud trumpet call, and they will gather his elect from the four winds, from one end of heaven to the other." (Matthew 24:29-31)

When the gospel is preached "throughout the whole world," the end will come, and Jesus will return! But no one knows when this will be. It will be sudden and unexpected—especially to those who do not have faith in Jesus. It will be like when the flood came. Even though Noah warned the people, no one really paid attention to his warning.

"For as in those days before the flood they were eating and drinking, marrying and giving in marriage, until the day when Noah entered the ark, and they were unaware until the flood came and swept them all away, so will be the coming of the Son of Man. Then two men will be in the field; one will be taken and one left. Two women will be grinding at the mill; one will be taken and one left." (Matthew 24:38-41)

What other situations can you imagine? Two people could be riding in a car... and the driver taken. A doctor could be performing an operation...and all of a sudden, the doctor will be gone. *"Therefore you also must be ready, for the Son of Man is coming at an hour you do not expect."*

What does Jesus mean when He tells us to "be ready"? Jesus is telling Christians to keep on trusting in Him all our lives, to be faithful in obeying God's will, and to zealously do the work of His Kingdom.

Jesus told a story to help His disciples understand what it means to be faithful. It is called the Parable of the Talents, and it is about a man who went on a journey.

He called three of his servants and trusted each of them with different amounts of money. Two were "faithful and wise" with what the master had given them. They took the master's money and traded and invested well so that they had a double amount to present to the master when he returned. The master was so pleased with each of them that he praised each one, *"Well done, good and faithful servant."* Then he joyfully rewarded them both greatly. But the other servant was wicked and decided that the master would not be returning for a while. He believed the master was mean, and he was afraid of him. So he dug a hole to hide what he had been given. He made no effort at all to increase what the master had given him. When the master got home, the servant returned only what he had been given. The master was disappointed with the wicked, lazy servant, and he punished him. Jesus ended His parable describing this punishment: *"And [the master] cast the worthless servant into the outer darkness. In that place there will be weeping and gnashing of teeth."*

When Jesus comes back to earth, He will come to reward and to punish. Those who have been faithful will be rewarded, and those who have been wicked will be punished. It will be too late then to change anything. That is why Jesus tells us to be ready now. This is the picture Jesus gave us of that day.

> *"When the Son of Man comes in his glory, and all the angels with him, then he will sit on his glorious throne. Before him will be gathered all the nations, and he will separate people one from another as a shepherd separates the sheep from the goats. And he will place the sheep on his right, but the goats on the left.*
>
> *"Then the King will say to those on his right, 'Come, you who are blessed by my Father, inherit the kingdom prepared for you from the foundation of the world. For I was hungry and you gave me food, I was thirsty and you gave me drink, I was a stranger and you welcomed me, I was naked and you clothed me, I was sick and you visited me, I was in prison and you came to me.'*
>
> *"Then the righteous will answer him, saying, 'Lord, when did we see you hungry and feed you, or thirsty and give you drink? And when did we see you a stranger and welcome you, or naked and clothe you? And when did we see you sick or in prison and visit you?' And the King will answer them, 'Truly, I say to you, as you did it to one of the least of these my brothers, you did it to me.'*
>
> *"Then he will say to those on his left, 'Depart from me, you cursed, into the eternal fire prepared for the devil and his angels.'"* (Matthew 25:31-41)

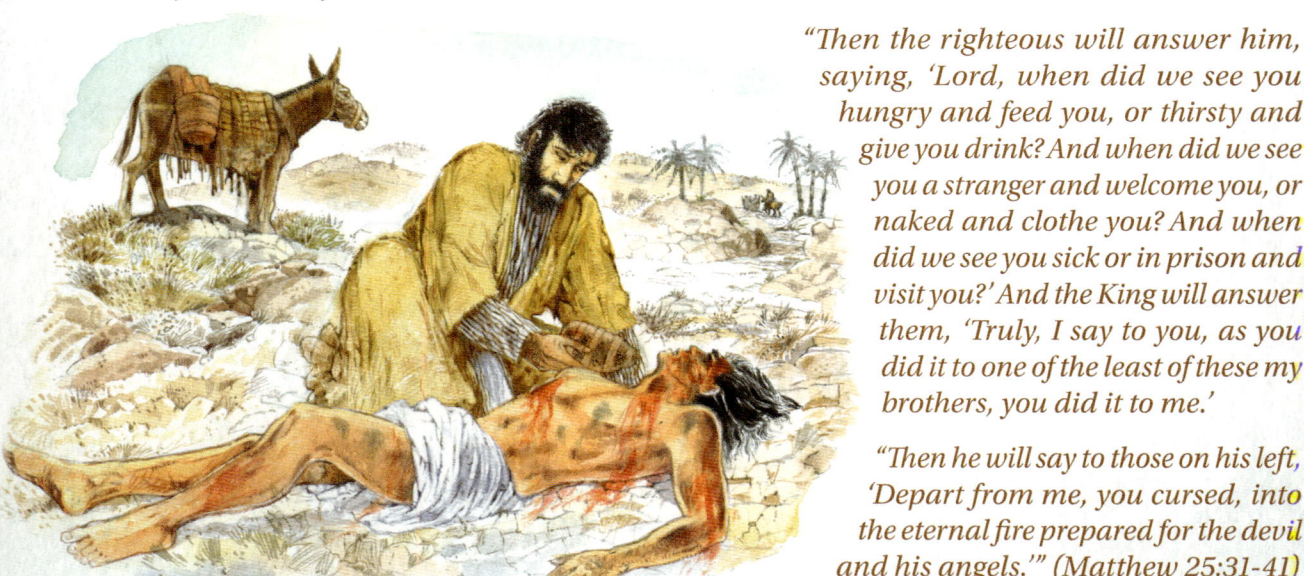

What joy must there be in hearing Jesus say, *"Come, you who are blessed by my Father, inherit the kingdom prepared for you from the foundation of the world."* What an amazing reward it will be to live in God's Kingdom forever, seeing Jesus face to face, rejoicing forever and ever and ever! That is what Jesus offers to those who repent, trust in Him, and receive His salvation! Those who are trusting in Jesus have a changed heart that responds to others with love, kindness, and unselfishness.

But others will never hear these words of welcome. They will be cursed forever. Their rebellious, selfish, evil, sinful hearts will condemn them to hell because they did not trust in Jesus' payment for their sin.

Does the thought of that day scare you? If you belong to Jesus, you have nothing to be afraid of. You will be overjoyed to see Him return. But if you do not belong to Jesus, it will be a dreadful day.

> **The sun shall be turned to darkness, and the moon to blood, before the great and awesome day of the LORD comes...The LORD roars from Zion, and utters his voice from Jerusalem, and the heavens and the earth quake. But the LORD is a refuge to his people, a stronghold to the people of Israel. (Joel 2:31; 3:16)**

THAT YOU MAY BELIEVE

What does this chapter tell us about God?

Talk about and apply the **biblical truths** in **bold** text. Make them personal and apply them to what is happening in your family, church, community, or the world today.

How can you be ready for the coming of Christ?

Read and discuss the Parable of the Talents (Matthew 25:14-30).

Talk About: *The LORD roars from Zion, and utters his voice from Jerusalem, and the heavens and the earth quake. But the LORD is a refuge to his people, a stronghold to the people of Israel. (Joel 3:16)*

How is God like a "lion" and a "lamb"—both tough and tender? What does this mean at the end of the age? What does this mean in daily life?

Pray: Praise Jesus for being the victorious King who will conquer Satan, death, and evil. Thank God for Jesus' faithful witness and sober warnings. Thank God for offering salvation to whoever comes to Jesus. Ask God to show you if you are ready for Christ's return.

Think About: *Does the thought of Jesus' return excite me or scare me?*

CHAPTER 123

JESUS IS THE PERFECT PASSOVER LAMB

Jesus Eats the Passover Meal with His Disciples— Luke 22:1-34; Matthew 26:1-35; John 13; Mark 14:1-31

"...for this is my blood of the covenant, which is poured out for many for the forgiveness of sins." (Matthew 26:28)

Jesus had just finished having His private conversation with His disciples on the Mount of Olives. The Passover was just two days away. The Passover is the day when the Jews remembered the rescue of God's people through the blood of the lamb painted on their doorframes. In just two days, Jesus would be crucified. He could have left Jerusalem and turned away from the cross...but He didn't. *Why didn't He?*

The chief priests and elders met with the high priest, Caiaphas, to plot how they would arrest Jesus and kill Him. They needed to have a clever plan, a secret plan to arrest Jesus privately. They didn't want the people in Jerusalem to cause problems. Then Judas Iscariot, one of Jesus' own disciples, gave them the opportunity they were looking for. "Satan entered into Judas," who went to the chief priests and said, *"What will you give me if I deliver him over to you?"* What a despicable, evil thing for Judas to do. How greed had taken over his heart! But the chief priests were delighted. They paid Judas thirty pieces of silver. *And from that moment he sought an opportunity to betray [Jesus].*

Then came the day of Unleavened Bread, on which the Passover lamb had to be sacrificed. This was Thursday, and Jesus sent Peter and John to get the Passover meal ready. But they didn't know where Jesus wanted to have the Passover meal. *He said to them, "Behold, when you have entered the city, a man carrying a jar of water will meet you. Follow him into the house that he enters and tell the master of the house, 'The Teacher says to you, Where is the guest room, where I may eat the Passover with my disciples?' And he will show you a large upper room furnished; prepare it there." And they went and found it just as he had told them, and they prepared the Passover.* Jesus knew about the upper room...and He knew what would happen that night...but He did not turn away.

At the Passover meal, the disciples got into an argument about which of them was the greatest. But Jesus told them they were thinking like the world. In God's Kingdom, a leader has a servant heart. But Jesus did more than just talk and teach, He was an example. Jesus, the King of the Universe, tied a towel around His waist, poured water into a washbowl, and began to wash the disciples' feet. **Jesus has a servant heart.** When He had finished, He taught them about true greatness and humble love.

> *…"Do you understand what I have done to you? You call me Teacher and Lord, and you are right, for so I am. If I then, your Lord and Teacher, have washed your feet, you also ought to wash one another's feet. For I have given you an example, that you also should do just as I have done to you. Truly, truly, I say to you,* **a servant is not greater than his master,** *nor is a messenger greater than the one who sent him. If you know these things,* **blessed are you if you do them.***" (John 13:12b-17)*

As they were eating the Passover meal, Jesus said something very startling: *"Truly, I say to you, one of you will betray me."* Not only did this shock the disciples, but it also made them very sad and troubled. Who would do this? The disciples began to ask Jesus one by one, "Is it I, Lord?" Who could the traitor be? They discussed among themselves which of them could possibly betray Jesus. It was almost unbelievable. These men had been Jesus' closest friends. Finally, one of the disciples asked Jesus, "Lord, who is it?" Jesus knew who it was and even spoke a warning,

> *"The Son of Man goes as it is written of him, but woe to that man by whom the Son of Man is betrayed! It would have been better for that man if he had not been born." (Matthew 26:24)*

Jesus knew He must be betrayed and die. He would not turn away from the cross. He would be the **perfect sin-bearer** and die to take away man's sin. He knew from the beginning that Judas was not a true disciple. *Jesus answered, "It is he to whom I will give this morsel of bread when I have dipped it." So when he had dipped the morsel, he gave it to Judas, the son of Simon Iscariot. Then after he had taken the morsel, Satan entered into him. Jesus said to him, "What you are going to do, do quickly."*

Judas got up and left the supper. None of the disciples tried to stop Judas! No one grabbed him or blocked his way. Didn't they love Jesus and want to protect Him? Yes, they did, but they were confused. They hadn't understood what Jesus was saying to Judas. Judas had the money bag, so some of the disciples thought Jesus wanted him to buy more food for the meal or to give some money to the poor.

Jesus knew this was His last Passover meal with His disciples. He would not eat another until His return at the end of history where they would eat together at the "wedding feast of the Lamb." *And he said to them, "I have earnestly desired to eat this Passover with you before I suffer. For I tell you I will not eat it until it is fulfilled in the kingdom of God."*

> *And he took bread, and when he had given thanks, he broke it and gave it to them, saying, "This is my body, which is given for you. Do this in remembrance of me"…And he took a cup, and when he had given thanks he gave it to them, saying, "Drink of it, all of you, for this is my blood of the covenant, which is poured out for many for the forgiveness of sins. I tell you I will not drink again of this fruit of the vine until that day when I drink it new with you in my Father's kingdom." (Luke 22:19; Matthew 26:27-29)*

Jesus was using the bread as a symbol of His body, which would be killed on the cross. The wine in the cup was a symbol of His blood, which would be poured out for man's sin. **God was making a new covenant through the death of His Son**, through the death of the perfect Lamb of God. This was the covenant God had promised through the prophet Jeremiah:

> *"For this is the covenant that I will make with the house of Israel after those days, declares the LORD:* **I will put my law within them, and I will write it on their hearts.** *And I will be their God, and they shall be my people." (Jeremiah 31:33)*

Moses had been a mediator between God and Israel teaching them God's Law and asking God to be merciful to sinful Israel. Now Jesus would be the mediator between God and man. He would establish a new covenant with His people through his death, a covenant that would bring salvation to all who trust in Him. Jesus' death would not just cover sin. It would take away sin.

> *Therefore he is the mediator of a new covenant, so that those who are called may receive the promised eternal inheritance, since a death has occurred that redeems them from the transgressions committed under the first covenant. (Hebrews 9:15)*

In the Old Testament, animals were sacrificed to cover man's sin. But the blood of an animal could never be the perfect sacrifice for sin. It was only temporary. An animal is not made in the image of God. Jesus, the Perfect Law-Keeper, the sinless Son of Man, is the perfect substitute to die in the place of sinners. God was working out His sovereign plan of salvation through the death of His own Son. **Jesus is the Perfect Passover Lamb whose blood would save His people.**

God will "pass over" sins, not through the blood of a lamb painted on your door frame, but through the blood of His Son poured out on the cross. Do you understand that you deserve the severe anger of God because of your sin? Are you able to keep God's good laws perfectly, or do you need a Passover Lamb to rescue you, a Scapegoat to carry your sins away, a Savior to give you His perfect righteousness? Are you thankful that Jesus gave His body and His blood to make peace between God and man?

> For in him all the fullness of God was pleased to dwell, and through him to reconcile to himself all things, whether on earth or in heaven, making peace by the blood of his cross. (Colossians 1:19-20)

THAT YOU MAY BELIEVE

What does this chapter tell us about God?

Talk about and apply the **biblical truths** in **bold** text. Make them personal and apply them to what is happening in your family, church, community, or the world today.

Why do we have communion in our churches? How does it remind us of how much Jesus suffered and how much He loves His people?

Talk About: *For in him all the fullness of God was pleased to dwell, and through him to reconcile to himself all things, whether on earth or in heaven, making peace by the blood of his cross. (Colossians 1:19-20)*

Why was the death of Jesus necessary? How does the Old Testament show the need for a Savior? How was it a picture or shadow of the new covenant? (Help your child to understand the Old Testament references of the Passover Lamb, the Scapegoat, the priest, the temple, etc. and to understand the difference between a covenant of law and works versus a covenant of faith and grace. See Galatians 3:7-14.)

Pray: Thank God for sending His Son to die on the cross. Thank Jesus for His obedience to the Father. Confess your sin that put Jesus on the cross. Ask God to give you a deep sorrow for sin.

Think About: *Am I at peace with God? How do I know this?*

CHAPTER 124
YOUR SORROW WILL TURN INTO JOY

Jesus Predicts Peter's Denial; Jesus Instructs His Disciples; Jesus' High Priestly Prayer— Luke 22:28-34; Matthew 26:30-35, John 14-17

"Truly, truly, I say to you, you will weep and lament, but the world will rejoice. You will be sorrowful, but your sorrow will turn into joy." (John 16:20)

After the Passover meal, Jesus was with His eleven disciples who had remained faithful to Him through many trials. But this Passover night, He told them that they would "all fall away," just as the prophet Zechariah had predicted—*"Strike the shepherd, and the sheep will be scattered."*

However, Peter was certain he would never desert Jesus! He firmly declared that even if everyone else left Jesus, he would never "fall away." He would die with Jesus before he would ever deny Jesus. But Jesus knew the future, and He knew Peter better than Peter knew himself.

"Simon, Simon, behold, Satan demanded to have you, that he might sift you like wheat, but I have prayed for you that your faith may not fail. And when you have turned again, strengthen your brothers." Peter said to him, "Lord, I am ready to go with you both to prison and to death." Jesus said, "I tell you, Peter, the rooster will not crow this day, until you deny three times that you know me." (Luke 22:31-34)

Oh, how strong we think we are... when really, we are very weak. **Jesus understands our weakness.** Jesus knew His disciples were weak,

171

so He spoke some last words of comfort, warning, and counsel to them. Jesus told them not to be troubled. Yes, He would be leaving, but He would "go and prepare a place" for them in His Father's house, heaven. *"And if I go and prepare a place for you, I will come again and will take you to myself, that where I am you may be also."* Thomas wasn't so sure about this. They didn't know where Jesus was going, so how would they know the way to get to Him? Jesus answered him, *"I am the way, and the truth, and the life. No one comes to the Father except through me."* Then Philip asked Jesus to show them the Father. The disciples were so slow to truly understand who Jesus is. But Jesus once again patiently explained, *"Whoever has seen me has seen the Father…I am in the Father and the Father is in me."* It is hard to understand that there is one God, but three persons in the one God—God the Father, God the Son, and God the Holy Spirit.

Because of man's weakness, Jesus would send a Helper, the Holy Spirit. The Holy Spirit would be with the disciples and all believers forever. He would help the disciples keep Jesus' commandments, teach them all things, and help them to remember what Jesus taught them. Jesus tenderly told the disciples not to be troubled or afraid because He was going away. Jesus was going back to be with His Father. Why did Jesus explain all this? *"And now I have told you before it takes place, so that when it does take place you may believe."*

After this conversation, the disciples sang a hymn, left the upper room, and went to the Mount of Olives. On the way, Jesus gave them a "picture" for them to know who He is and who they were.

> *"I am the true vine, and my Father is the vinedresser. Every branch in me that does not bear fruit he takes away, and every branch that does bear fruit he prunes, that it may bear more fruit"…***"Abide in me, and I in you.*** *As the branch cannot bear fruit by itself, unless it abides in the vine, neither can you, unless you abide in me. I am the vine; you are the branches. Whoever abides in me and I in him, he it is that bears much fruit, for* **apart from me you can do nothing***."* (John 15:1-2, 4-5)

Jesus knew His disciples would face much persecution. The world would hate them, just as it had hated Jesus. But He had told them the way to stay strong—to be connected to Him, to abide or trust in Him. The Helper would come to strengthen them. They would have many troubles in the world, but they should not despair because Jesus has "overcome the world." **Jesus is victorious!** They may be scared and sad that Jesus was leaving, but Jesus promised that their sorrow would "turn to joy." Jesus even gave them an example to help them understand and believe that their sorrow could turn to joy.

> *"Truly, truly, I say to you, you will weep and lament, but the world will rejoice. You will be sorrowful, but your sorrow will turn into joy. When a woman is giving birth, she has sorrow because her hour has come, but when she has delivered the baby, she no longer remembers the anguish, for joy that a human being has been born into the world. So also you have sorrow now, but I will see you again, and your hearts will rejoice, and no one will take your joy from you." (John 16:20-22)*

After Jesus spoke these encouraging words, He prayed to His Father. *Do you remember what the "Remembrance Stones" were?* These were the stones on the high priest's special ephod garment that had the names of the twelve tribes of Israel engraved on them. When the high priest went into the Most Holy Place once a year, God saw the names of all the tribes of Israel on the ephod. The high priest represented the people before God and pleaded for His mercy on His people because of the covenant relationship He had with them. Unlike the high priest, **Jesus is continually in the presence of His Father, as a Perfect High Priest.** Jesus could come boldly before God and pray. He prayed for Himself, for His disciples, and for all believers. What did Jesus pray?

For Himself: *"glorify your Son that the Son may glorify you."* Jesus had faithfully done the work God had given Him to do. Now Jesus prayed that He would finish the work—that His Father would help Jesus in His suffering on the cross, that His payment for sin would be accepted, that the Father would raise Him from the dead, and that God would bring Him back to heaven. This would show the power, wisdom, and love of God to the world.[19]

For His disciples: Jesus had faithfully taught His disciples, giving them the words His Father gave Him. He would be leaving the world, but the disciples would remain. So Jesus asked the Father to keep them or protect them—that He would keep them believing, keep them from sin, keep them doing the work of the Kingdom. *"I do not ask that you take them out of the world, but that you keep them from the evil one."*

For future believers: Jesus prayed that believers would be united together and joined to God—that they would have friendship with each other and would truly know the one true God. He prayed that God's people would someday be with Him forever and have eternal life.

If you are a Christian, you have the same work as the disciples had—to faithfully represent Christ here on earth. You are called to live in a way that shows He is good, loving, powerful, and alive—to bring glory to Him. Your mission is to show the world what God is like and tell others about the saving work of Jesus. You can only do this by abiding or trusting in Jesus. Are you trusting Jesus today?

> "Whoever has my commandments and keeps them, he it is who loves me. And he who loves me will be loved by my Father, and I will love him and manifest myself to him." (John 14:21)

THAT YOU MAY BELIEVE

What does this chapter tell us about God?

Talk about and apply the **biblical truths** in **bold** text. Make them personal and apply them to what is happening in your family, church, community, or the world today.

What temptations make it hard to speak boldly about God? How are you weak?

Talk About: *"Whoever has my commandments and keeps them, he it is who loves me. And he who loves me will be loved by my Father, and I will love him and manifest myself to him." (John 14:21)*

What are some ways that your family can show others what God is like?

Pray: Thank God that He understands our weakness. If you are not a Christian, ask God to save you. If you are a Christian, thank God for His promise to "keep" you. Praise God for His wisdom, power, and love.

Think About: *Do I "abide" in Christ—do I trust Him in all kinds of situations?*

---

19 Paraphrased from E. A. Blum, as quoted by J. F. Walvoord & R. B. Zuck, editors, *The Bible Knowledge Commentary: An Exposition of the Scriptures*, on John 17:1, (Wheaton, Ill. Victor Books, 1985).

CHAPTER 125

SAD BETRAYALS AND WILLING FAITHFULNESS

Jesus Prays in the Garden and Is Arrested; Peter Denies Christ—
Mark 14:32-72; Luke 22:39-71; Matthew 26:36-56; John 18:1-27

..."Father, if you are willing, remove this cup from me. Nevertheless,
not my will, but yours, be done." (Luke 22:42)

We already know about the Garden of Eden. *What was the result of what happened there?* Jesus and His disciples went to another garden—the garden of Gethsemane. But the results in this garden were very different. Jesus asked all the disciples except Peter, James, and John to stay behind while He prayed. As He walked on with the three disciples, He became very sad and troubled. Jesus knew the temptation and the agony that was coming: *"My soul is very sorrowful, even to death. Remain here and watch."*

Leaving Peter, James, and John behind, Jesus walked a little bit farther alone and fell to the ground. He poured out His heart to His Father in prayer. *"Abba, Father, all things are possible for you. Remove this cup from me. Yet not what I will, but what you will."* The "cup" was God's wrath or extreme anger—the judgment or the punishment God's sinful people deserved. Jesus had a close, tender relationship with His Father. "Abba" is a word for father that shows affection and trust. Jesus trusted that His Abba Father would not ask Him to "drink" this cup of suffering if it were not necessary.

After an hour, Jesus went back to the three disciples. They were not watching or praying. They were sleeping! Jesus was going to face excruciating suffering. The disciples were facing great temptations and sorrow, but they could not stay awake and pray. When Jesus found them sleeping, He was disappointed and said to Peter, *"Watch and pray that you may not*

enter into temptation. *The spirit indeed is willing, but the flesh is weak."* Then Jesus went back to pray, "saying the same words."

> *..."Father, if you are willing, remove this cup from me. Nevertheless, **not my will, but yours, be done.**" And there appeared to him an angel from heaven, strengthening him. And being in an agony he prayed more earnestly; and his sweat became like great drops of blood falling down to the ground. (Luke 22:42-44)*

Why did Jesus need "strengthening"? Jesus is God, but He was also man. The physical, emotional, and spiritual torment Jesus would face on the cross would be horrific. Yet Jesus would not disobey and rebel against God. Jesus, the "second Adam," would perfectly obey where the first Adam had failed.

Again, Jesus returned to find the three disciples sleeping. After praying another time, Jesus came back a third time to find them sleeping—*"Are you still sleeping and taking your rest?*

It is enough the hour has come. The Son of Man is betrayed into the hands of sinners. Rise, let us be going; see my betrayer is at hand." While Jesus was speaking to them, there was a commotion. A crowd of chief priests, scribes, elders, and soldiers led by Judas came with swords and clubs! Their evil plot was unfolding…Judas had told them that he would identify Jesus to them by giving Jesus a kiss. In Jesus' day, it was common to greet one another with a kiss on the cheek. It was a sign of respect and friendship. As Judas came near to kiss Jesus, Jesus knew what was in his heart and said to him, *"Judas, would you betray the Son of Man with a kiss?"* How could a person betray someone using a sign of friendship? Yet this is just what Judas did. Then the soldiers grabbed Jesus to arrest Him. But Peter drew out a sword and cut off the ear of the servant of the high priest. *What did Jesus think of this?*

Jesus said, *"No more of this!"* Then He touched the servant's ear and healed him! Jesus told Peter to put the sword away. *"Shall I not drink the cup that the Father has given me?"…"Do you think that I cannot appeal to my Father and he at once will send me more than twelve legions of angels? But how then should the Scriptures be fulfilled, that it must be so?"* Jesus didn't need Peter to protect Him! Besides that, Jesus didn't want protection. **Jesus was determined to fulfill God's plan and go to the cross**.

But Jesus did scold the crowd. Many days He had taught in the temple, and they never came to arrest Him. Now they came with clubs and swords secretly in the middle of the night. They acted as if they were arresting a robber! The soldiers seized Jesus, tied Him up, and took Him away. *What happened to the disciples? Were they arrested, too?* All of Jesus' disciples left Him and ran away. But Peter stopped and followed some distance behind the crowd.

They brought Jesus first to Annas, the father-in-law of Caiaphas. *Do you remember who Caiaphas was?* He was the high priest who said that Jesus must die. Annas asked Jesus what He had taught. Jesus replied that He had taught openly in the synagogue, not in secret, where all Jews could hear His teaching—*"Why do you ask me? Ask those who have heard me what I said to them; they know what I said."* At this comment, one of the officers became indignant that Jesus would speak to the high priest in such a way, and he hit Jesus!

Then they brought Jesus to Caiaphas himself. Many of the leaders told lies about Jesus. They even told lies that didn't agree with each other. It was very obvious that they were lying. But Jesus said nothing. He would not reply to their lies. Then Caiaphas asked Jesus if He was the Son of God. This Jesus would answer and answer boldly. *"I am, and you will see the Son of Man seated at the right hand of Power, and coming with the clouds of heaven."* Caiaphas got so angry at Jesus' answer that he tore his clothes. This was enough for him to hear! He asked the council their decision about Jesus. And they all condemned Jesus, saying that Jesus should be put to death. Some even spit at Him; others hit Him. They mocked Jesus—blindfolding Him and telling Him to "prophesy" who had hit Him. The guards beat Jesus. Jesus had shown compassion, healing the sick, freeing those tormented by demons, raising the dead…and now He was being treated like a criminal!

What was Peter doing in the meantime? He had followed the crowd into the courtyard of the high priest. Peter was warming himself by the fire with the guards when a servant girl saw him there. She looked at Peter closely and said, *"You also were with Jesus."*

But he denied it, saying, "Woman, I do not know him." And a little later someone else saw him and said, "You also are one of them." But Peter said, "Man, I am not." And after an interval of about an hour still another insisted, saying, "Certainly this man also was with him, for he too is a Galilean." But Peter said, "Man, I do not know what you are talking about." And immediately, while he was still speaking, the rooster crowed. And the Lord turned and looked at Peter. And Peter remembered the saying of the Lord, how he had said to him, "Before the rooster crows today, you will deny me three times." And he went out and wept bitterly. (Luke 22:57-62)

How this must have wounded Jesus! Peter, the person Jesus said would build the church, had just denied Him. Yet Jesus was willing to die for Peter's sins… and the sins of all God's people. Can you imagine how Peter felt when Jesus looked at him? This is the way we should feel every time we sin against the Lord. Do you grieve over your sin?

…but God shows his love for us in that while we were still sinners, Christ died for us. (Romans 5:8)

"Greater love has no one than this, that someone lay down his life for his friends." (John 15:13)

THAT YOU MAY BELIEVE

What does this chapter tell us about God?

Talk about and apply the **biblical truths** in **bold** text. Make them personal and apply them to what is happening in your family, church, community, or the world today.

What does this story tell you about Jesus' character?

Talk About: *…but God shows his love for us in that while we were still sinners, Christ died for us. (Romans 5:8)*

How have you offended Jesus?

Pray: Ask God to forgive the times you have been ashamed to speak up for Him. Thank Jesus for His willingness to die for sinners.

Think About: *Why would Jesus take the punishment I deserve?*

CHAPTER 126
"CRUCIFY HIM!"
Jesus Is Put on Trial—Matthew 27:1-33; Mark 15:1-22; Luke 23:1-31; John 18:28-19:17

..."My kingdom is not of this world. If my kingdom were of this world, my servants would have been fighting, that I might not be delivered over to the Jews. But my kingdom is not from the world." (John 18:36)

It was now early Friday morning, the day of Passover, and Jesus had been up the entire night before—eating the Passover meal with His disciples, praying in the garden, being arrested, and being condemned to death by the Jewish council. Now the whole group of Jewish leaders brought Jesus to the home of Pilate, the Roman governor. *Why do you think they went to see Pilate?*

The Jewish leaders did not have the authority or the right to put someone to death. They needed the Roman governor to order that. But when the leaders got to Pilate's home, they would not go inside. *Do you know why they would not go inside?* Pilate was a Gentile, so if the religious leaders went inside Pilate's house, they would be "unclean." *What is so utterly foolish about this?*

The Jewish leaders were worried about being unclean or impure and unable to approach a Holy God by simply going into a Gentile home...while they were *plotting the death of Jesus! Which is the greater offense to God?* They could not see their great sin of hatred, envy, rebellion, and murder. No wonder Jesus called them blind guides. Jesus had once said to them, *"You blind guides, straining out a gnat and swallowing a camel"*! A gnat is a very tiny bug. The Pharisees and scribes were so concerned about keeping the "gnats" of the law—the less important parts of the law. But they "swallowed camels"—they disobeyed the great or "weightier" commands like justice, mercy, and faithfulness. They not only did this themselves but, as teachers and leaders, they were leading the Jews to live the same way.

When Pilate came outside, the Jewish leaders started accusing Jesus of wanting to overthrow the government and be king. So Pilate asked Jesus, "Are you the king of the Jews?" Jesus answered, "You have said so." *Then Pilate said to the chief priests and the crowds, "I find no fault in this man."* But the Jews would not give up. They made up all kinds of lies about Jesus. But Pilate found a way out of having to decide about Jesus. Since Jesus was from Galilee, he sent Jesus to Herod, who ruled over Galilee. *Do you remember who this Herod was?* He was the man who had John the Baptist beheaded.

Herod was actually glad to see Jesus because he had heard about Jesus and was hoping Jesus would do some miracles. *What was wrong with Herod's thinking?* Jesus was not some kind of magician performing miracles to entertain people. **Jesus' miracles were signs that He is the all-powerful God.** The signs were to show that Jesus was more than a man. He was God in the form of man. Herod asked Jesus many questions, but Jesus would not answer him. The Jewish leaders accused Jesus "vehemently." *Do you know what "vehemently" means?* It means fiercely. They were getting bolder and angrier, and they wanted to make sure Jesus was put to death!

Herod and his soldiers mocked Jesus and sent Him back to Pilate. Again, Pilate told the crowd that Jesus had done nothing deserving death. He would punish Jesus and let Him go. But the crowd was not satisfied. So Pilate questioned Jesus again—"What have you done? Are you the King of the Jews?"

> *Jesus answered,* **"My kingdom is not of this world**. *If my kingdom were of this world, my servants would have been fighting, that I might not be delivered over to the Jews. But my kingdom is not from the world." (John 18:36)*

It was a tradition that during the feast of the Passover the governor would set one prisoner free. Pilate was nervous. His wife had sent him a message saying that she had been troubled by a dream. Her dream warned her that Jesus was innocent. So Pilate offered to release either Jesus or Barabbas. He knew the Jewish leaders had accused Jesus because they were envious that people were following Jesus. But Barabbas was a well-known thief and a murderer. Surely, Jesus would be released, and Pilate would be rid of this problem. *But they all cried out together, "Away with this man, and release to us Barabbas."*

Then Pilate had Jesus whipped. The whips had jagged pieces of metal in them. The soldiers twisted a vine of thorns together to make a crown for Jesus. They pushed the crown onto Jesus' head and dressed him in a purple robe. They spit on Him and mocked Him. *They came up to him saying, "Hail, King of the Jews!" and struck him with their hands.* Then Pilate brought Jesus out to the Jews. Surely, they would be satisfied when they saw that Jesus had been punished, Pilate announced to the crowd, *"See, I am bringing him out to you that you may know that I find no guilt in him"*...When the chief priests and the officers saw him, they cried out, *"Crucify him, crucify him!"*

Pilate brought Jesus inside again and questioned Him. But Jesus didn't answer Pilate. *So Pilate said to him, "You will not speak to me? Do you not know that I have authority to release you and authority to crucify you?" Jesus answered him, "You would have no authority over me at all unless it had been given you from above."* Pilate was not in charge. **God is sovereign over all things.** Nothing that happens is outside of God's purposes, and nothing can stop God's plan. No governor, king, or ruler is greater than God…and any power they have has been given to them by God.

Pilate went out to the people again. He was hoping to release Jesus. But the Jews were determined to crucify Jesus. They said that if Pilate released Jesus, he was not a friend of Caesar, the emperor of Rome. The crowd was getting out of control, screaming at Pilate to crucify Jesus.

> *So when Pilate saw that he was gaining nothing, but rather that a riot was beginning, he took water and washed his hands before the crowd, saying, "I am innocent of this man's blood; see to it yourselves." And all the people answered, "His blood be on us and on our children!"…So Pilate, wishing to satisfy the crowd, released for them Barabbas, and having scourged Jesus, he delivered him to be crucified. (Matthew 27:24-25; Mark 15:15)*

Pilate knew Jesus was innocent...but he was afraid of the crowd. He wanted to please them rather than do what he knew was right. So he sent an innocent man, the Son of God, to be killed. The soldiers took Jesus inside and *began to salute him, "Hail, King of the Jews!" And they were striking his head with a reed and spitting on him...And when they had mocked him, they stripped him of the purple cloak and put his own clothes on him. And they led him out to crucify him.* The sinless Jesus was being put to death for a crime He did not commit, for evils He did not do, and for sins that were not His own.

He went out, bearing his own cross. At some point, the soldiers grabbed a man named Simon of Cyrene and forced him to carry the cross behind Jesus to a place called Golgotha. A great crowd of people followed Jesus, including women who were crying for Jesus. Jesus turned to them and said, *"Daughters of Jerusalem, do not weep for me, but weep for yourselves and for your children."* Jesus warned them that days of greater persecution were coming. His message of repentance and faith had been rejected when He spoke it in person. It would be rejected even more when He was not in person on earth.

Just like the trip Abraham and Isaac took up Mount Moriah, so another Father brought His Son to be the sacrifice for sin. God gave Abraham a substitute ram to take Isaac's place, but **God's Son was the sacrificial lamb who was the substitute for man's sin.**

Who put Jesus on the cross? Was it Pilate? Or the Jews? Or Satan? God did. God planned the cross and permitted evil men to kill His Son. But it was our sin that made the cross necessary.

Unless you truly trust in Jesus' payment for your sin on the cross, you will bear the punishment for your sin. Have you come to Jesus, the spotless Lamb of God, for the forgiveness of your sin?

All we like sheep have gone astray; we have turned—every one—to his own way; and the LORD has laid on him the iniquity of us all. (Isaiah 53:6)

He himself bore our sins in his body on the tree, that we might die to sin and live to righteousness. By his wounds you have been healed. (1 Peter 2:24)

THAT YOU MAY BELIEVE

What does this chapter tell us about God?

Talk about and apply the **biblical truths** in **bold** text. Make them personal and apply them to what is happening in your family, church, community, or the world today.

Explain John 18:36.

What is so wrong about the religious leaders being envious of Jesus? (Make sure your child understands not only the sin of envy, but also the sins of not believing in Jesus and treasuring the kingdom of this world more than the Kingdom of God. The religious leaders should have rejoiced that people were following Jesus—that the Son's ministry was fruitful, and people were believing in Christ.)

Talk About: *He himself bore our sins in his body on the tree, that we might die to sin and live to righteousness. By his wounds you have been healed. (1 Peter 2:24)*

What sin do you see in the Jews? In Pilate? In the soldiers? In yourself?

Pray: Thank Jesus for enduring shame and suffering for sinners. Confess your sin. Thank God that He is a forgiving God.

Think About: *How did my sin put Jesus on the cross?*

MAN OF SORROWS

Isaiah 53

Who has believed what he has heard from us? And to whom has the arm of the LORD been revealed? ²For he grew up before him like a young plant, and like a root out of dry ground; he had no form or majesty that we should look at him, and no beauty that we should desire him. ³He was despised and rejected by men; a man of sorrows, and acquainted with grief; and as one from whom men hide their faces he was despised, and we esteemed him not. ⁴Surely he has borne our griefs and carried our sorrows; yet we esteemed him stricken, smitten by God, and afflicted. ⁵But he was pierced for our transgressions; he was crushed for our iniquities; upon him was the chastisement that brought us peace, and with his wounds we are healed. ⁶All we like sheep have gone astray; we have turned—every one—to his own way; and the LORD has laid on him the iniquity of us all. ⁷He was oppressed, and he was afflicted, yet he opened not his mouth; like a lamb that is led to the slaughter, and like a sheep that before its shearers is silent, so he opened not his mouth. ⁸By oppression and judgment he was taken away; and as for his generation, who considered that he was cut off out of the land of the living, stricken for the transgression of my people? ⁹And they made his grave with the wicked and with a rich man in his death, although he had done no violence, and there was no deceit in his mouth. ¹⁰Yet it was the will of the LORD to crush him; he has put him to grief; when his soul makes an offering for guilt, he shall see his offspring; he shall prolong his days; the will of the LORD shall prosper in his hand. ¹¹Out of the anguish of his soul he shall see and be satisfied; by his knowledge shall the righteous one, my servant, make many to be accounted righteous, and he shall bear their iniquities. ¹²Therefore I will divide him a portion with the many, and he shall divide the spoil with the strong, because he poured out his soul to death and was numbered with the transgressors; yet he bore the sin of many, and makes intercession for the transgressors.

CHAPTER 127
FATHER, FORGIVE THEM

Jesus Is Crucified—Matthew 27:34-44; Mark 15:23-32; Luke 23:32-43; John 19:18-27

And Jesus said, "Father, forgive them, for they know not what they do." (Luke 23:34a)

Why did Jesus have to die?

Suppose there was a very cute, cuddly little puppy…and someone started kicking the puppy over and over. The puppy was yelping with pain and fear, but the person kept kicking the puppy until it lay bleeding and unmoving on the ground. *How would you feel?*

You would feel so angry at the cruel, harsh, sinful treatment of the puppy. **It is right to be angry at sin and cruelty**. But the meanness that you would see is a very, very, very tiny, itty-bitty part of all the sin that God sees. And the anger that you would feel is a very, very, very weak anger compared to God's fierce anger—His wrath—that He feels toward sin. **God is holy, and He cannot tolerate sin**. There has to be punishment for rebelling against God and breaking God's good and loving commands. God could punish every person for his sin…but He chose to provide a sin-bearer for His people—for those who would trust in Jesus. God paid for those sins Himself by pouring out His wrath on His Son. **Jesus died to receive the punishment sinners deserve. Jesus, who kept all of God's righteous Laws, didn't deserve punishment…but He willingly died for the sins of His people—for those who would trust in Him.**

Jesus was taken with two other men, men who were criminals, to a place called Golgotha or Calvary to be crucified.[20] The soldiers stretched Jesus' arms out on the cross. Then they took nails and drove them in His hands near His wrists. What excruciating pain this must have been for Jesus! Then they took His feet and nailed them to the cross, causing even more extreme pain. A sign written by Pilate was hung on the cross in three languages saying, "This is Jesus, the King of the Jews." The crowd around Jesus was made up of soldiers, religious rulers, Jews, Gentiles, men, women, children…and Jesus' followers, too. How differently the people in the crowd must have felt. Some were angry; others were mocking; some were probably scared; and surely, some were crying. Jesus looked down on it all. *What did Jesus see as He looked down from the cross?*

The soldiers took Jesus' clothes and divided them into four parts—one part for each soldier. But His tunic, the inner garment, was woven in one piece so the soldiers decided to "cast lots" (like rolling dice) to see who would win it. This was to fulfill the Old Testament Scripture, *"They divided my garments among them and for my clothing they cast lots."* Jesus was in agonizing pain, sacrificing Himself for sinners, and the soldiers ignored His suffering. They were more interested in His clothing.

The crowd spit out many insults at Jesus. *"You who would destroy the temple and rebuild it in three days, save yourself! If you are the Son of God, come down from the cross!"* The chief priests, scribes, and elders mocked Him. *"He saved others; he cannot save himself. He is the King of Israel; let him come down now from the cross, and we will believe in him. He trusts in God; let God deliver him now, if he desires him. For he said, 'I am the Son of God.'"* Jesus could have broken loose from the cross; He could have called thousands of angels to wipe those people out; He could have stopped the mocking in one second. But He didn't.

Can you imagine what it must have been like for Jesus to hear all the mocking and insults, knowing He could stop it...but instead He endured it all? Jesus looked down on all this—the cruelty, the insults, the disrespect, the greed, the envy, the hatred...and He said, *"Father, forgive them, for they know not what they do."* Jesus' response was love! Jesus' response was forgiveness! Jesus' response was to pray for others!

Even one of the criminals hanging beside Jesus insulted Him saying, *"Are you not the Christ? Save yourself and us!"* This man, in his last hours of life, was hatefully sinning. But the other criminal scolded him.

> *"Do you not fear God, since you are under the same sentence of condemnation? And we indeed justly, for we are receiving the due reward of our deeds; but this man has done nothing*

said to him, "Truly, I say to you, today you will be with me in paradise." (Luke 23:40-43)

Jesus willingly forgives anyone who comes to Him in faith. Even a criminal who repents at the end of his life finds forgiveness from Jesus. Jesus spoke truthfully when He had said, *"I have come into the world as light, so that whoever believes in me may not remain in darkness."*

Jesus saw something else when He looked down from the cross. He saw His mother, His aunt, another woman, and Mary Magdalene. How heartbroken they must have been. Jesus, whom they loved, was nailed to a cross dying! He was bleeding from the thorns pierced into His head and the nails driven into His feet and hands. He was bruised and bleeding from the beatings He had endured. He was insulted and mocked. How they must have grieved to see Jesus on the cross.

Jesus also saw the disciple John, His trusted and beloved friend. *When Jesus saw his mother and the disciple whom he loved standing nearby, he said to his mother, "Woman, behold, your son!" Then he said to the disciple, "Behold, your mother!" And from that hour the disciple took her to his own home.* Even in His time of greatest agony, Jesus cared about others.

The physical suffering that Jesus felt on the cross was extremely painful. The emotional sadness He felt in seeing His followers mourning and others sinfully mock and reject Him was agonizing. But there was an even greater suffering that Jesus experienced on the cross—the agony of bearing the sin of His people and experiencing the wrath of God.

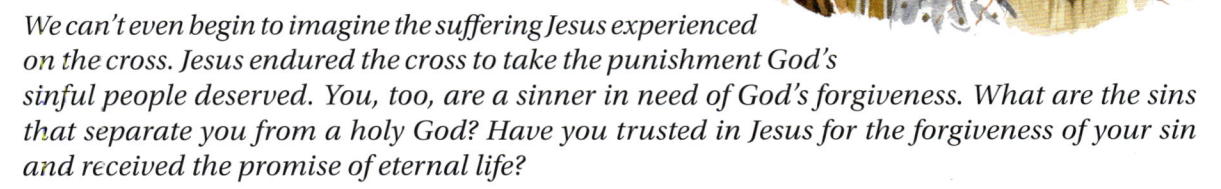

We can't even begin to imagine the suffering Jesus experienced on the cross. Jesus endured the cross to take the punishment God's sinful people deserved. You, too, are a sinner in need of God's forgiveness. What are the sins that separate you from a holy God? Have you trusted in Jesus for the forgiveness of your sin and received the promise of eternal life?

> But he was pierced for our transgressions; he was crushed for our iniquities; upon him was the chastisement that brought us peace, and with his wounds we are healed. (Isaiah 53:5)

THAT YOU MAY BELIEVE

What does this chapter tell us about God?

Talk about and apply the **biblical truths** in **bold** text. Make them personal and apply them to what is happening in your family, church, community, or the world today.

Does sin make you angry? Explain. Why does God have the right to be angry at sin and punish sinners?

Talk About: *But he was pierced for our transgressions; he was crushed for our iniquities; upon him was the chastisement that brought us peace, and with his wounds we are healed. (Isaiah 53:5)*

What is the consequence of not accepting Jesus as your sin-bearer and Savior? Explain.

Pray: Thank Jesus for dying on the cross. Confess your sin and ask Jesus to give you a heart of faith.

Think About: *How can I tell if I am trusting in Jesus as my Savior?*

---

20 Golgotha is Aramaic for "Place of a Skull." Calvary is the Latin translation. Calvary is a skull-shaped hill outside Jerusalem.

CHAPTER 128
"IT IS FINISHED"

Jesus Dies and Is Buried—Matthew 27:45-66; Mark 15:33-47; Luke 23:44-56; John 19:28-42

And behold, the curtain of the temple was torn in two from top to bottom. (Matthew 27:51a)

"Truly this was the Son of God!" (Matthew 27:54b)

It was now about noon, a time when it is usually light outside, but "darkness came over the whole land" until about 3:00 in the afternoon. It was as dark as night, in the middle of the day. Surely, something very strange was happening. **The wrath of God toward sin was being poured out on Jesus, the substitute sacrifice for His people. God's love was being poured on His people as Jesus took God's punishment for their sin.** Jesus had always enjoyed perfect fellowship with God, but now He cried out with a loud voice, *"Eloi, Eloi, lema sabachthani?" which means, "My God, my God, why have you forsaken me?"* We can't even imagine the darkness of that hour, the agony Jesus suffered, the rejection He felt.

After this, Jesus, knowing that all was now finished, said (to fulfill the Scripture), "I thirst." There was a jar of sour wine nearby, and someone dipped a sponge on a branch into the sour wine and held the sponge up to Jesus' mouth. *When Jesus had received the sour wine, he said,* **"It is finished"***...Then Jesus, calling out with a loud voice, said, "Father, into your hands I commit my spirit!" And having said this, he breathed his last. And behold, the curtain of the temple was torn in two, from top to bottom,*

What a shocking thing it must have been that the temple curtain tore when Jesus died! *What did it mean? What was the significance of the curtain being torn in two—from top to bottom?* The temple curtain separated the Holy Place from the Most Holy Place. It was a symbol of man's separation from God because of sin. The high priest was allowed to enter the Most Holy Place only once a year, entering the presence of God to make "atonement" or payment for sin so that Israel could be at peace with God. But now this curtain was torn in two... from *top to bottom*. God had torn the curtain! Jesus is the final sacrifice for sin. There is no need for temple sacrifices any more. Jesus' blood is the eternal sacrifice that redeems forever those who trust in Him. **Jesus is the perfect and final sacrifice.** There is no more need to sprinkle blood on the mercy seat because Jesus' blood takes away man's sin. No longer is there just a temporary covering for sin, but Jesus provides atonement for sin—not just a covering but a taking away of sin. Jesus *takes away* sin and *gives* His perfect righteousness to those who trust in Him as their Savior. Sin is removed and **a perfect covering of righteousness over us is given. Jesus is the Perfect High Priest** who is the "go between" or mediator between man and God. Through faith in Jesus, God's people can go directly to Him in prayer and confession. What an amazing thing it was that the curtain of the temple was torn in two! What a gloriously wonderful thing it is that those who are trusting in Jesus can come into God's very presence through prayer!

> *And behold, the curtain of the temple was torn in two, from top to bottom.*
>
> *And the earth shook, and the rocks were split. The tombs also were opened. And many bodies of the saints who had fallen asleep were raised, and coming out of the tombs after his resurrection they went into the holy city and appeared to many. When the centurion and those who were with him, keeping watch over Jesus, saw the earthquake and what took place, they were filled with awe and said,* **"Truly this was the Son of God!"** *(Matthew 27:51b-54)*

To those with blind eyes, Jesus was just a good teacher, a miracle-worker, a prophet…or even a troublemaker. But to those whose eyes were opened by the Holy Spirit, it was clear—**JESUS IS THE SON OF GOD!** The centurion was one whose eyes were opened. When he saw the earthquake and all the other happenings, his response was, *"Truly this was the Son of God!"*

Since it was late on Friday, the Jews asked Pilate to order the soldiers to break the legs of the men who were crucified. By breaking the legs, those on the cross could no longer push themselves up in order to let the air out of their lungs to take another breath. Since they couldn't breathe, they would die. This way the bodies could be taken down before the Sabbath. But when the soldiers got to Jesus, He was already dead, so they did not break His legs. But one of the soldiers stabbed Jesus' side with a spear, and blood and water flowed out. This was a fulfillment of Scripture that not one bone would be broken, and that Jesus' side would be pierced. Jesus fulfilled every word of prophecy—even in His death.

Now there was a man named Joseph, from the Jewish town of Arimathea. He was a member of the council, a good and righteous man, who had not consented to their decision and action; and he was looking for the kingdom of God. This man went to Pilate and asked for the body of Jesus. Do you know who helped Joseph of Arimathea? It was Nicodemus the Pharisee who had come to Jesus at night. Nicodemus brought spices, and the two men wrapped Jesus' body and the spices in strips of cloth. Then they put Jesus's body in Joseph's own new tomb and rolled a stone over the opening.

But the chief priests and Pharisees remembered that Jesus had said that He would rise after three days. Even after all they had seen, these men still believed that Jesus was a fake or an imposter. They were afraid that Jesus' disciples might steal his body and tell the people that Jesus had risen from the dead. So they asked Pilate to seal the tomb and order soldiers to guard it. The tomb was sealed; the guards were on duty. The disciples would not fool the people! How foolishly unbelieving these men were.

When Jesus said, *"It is finished!"* Jesus had accomplished what He came to do. He took the wrath of God and paid the price for man's sin. He defeated sin and evil. He crushed the head of the serpent. He gained forgiveness, perfect righteousness, and eternal life for those who trust in Him.

The cross is good news for sinners! We have a place to go to get rid of our sin and guilt and shame! God has made a way for us to be at peace with Him and have our sins forgiven. You can have a right relationship with God and receive the promise of eternal life with God. But this is only possible through faith in Jesus. Do you want a right relationship with God? Will you receive Jesus as your Savior?

> **Therefore, since we have been justified by faith, we have peace with God through our Lord Jesus Christ. (Romans 5:1)**

THAT YOU MAY BELIEVE

What does this chapter tell us about God?

Talk about and apply the **biblical truths** in **bold** text. Make them personal and apply them to what is happening in your family, church, community, or the world today.

How can you be seen by God as forgiven, righteous, and "not guilty"?

Talk About: *Therefore, since we have been justified by faith, we have peace with God through our Lord Jesus Christ. (Romans 5:1)*

What does true faith in Jesus look like?

Pray: Praise God for being a gracious and forgiving God. Thank Jesus for His sacrifice on the cross. Confess that you are a sinner in need of God's grace. Ask Jesus to be your Savior and commit yourself to follow Him.

Think About: *Have I received Jesus as my Lord and Savior?*

The OLD TESTAMENT POINTED to CHRIST

Jesus is the second Adam who perfectly kept the Law and clothes those who trust in Him with His perfect righteousness.

For as by the one man's disobedience the many were made sinners, so by the one man's obedience the many will be made righteous. (Romans 5:19)

Jesus is the one way of salvation.

Jesus said to him, "I am the way, and the truth, and the life. No one comes to the Father except through me." (John 14:6)

Jesus is the Promised Son born through the power of the Holy Spirit, belonging to the line of Abraham, whom God the Father offered as a sacrifice to redeem a people for Himself, a holy nation to bless the world.

"For God so loved the world, that he gave his only Son, that whoever believes in him should not perish but have eternal life." (John 3:16)

But you are a chosen race, a royal priesthood, a holy nation, a people for his own possession, that you may proclaim the excellencies of him who called you out of darkness into his marvelous light. (1 Peter 2:9)

Jesus is the substitute—a sacrifice who has paid the price for the sins of those who have faith in Him so that we might live.

"Behold, the Lamb of God, who takes away the sin of the world!" (John 1:29b)

Jesus is the perfect and final prophet through whom God has spoken.

Long ago, at many times and in many ways, God spoke to our fathers by the prophets, but in these last days he has spoken to us by his Son, whom he appointed the heir of all things, through whom also he created the world. (Hebrews 1:1-2)

Jesus is the Passover Lamb, who has provided a way for those who believe in Him to have their sins passed over and to be freed from the slavery of sin.

For Christ, our Passover lamb, has been sacrificed. (1 Corinthians 5:7b)

…you were ransomed from the futile ways inherited from your forefathers, not with perishable things such as silver or gold, but with the precious blood of Christ, like that of a lamb without blemish or spot. (1 Peter 1:18-19)

Jesus has rescued His people from the slavery of sin and darkness to His Kingdom of freedom and forgiveness.

He has delivered us from the domain of darkness and transferred us to the kingdom of his beloved Son, in whom we have redemption, the forgiveness of sin. (Colossians 1:13-14)

Jesus is the Perfect Law-Keeper who justifies (declares righteous) those who come to Him by faith.

For our sake he made him to be sin who knew no sin, so that in him we might become the righteousness of God. (2 Corinthians 5:21)

Now before faith came, we were held captive under the law, imprisoned until the coming faith would be revealed. So then, the law was our guardian until Christ came, in order that we might be justified by faith. But now that faith has come, we are no longer under a guardian, for in Christ Jesus you are all sons of God, through faith. (Galatians 3:23-26)

By His blood on the cross, Jesus replaced the temporary old covenant of the Law and made an eternal new covenant between man and God—a covenant of salvation by faith through grace.

But as it is, Christ has obtained a ministry that is as much more excellent than the old as the covenant he mediates is better, since it is enacted on better promises. (Hebrews 8:6)

There is therefore now no condemnation for those who are in Christ Jesus. For the law of the Spirit of life has set you free in Christ Jesus from the law of sin and death. (Romans 8:1-2)

For by grace you have been saved through faith. And this is not your own doing; it is the gift of God, not a result of works, so that no one may boast. (Ephesians 2:8-9)

Now it is evident that no one is justified before God by the law, for "The righteous shall live by faith."…Christ redeemed us from the curse of the law by becoming a curse for us…so that in Christ Jesus the blessing of Abraham might come to the Gentiles, so that we might receive the promised Spirit through faith. (Galatians 3:11, 13a, 14)

Jesus is the Bread of Life who satisfies and gives eternal life.

Jesus then said to them, "Truly, truly, I say to you, it was not Moses who gave you the bread from heaven, but my Father gives you the true bread from heaven. For the bread of God is he who comes down from heaven and gives life to the world." (John 6:32-33)

Jesus said to them, "I am the bread of life; whoever comes to me shall not hunger, and whoever believes in me shall never thirst." (John 6:35)

Jesus is the perfect and permanent High Priest, who has made a single sacrifice for all time and is seated at the right hand of God as the mediator of a better covenant.

The former priests were many in number, because they were prevented by death from continuing in office, but he holds his priesthood permanently, because he continues forever. Consequently, he is able to save to the uttermost those who draw near to God through him, since he always lives to make intercession for them. (Hebrews 7:23-25)

We have this as a sure and steadfast anchor of the soul, a hope that enters into the inner place behind the curtain, where Jesus has gone as a forerunner on our behalf... (Hebrews 6:19-20a)

For Christ has entered, not into holy places made with hands, which are copies of the true things, but into heaven itself, now to appear in the presence of God on our behalf. (Hebrews 9:24)

Jesus is God dwelling among His people in human form, and we go to Jesus Christ to experience the blessing of God's presence.

And the Word became flesh and dwelt among us, and we have seen his glory, glory as of the only Son from the Father, full of grace and truth. (John 1:14)

Jesus is the final Scapegoat who has carried away our sins so that they are remembered no more.

All we like sheep have gone astray; we have turned—every one—to his own way; and...the LORD has laid on him the iniquity of us all. (Isaiah 53:6)

Jesus died on the cross to save all those who believe in Him.

And as Moses lifted up the serpent in the wilderness, so must the Son of Man be lifted up, that whoever believes in him may have eternal life. (John 3:14-15)

Jesus is the everlasting King from the line of David who will reign with righteousness forever.

"He will be great and will be called the Son of the Most High. And the Lord God will give to him the throne of his father David, and he will reign over the house of Jacob forever, and of his kingdom there will be no end." (Luke 1:32-33)

"When the Son of Man comes in his glory, and all the angels with him, then he will sit on his glorious throne." (Matthew 25:31)

Jesus has made a way for those who trust in Him to enter into the presence of God.

Since then we have a great high priest who has passed through the heavens, Jesus, the Son of God, let us hold fast our confession...Let us then with confidence draw near to the throne of grace, that we may receive mercy and find grace to help in time of need. (Hebrews 4:14, 16)

Therefore, brothers, since we have confidence to enter the holy places by the blood of Jesus, by the new and living way that he opened for us through the curtain, that is, through his flesh, (Hebrews 10:19-20)

CHAPTER 129
IMPOSTER OR THE SON OF GOD?

Resurrection Appearances—
Matthew 28:1-10, 16-20; John 20:11-29; John 21:1-17

..."Why do you seek the living among the dead? He is not here, but has risen." (Luke 24:5b-6a)

Do you know what an "impostor" is? An impostor is someone who pretends to be someone else in order to fool or deceive others. An impostor is a fake. Jesus' tomb was sealed and guarded because the chief priests and Pharisees said that Jesus—*"that impostor"*—claimed He would rise from the dead. So they wanted to make very sure that the disciples did not steal Jesus' body and claim that He had risen from the dead.

Was Jesus an impostor? Was Jesus simply a dead man who had made outlandish or ridiculous claims? Or was Jesus the Son of God who would truly rise from the dead? While the soldiers were guarding the tomb, something amazing happened!

> *And behold, there was a great earthquake, for an angel of the Lord descended from heaven and came and rolled back the stone and sat on it. His appearance was like lightning, and his clothing white as snow. And for fear of him the guards trembled and became like dead men. (Matthew 28:2-4)*

Can you imagine how amazed and how scared the guards were? They couldn't even move! The stone was rolled away, and they could see inside the tomb. But Jesus wasn't there!

After the Sabbath, on Sunday morning, Mary Magdalene and some other women were on the way to Jesus' tomb with some spices. They wanted to anoint Jesus' body—to rub oil on it to keep the dead body from smelling. But there was a big problem. *Do you know what it was?* How would they move the big stone from the entrance? But when the women got to the tomb...the stone was already rolled away! What had happened? The women entered the tomb and saw an angel. What an astonishing surprise! The angel told them not to be afraid. *"I know you seek Jesus who was crucified.* **He is not here, for he has risen as he said.***"* Then the angel told them to go quickly and tell the disciples that Jesus had risen! Jesus was going to Galilee, and they would see Him there!

So they departed quickly from the tomb with fear and great joy, and ran to tell his disciples. And behold, Jesus met them and said, "Greetings!" And they came up and took hold of his feet and worshiped him. Then Jesus said to them, "Do not be afraid; go and tell my brothers to go to Galilee, and there they will see me." (Matthew 28:8-10)

Jesus appeared to Mary Magdalene alone near the tomb. She was weeping outside the tomb and turned around and saw a man. She thought he was the gardener until He called her by name—*"Mary."* Then she knew he was Jesus, and she went to tell the disciples, *"I have seen the Lord."*

Later in the day, two disciples were talking together as they were walking to the village of Emmaus. Jesus caught up to them, but they didn't recognize Him—"Their eyes were kept from recognizing him." He asked them what they were talking about. Naturally, they were surprised! The events of the past few days were big news! So they told Him about Jesus'

crucifixion and the women's report of His resurrection. *And he said to them, "O foolish ones, and slow of heart to believe all that the prophets have spoken! Was it not necessary that the Christ should suffer these things and enter into his glory?" And beginning with Moses and all the Prophets, he interpreted to them in all the Scriptures the things concerning himself.*

When they got to the village, they invited the "stranger" to stay with them. As they were eating their meal, Jesus "took the bread and blessed it and broke it and gave it to them." *What is this a reminder of? And their eyes were opened, and they recognized him. And he vanished from their sight. They said to each other, "Did not our hearts burn within us while he talked to us on the road, while he opened to us the Scriptures?" And they rose that same hour and returned to Jerusalem. And they found the eleven and those who were with them gathered together, saying,* **"The Lord has risen indeed***, and has appeared to Simon!" (Luke 24:31-34)*

As the two disciples were telling the others about what had happened on the road to Emmaus, *Jesus appeared* in the room! *"Peace be with you,"* He said. The disciples were startled and afraid, thinking they were seeing a spirit. But Jesus showed them His hands and His side, and they were full of joy! They had witnessed His death and resurrection. Jesus told them to spread the news to all nations but to wait in Jerusalem until the coming of the Holy Spirit.

However, Thomas was not with them when Jesus came, so when the other disciples told him, *"We have seen the Lord,"* he didn't believe it. *"Unless I see in his hands the mark of the nails, and place my finger into the mark of the nails, and place my hand into his side, I will never believe."* Thomas was not convinced. He doubted that Jesus had risen from the dead...but eight days later when the doors were locked, *Jesus appeared in the room with them again!*

Then he said to Thomas, "Put your finger here, and see my hands; and put out your hand, and place it in my side. Do not disbelieve, but believe." Thomas answered him, "My Lord and my God!" Jesus said to him, "Have you believed because you have seen me? Blessed are those who have not seen and yet have believed." (John 20:27-29)

Jesus appeared yet another time. Peter, Thomas, Nathanael, James, John, and two other disciples went fishing. But they didn't catch anything that night. As morning came and they got closer to the shore, a man stood on the beach. He called to them and asked if they had caught any fish. When they told Him they hadn't, He told them, *"Cast the net on the right side of the boat, and you will find some."* Sure enough, they threw in the net, and it was so full of fish they could not drag it into the boat. John said to Peter, *"It is the Lord!"*

What do you think Peter did? He jumped out of the boat and swam to shore where Jesus was cooking fish over a fire. Jesus invited the disciples to eat breakfast, and none of them asked who He was…They all knew it was Jesus. While they were eating, Jesus asked Peter three times, *"Simon…do you love me?"* Each time Simon Peter said he did…and each time Jesus told him to care for the believers, to "feed His sheep." Peter was forgiven for denying Jesus. He would still be used of God to build the Church.

Jesus also "appeared to more than five hundred brothers at one time." So many people had seen the resurrected Christ—not just His disciples. Jesus appeared on a mountain in Galilee. He had told the disciples to meet Him there. *And Jesus came and said to them, "All authority in heaven and on earth has been given to me. Go therefore and make disciples of all nations, baptizing them in the name of the Father and of the Son and of the Holy Spirit, teaching them to observe all that I have commanded you. And behold, I am with you always, to the end of the age."*

The last time Jesus appeared to the disciples was near Bethany. He lifted up His hands and blessed them. *While he blessed them, he parted from them and was carried up into heaven. And they worshiped him and returned to Jerusalem with great joy, and were continually in the temple blessing God.* They would wait in Jerusalem as Jesus had told them to do until the Holy Spirit came upon them.

Was Jesus an impostor, or is He the Son of God? There were many witnesses of the resurrection—people who saw and spoke to Jesus. Angels testified that Jesus had risen from the dead. The resurrected Jesus took bread, blessed it, and broke it. He created another miracle of a great catch of fish. He showed the disciples the nail scars on His hands and the scar on His side.

Again and again, Jesus appeared in person. Jesus is not an imposter. **Jesus is the Son of God who was crucified, died, and was buried. On the third day, He rose from the dead, defeating death, sin, and Satan! He is the living Savior and permanent High Priest.** *Do you believe this?*

Now Jesus did many other signs in the presence of the disciples, which are not written in this book; but these are written so that you may believe that Jesus is the Christ, the Son of God, and that by believing you may have life in his name. (John 20:30-31)

THAT YOU MAY BELIEVE

What does this chapter tell us about God?

Talk about and apply the **biblical truths** in **bold** text. Make them personal and apply them to what is happening in your family, church, community, or the world today.

Read John 20:1-18. What does this account tell you about Jesus?

Talk About: *Now Jesus did many other signs in the presence of the disciples, which are not written in this book; but these are written so that you may believe that Jesus is the Christ, the Son of God, and that by believing you may have life in his name. (John 20:30-31)*

If someone told you that no one can rise from the dead, what would you tell that person?

Pray: Thank God for raising Jesus from the dead. Ask God for the gift of faith.

Think About: *What do you believe about Jesus? How do you know that you believe it?*

Memorize: Matthew 28:18-20

CHAPTER 130

YOU WILL RECEIVE POWER

The Holy Spirit Comes with Power—Acts 1-2

"But you will receive power when the Holy Spirit has come upon you, and you will be my witnesses in Jerusalem and in all Judea and Samaria, and to the end of the earth." (Acts 1:8)

Can you imagine what the disciples must have thought and felt when they saw Jesus taken into heaven? What reactions might they have had? They must have been amazed. Surely, they were sad to see Jesus leave. Some may have been excited, or they may have been nervous, confused, or even doubtful. They probably didn't understand the importance of the "Ascension"—of Jesus being taken up into heaven. Jesus went to heaven and "sat down at the right hand of God." His work on earth was done. Through His suffering on the cross and His resurrection, Jesus bought complete forgiveness and eternal life for those who are trusting in Him. Jesus returned to heaven to rule with the highest authority so that believers can *with confidence draw near to the throne of grace, that we may receive mercy and find grace to help in time of need.* Jesus is working to help and bless His people!

Before Jesus returned to heaven, the disciples received a promise that He would return. As they were looking up to heaven, two angels stood by them and said, *"This Jesus, who was taken up from you into heaven, will come in the same way as you saw him go into heaven."* Someday, just as Jesus left in glory, He will return in glory to gather His people to Himself forever!

But in the meantime, Jesus is continuing His work on earth through the Holy Spirit and the

Church. Before He ascended into heaven, Jesus told the disciples to wait in Jerusalem: *"But you will receive power when the Holy Spirit has come upon you, and you will be my witnesses in Jerusalem and in all Judea and Samaria, and to the end of the earth."*

So the disciples were waiting—the eleven disciples, all but Judas. While they were waiting for the coming of the Holy Spirit, they were praying along with other believers. And Peter stood up and spoke to them about the missing disciple. The Scripture had been fulfilled—Judas betrayed Jesus for thirty pieces of silver. But what happened to Judas?

> *Then Judas, his betrayer, saw that Jesus was condemned, he changed his mind and brought back the thirty pieces of silver to the chief priests and the elders, saying, "I have sinned by betraying innocent blood." They said, "What is that to us? See to it yourself." And throwing down the pieces of silver into the temple, he departed, and he went and hanged himself.* (Matthew 27:3-5)

Another man must be chosen to take Judas's place. But he had to be someone who had been a disciple since the baptism of Jesus and had witnessed the resurrection. The disciples came up with two names, Justus and Matthias. But how could they make this choice? They were only men. How could they know who would be the right person? *And they prayed and said, "You, Lord, who know the hearts of all, show which one of these two you have chosen to take the place in this ministry and apostleship from which Judas turned aside to go to his own place." And they cast lots for them, and the lot fell on Matthias, and he was numbered with the eleven apostles.*

While the disciples were still waiting in Jerusalem, the day of Pentecost arrived. In the Old Testament, the Jews celebrated the Feast of Weeks (also called the Feast of Harvest). It was to celebrate the beginning of the early weeks of the first harvest season. In Greek, the name of this festival is "Pentecost." The apostles were all together celebrating Pentecost when suddenly "there came from heaven a sound like a mighty rushing wind." It filled the whole room and "tongues as of fire" appeared resting on each of them. *And they were all filled with the Holy Spirit and began to speak in other tongues.* They were speaking in languages they had never learned!

Do you think this would seem a bit strange and amazing? Well, it was quite amazing! And it was amazing to some other people, too. Because it was the celebration of Pentecost, there were many Jews who had come for the feast from other nations. These Jews from other nations spoke many different languages. These Jews heard the noise of the apostles and they gathered together to find out what was going on. "And they were amazed and astonished" because all the apostles were from Galilee, but each person was hearing them in their own language! Some were confused but amazed. But others mocked the apostles, saying that they were drunk.

But then Peter stood up and preached to the crowd. The apostles were not drunk, but God was fulfilling a prophecy He had spoken through the prophet Joel.

> "And in the last days it shall be, God declares, that **I will pour out my Spirit** on all flesh… And it shall come to pass that **everyone who calls upon the name of the Lord shall be saved.**" (Acts 2:17a, 21)

Then Peter began to speak about Jesus. *"Men of Israel, hear these words: Jesus of Nazareth, a man attested to you by God with mighty works and wonders and signs that God did through him in your midst, as you yourselves know—this Jesus, delivered up according to the definite plan and foreknowledge of God, you crucified and killed by the hands of lawless men. God raised him up, loosing the pangs of death, because it was not possible for him to be held by it."*

Peter told the Jews that God had proven that Jesus is His Son, the Messiah, by the mighty wonders and signs Jesus did on earth. But the Jews had killed Jesus. Even though this was part of God's plan, it was the evil acts of man that actually killed Jesus. However, God raised

Jesus from the dead because Jesus is life and could not stay dead. Jesus' resurrection proved that He is the Messiah. The apostles had witnessed the resurrection—they saw Jesus and spoke with Him. Jesus is sitting at the right hand of God, and the pouring out of the Holy Spirit showed His authority. He is the promised descendant of King David who would sit on the eternal throne.

Peter boldly told the Jews that the man they crucified is the Lord and Savior God sent to them. **Jesus is God**. When the people heard this, they were in anguish and said, *"Brothers what shall we do?"*

> *And Peter said to them, "Repent and be baptized every one of you in the name of Jesus Christ for the forgiveness of your sins, and you will receive the gift of the Holy Spirit. For the promise is for you and for your children and for all who are far off, everyone whom the Lord our God calls to himself." (Acts 2:38-39)*

Think of how many times the Jews had heard the truth about Jesus. How often they responded with anger, mocking, and even wanting to kill Him. But at Pentecost, about 3,000 people believed and were baptized, declaring to others that they had put their faith in Christ. The Holy Spirit had come with power to show them their guilt and cause them to believe. And, just as Jesus had said, the apostles were His witnesses in Jerusalem.

Has the Holy Spirit shown you your need for a Savior? Are you trusting in Jesus?

> **...if you confess with your mouth that Jesus is Lord and believe in your heart that God raised him from the dead, you will be saved. For with the heart one believes and is justified, and with the mouth one confesses and is saved. (Romans 10:9-10)**

THAT YOU MAY BELIEVE

What does this chapter tell us about God?

Talk about and apply the **biblical truths** in **bold** text. Make them personal and apply them to what is happening in your family, church, community, or the world today.

You can believe in your head that Jesus is the Savior, but is He your Savior?

Talk About: *If you confess with your mouth that Jesus is Lord and believe in your heart that God raised him from the dead, you will be saved. For with the heart one believes and is justified, and with the mouth one confesses and is saved. (Romans 10:9-10)*

How can you and your family be God's witnesses where you live? What ideas do you have to share the gospel?

Pray: Praise God for sending the Holy Spirit to be the Helper. If Jesus is not your Savior, consider receiving Him. If Jesus is your Savior, thank God that He has given you the Holy Spirit to fill and empower you for worship, obedience, and ministry.

Think About: *Do I see the Holy Spirit working in my life?*

CHAPTER 131

A SECOND CHANCE TO BELIEVE IN JESUS AND BE SAVED

A Lame Man Is Healed in Jesus' Name; Peter Preaches Boldly—Acts 3:1-4:31

"we cannot but speak of what we have seen and heard." (Acts 4:20)

"Repent therefore, and turn again, that your sins may be blotted out," (Acts 3:19)

Can you imagine what it would be like to be born lame—to never have been able to walk? What couldn't you do? That is what it was like for a man who lay every day at the temple gate in Jerusalem. Every day he hoped people would give him some coins—some money for food and other things he needed. He was there when Peter and John went to the temple to pray. He saw them and asked them for money.

Peter and John stopped. They looked at the man. "Look at us," they told him. His hopes were high. They had noticed him. Maybe they would give him some money. *But Peter said, "I have no silver and gold, but what I do have I give to you. In the name of Jesus Christ of Nazareth, rise up and walk!"* Peter took the man by the hand, pulled him up, "and immediately his feet and ankles were made strong." *And leaping up he stood and began to walk, and entered the temple with them, walking and leaping and praising God.*

Can you imagine what people thought when they saw him walking and praising God? They recognized him as the lame man from the temple gate. How could he be walking? And leaping? The people were "filled with

209

wonder and amazement." The man hung on to Peter and John and all the people rushed toward them.

Peter had an audience! He would tell them about Jesus! *"Men of Israel, why do you wonder at this, or why do you stare at us, as though by our own power or piety we have made him walk?"* Then Peter began to tell the people whose power healed the man. Just like John the Baptist, Peter, and the other apostles pointed people to Jesus, not to themselves. This is how Peter started his sermon:

> ..."Men of Israel, why do you wonder at this, or why do you stare at us, as though by our own power or piety we have made him walk? The God of Abraham, the God of Isaac, and the God of Jacob, the God of our fathers, glorified his servant Jesus, whom you delivered over and denied in the presence of Pilate, when he had decided to release him. But you denied the Holy and Righteous One, and asked for a murderer to be granted to you, and you killed the Author of life, whom God raised from the dead. To this we are witnesses." (Acts 3:12-15)

Jesus had said that the apostles would be His witnesses, and now Peter was speaking boldly in the temple. God had sent the Messiah first to the Jews, but the Jews in Jerusalem rejected God's Messiah. They had let a murderer go free and had murdered **God's Son, the Holy and Righteous One**. They killed the **Author of life**, but **God raised Jesus from the dead.** Peter continued to tell them that they had "acted in ignorance"—they didn't know what they were doing. If they had truly known who Jesus was, they would not have crucified Him. But God was giving the people of Jerusalem another chance! **God is slow to anger, abounding in steadfast love.** *"Repent therefore, and turn again, that your sins may be blotted out, that times of refreshing may come from the presence of the Lord."*

All the prophets had pointed to Jesus as the Messiah. God had fulfilled all He had foretold through the prophets about the suffering of Christ. The covenant God made to Abraham—that through him all the families of the earth will be blessed—was fulfilled in Jesus. The Jews had waited for hundreds of years for this servant of God...and they totally missed who Jesus is. Though Jesus had been rejected, **Jesus will come again and establish God's Kingdom**. If the Jews accepted Jesus as the Messiah, they could be a part of God's eternal Kingdom. They must turn to God by receiving

Jesus as their Savior. But if the Jews refused to believe in Christ, there would be no forgiveness for them, and they would be "rooted out" or removed from God's people. How kind and merciful of God to give these Jews a second chance. A chance to repent and trust in Jesus! This was very good news—this was amazing news!

As Peter was preaching to the people, the priests, the captain of the temple, and the Sadducees (a powerful political-religious group) came to check out what he was saying. They were very upset because Peter and John were teaching the people and telling them about the resurrection of Jesus. The Sadducees did not believe in any resurrection at all. *Do you know what they did?* They arrested Peter and John. But they could not stop the Holy Spirit from working in the hearts of men. Many people who heard the preaching of Peter believed in Jesus, the Messiah! *Do you know how many people believed?* About 5,000 men!

After a night in jail, Peter and John were brought before Annas, Caiaphas, and other chief priests. These priests demanded to know, "By what power or by what name did you do this?"

Peter, "filled with the Holy Spirit," boldly proclaimed that the crippled man was healed *"by the name of Jesus Christ of Nazareth whom you crucified, whom God raised from the dead...This Jesus, is the stone that was rejected by you, the builders, which has become the cornerstone."*

> **"And there is salvation in no one else, for there is no other name under heaven given among men by which we must be saved." (Acts 4:12)**

Buildings were built in ancient times by first putting the largest, strongest, and most carefully shaped stone at the corner of the building. It was the most important stone. Jesus is like the cornerstone because He is most important. The only way to have salvation from sin and judgment is to build your faith on Jesus.

These leaders were amazed at the boldness of Peter and John, who were common, uneducated men. How could Peter and John teach like this? But the leaders could not argue with Peter and John because the evidence of the work of Jesus was standing there—a crippled man was healed! The only thing the leaders could do was to warn Peter and John not to "speak or teach at all in the name of Jesus."

What do you think Peter and John, who had fled in fear when Jesus was arrested, said? Peter and John boldly announced, *"We cannot but speak of what we have seen and heard."* They would obey God, not these men! Peter had denied even knowing Christ, and now he was standing up to the same men who plotted Jesus' death. The Holy Spirit, the Helper, was making Peter strong. All the leaders could do was to threaten them and let them go. They couldn't punish Peter and John because all the people were praising God for what had happened. Only God could heal someone who had been crippled for more than forty years!

When Peter and John were released, they went to their friends and held a prayer meeting, asking God to give them boldness. *"And now, Lord, look upon their threats and grant to your servants to continue to speak your word with all boldness while you stretch out your hand to heal, and signs and wonders are performed through the name of your holy servant Jesus."* When they had finished praying, the building they were in was "shaken, and they were all filled with the Holy Spirit and continued to speak the word of God with boldness."

Peter's message is for you and for everyone you know. Repent and turn to Jesus and your sins will be blotted out. Do you want your sins to be erased? Trust in Jesus and embrace His salvation!

> **"And there is salvation in no one else, for there is no other name under heaven given among men by which we must be saved." (Acts 4:12)**

THAT YOU MAY BELIEVE

What does this chapter tell us about God?

Talk about and apply the **biblical truths** in **bold** text. Make them personal and apply them to what is happening in your family, church, community, or the world today.

How did Peter and John bring glory to Jesus? What temptations to sin could there have been? How can you fight these temptations and bring glory to Jesus?

Talk About: *"And there is salvation in no one else, for there is no other name under heaven given among men by which we must be saved." (Acts 4:12)*

Why were Peter and John so different than they had been when Jesus was arrested? Explain.

Pray: Thank God for answering prayer. If you have not received Christ as your Savior and Lord, ask God to help you repent and receive Christ today. Ask God for boldness in being His witness. Pray that others will come to trust in Jesus as their Savior and Lord.

Think About: *Am I fully convinced that Jesus is the Savior? Am I convinced enough to spend my life making Him known?*

CHAPTER 132
THE HOLY SPIRIT GIVES BELIEVERS LOVE AND COURAGE

The Church Grows in Love and in Number; Ananias and Sapphira Die; and the Apostles Preach—Acts 5

…*"We must obey God rather than men."* (Acts 5:29)

One of the things that Jesus prayed for believers is that they would be one—that they would be unified and love one another. This is just what was happening in Jerusalem among the Jesus-believers. They were "of one heart and soul" and shared everything. People freely sold some of their possessions—even land or houses—and brought the money to the apostles. Then they gave it to those who needed money. Everyone had what they needed; no one was needy. Jesus had said, *"By this all people will know that you are my disciples, if you have love for one another."*

Why did these people live this way? **Faith in Jesus gives His followers a greater love for people than for things**. No one made these believers give their money and share their things. They didn't give because they *had* to; they had changed hearts and *wanted* to give. They had a new love—a love for Jesus and His Kingdom that made this world and its things unimportant to them. This was not a new idea—this way of caring for one another was described in the Torah—in the commands of the first five books of the Bible written by Moses. The Jews had failed to fulfill God's commands on how to care for one another, but the followers of Christ had become a loving community.

A man named Barnabas sold a field and brought the money to the disciples. So then a man named Ananias and his wife, Sapphira, sold some land. They

213

agreed to keep some of the money for themselves. Ananias brought the rest of the money to the apostles. However, he lied and said it was the full amount they had received. *But Peter said, "Ananias, why has Satan filled your heart to lie to the Holy Spirit and to keep back for yourself part of the proceeds of the land? While it remained unsold, did it not remain your own? And after it was sold, was it not at your disposal? Why is it that you have contrived this deed in your heart? You have not lied to men but to God."* When Ananias heard these words...he dropped dead!

Sapphira didn't know what had happened, but three hours later she came to the apostles. Peter asked her if she had sold the land for the amount Ananias brought to them. And Sapphira lied, too. *But Peter said to her, "How is it that you have agreed together to test the Spirit of the Lord? Behold, the feet of those who have buried your husband are at the door, and they will carry you out."* Immediately, Sapphira dropped dead.

What was so wrong about what Ananias and Sapphira did? What they did showed what was really in their hearts. They loved money. They were hypocrites who wanted to look more generous than they really were, so they lied. They did not truly trust in Jesus or love His people...and they showed great disrespect for the Holy Spirit. The result of their sin was death. *And great fear came upon the whole church and upon all who heard of these things.*

God was warning the Church of the sin of hypocrisy and pretending to have faith. Not everyone who just pretends to be a Christian drops dead...but someday they will die eternally. God, in His kindness, gave the church in Jerusalem (and us) this example as a warning to think about what we truly love.

The apostles continued to do many signs and wonders—healing people and casting out demons. And more people became believers in Jesus. Of course, this was a big problem for the Sadducees, who were "filled with jealousy." Once again, they arrested the apostles and put them in prison.

But do you know what happened? ...during the night an angel of the Lord opened the prison doors and brought them out, and said, "Go and stand in the temple and speak to the people all the words of this Life." So the next day, when the high priest and the council asked to see the apostles, the guards came back with a very strange report. They found the prison locked and the guards outside the doors, but when they looked inside, the apostles were gone! That caused a lot of confusion. What could have happened?

Finally, someone came and told them that the apostles were teaching in the temple. So the council had them dragged in again. The high priest said to them,

> *"We strictly charged you not to teach in this name, yet here you have filled Jerusalem with your teaching, and you intend to bring this man's blood upon us." But Peter and the apostles answered, "**We must obey God rather than men**. **The God of our fathers raised Jesus**, whom you killed by hanging him on a tree. **God exalted him at his right hand as Leader and Savior**, to give repentance to Israel and forgiveness of sins. And we are witnesses to these things, and so is the Holy Spirit, whom God has given to those who obey him." (Acts 5:28-32)*

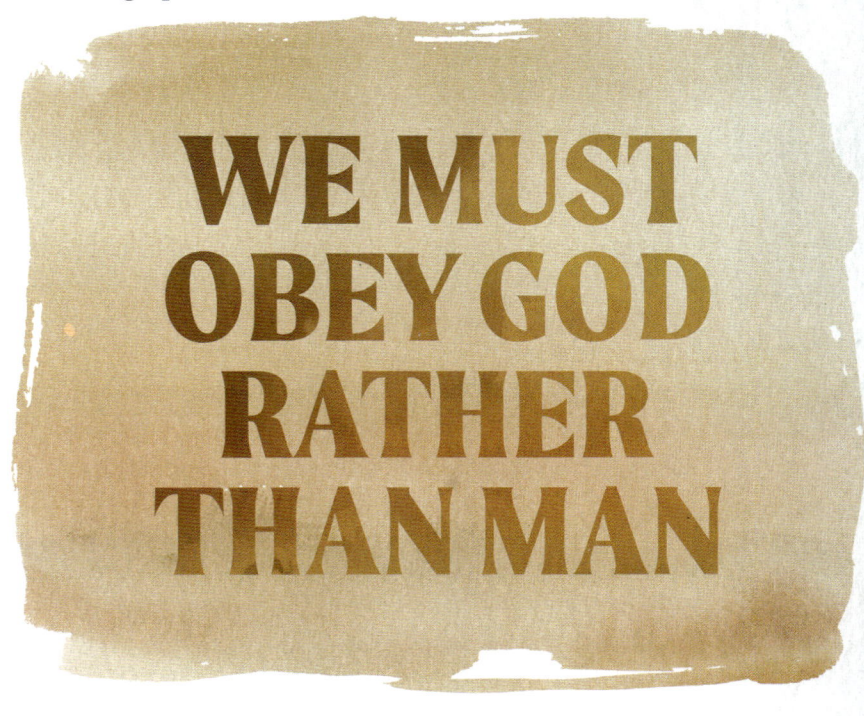

WE MUST OBEY GOD RATHER THAN MAN

This made the religious leaders FURIOUS, and they wanted to kill the apostles! But God had placed a teacher of the law named Gamaliel on the council. He was well respected, and he suggested that they have the apostles leave the room. Then Gamaliel spoke to the council about others who had come and had gathered followers. But after they died, their followers scattered and lost interest in their teaching.

> *"So in the present case I tell you, keep away from these men and let them alone, for if this plan or this undertaking is of man, it will fail; but **if it is of God, you will not be able to overthrow them**. You might even be found opposing God!" So they took his advice, (Acts 5:38-39)*

But first, they beat the apostles and told them again not to speak any more about Jesus. When the apostles left, they left *rejoicing that they were counted worthy to suffer dishonor for the name*. And they kept on preaching—every day. They preached in the temple and went from house-to-house preaching. And they did not stop.

Do you have a love for Jesus that makes your love for people greater than your love for things? Are you willing to suffer for the sake of Jesus? Is Jesus your greatest treasure?

Do not love the world or the things in the world. If anyone loves the world, the love of the Father is not in him. For all that is in the world—the desires of the flesh and the desires of the eyes and pride in possessions—is not from the Father but is from the world. And the world is passing away along with its desires, but whoever does the will of God abides forever. (1 John 2:15-17)

THAT YOU MAY BELIEVE

What does this chapter tell us about God?

Talk about and apply the **biblical truths** in **bold** text. Make them personal and apply them to what is happening in your family, church, community, or the world today.

Have you seen the kind of unity and love that the early church had? How can you be that kind of person to others?

Talk About: *Do not love the world or the things in the world. If anyone loves the world, the love of the Father is not in him. (1 John 2:15)*

Check out some stories of persecuted Christians on the Voice of the Martyrs website. Pray for persecuted Christians and ask God to give you a heart willing to suffer for Christ.

Pray: Thank God for His warnings in His Word that show us that judgment is real. Ask God to give you a unity and love for others in your family and church. Ask God to give you a willingness to suffer for His name.

Think About: *Is Christ my greatest treasure?*

CHAPTER 133
FULL OF GRACE AND POWER
Stephen Proclaims the Gospel and Is Martyred—Acts 6:1-8:3

*But they could not withstand the wisdom and the Spirit
with which he was speaking. (Acts 6:10)*

Satan loves to destroy the unity in the Church and the witness about Jesus. And this is just what he tried to do in the early church. He used a conflict, a disagreement, between two groups in the church. One group complained because no one was caring for their widows. However, if the apostles took time to serve the widows, they would not have as much time to preach the word of God. That would not be good.

But **God protected His Church** and gave the apostles the solution. They told the believers to choose seven godly men known to be "full of the Spirit and of wisdom" to serve the Church daily in practical ways. The apostles could still spend their time in prayer and preaching. So the believers chose Stephen, Philip, and five other men. The apostles "prayed and laid their hands on them." Laying on of hands was a way of appointing and giving authority to someone.

The Church continued to grow, and even some of the Jewish priests became believers. *And Stephen, full of grace and power, was doing great wonders and signs among the people.* Some of the unbelieving Jews from the synagogue disagreed with Stephen. *But they could not withstand the wisdom and the Spirit with which he was speaking.* So they did a sneaky thing. They convinced others to accuse Stephen of saying "blasphemous" or wrong things about Moses and God. These men were twisting the truth, and they got the people, elders, and scribes so upset that they brought Stephen before the council. Stephen was put on trial, *and they set up false witnesses who said, "This man never ceases to speak words against this holy place and the law, for we have heard him say that this Jesus of Nazareth will destroy this place and will change the customs that Moses delivered to us."* The council looked at Stephen to see how he would respond. *And gazing at him, all who sat in the council saw that his face was like the face of an angel.*

The high priest gave Stephen a chance to defend himself. *Do you know what Stephen did?* He gave them a history lesson! He talked about Israel's history with God—how they had, time after time, resisted and rejected God and about God's patience with Israel. He ended the history lesson with the building of the temple. Solomon had built the temple, *"yet the Most High does not dwell in houses made by hands."* God is everywhere—"heaven is [His] throne and the earth is [His] footstool." God's people would no longer need to go to a particular building in order to enjoy His special presence. The Holy Spirit would now dwell *in* God's people, all the time!

God's new "temple" is the Church—the community of those who believe in Jesus.

The problem was not that Stephen was speaking wrongly against God, Moses, and the temple. The problem was that **the Jews had a history of resisting God.** They rejected all the prophets...and they rejected God's Son, "the Righteous One." God had a covenant relationship with His people. True worship of God and obedience comes through faith. But the Jews were trusting in their religious acts or duties and in their own efforts to keep the law.

The Jews did not understand the new covenant that God made through Jesus. The old sacrificial system and the temple practices were no longer needed because **Jesus had fulfilled the Law.** He is the perfect, final sacrifice. He is the eternal High Priest praying for His people—the "go-between" or mediator between God and man. The glory of God rested on Jesus, not in the temple's Most Holy Place. **The old covenant of law-keeping is replaced by the new covenant of salvation by grace, through faith in Jesus.** When Jesus said He would destroy the temple, He was not talking about the building itself (even though the temple was later destroyed). He was talking about His death and resurrection, which would end the temple system of sacrifices. It would end the need to have priests and a scapegoat in order to receive forgiveness. Jesus said He would destroy the temple system...and build His Church. The Church, the people of faith in Jesus, is the new temple. The problem was with the stubbornness of the Jews. God was doing a new thing, but they would not accept it. The religious leaders and most of the Jews didn't understand who Jesus is and what He came to do. Stephen ended with these words:

> *"You stiff-necked people, uncircumcised in heart and ears, you always resist the Holy Spirit. As your fathers did, so do you. Which of the prophets did your fathers not persecute? And they killed those who announced beforehand the coming of the Righteous One, whom you have now betrayed and murdered, you who received the law as delivered by angels and did not keep it." (Acts 7:51-53)*

Do you know what happened next? The religious leaders and others understood that Stephen was saying that the Jews were guilty, and their temple worship was only temporary and now unnecessary. When they heard this, they became so angry with Stephen that they "ground their teeth at him." The Bible says they were "enraged." But the Bible tells us this about Stephen:

> *But he, full of the Holy Spirit, gazed into heaven and saw the glory of God, and Jesus standing at the right hand of God. And he said, "Behold, I see the heavens opened, and the Son of Man standing at the right hand of God." (Acts 7:55-56)*

Stephen was claiming that he had a vision of God! He was seeing heaven and Jesus welcoming him. The people screamed out, covered their ears, and attacked him. This was too much for the crowd! They forcefully dragged Stephen out of the city and stoned him. Those who were part of the angry mob threw off their outer clothing at the feet of a young rabbi named Saul. By guarding their clothing, Saul was agreeing with what they were doing. Saul was a very zealous Pharisee, and *Saul approved of [Stephen's] execution.*

As they were throwing stones at Stephen to kill him, he said two things that will sound very

219

familiar. He called out, *"Lord Jesus, receive my spirit."* Then he fell on his knees and loudly cried out, *"Lord, do not hold this sin against them."* And then he died. Stephen became the first martyr—the first person to die for his faith in Jesus.

This was the beginning of a great persecution of the believers in Jerusalem. Saul began to attack the Church of Jesus with great determination. Jesus' followers gathered every day in the courts of the temple and in homes. So Saul went to home after home of the believers and threw both men and women in prison. The fierce persecution caused many of the believers to leave Jerusalem and scatter throughout different areas. But the apostles stayed in Jerusalem.

Stephen loved Jesus more than life. He boldly proclaimed the truth about Jesus. Stephen was hated by the unbelieving Jews in Jerusalem...but he was loved by Jesus. His short life on earth ended, but he will spend all of eternity with Jesus and the believers. **God's new covenant is for any sinner who repents and trusts in Jesus for salvation.** *Are you trusting in Jesus for salvation? Do you love Jesus enough to boldly tell others about Him?*

"Blessed are you when others revile you and persecute you and utter all kinds of evil against you falsely on my account. Rejoice and be glad, for your reward is great in heaven, for so they persecuted the prophets who were before you." (Matthew 5:11-12)

Therefore, since we are surrounded by so great a cloud of witnesses, let us also lay aside every weight, and sin which clings so closely, and let us run with endurance the race that is set before us, looking to Jesus, the founder and perfecter of our faith, who for the joy that was set before him endured the cross, despising the shame, and is seated at the right hand of the throne of God. (Hebrews 12:1-2)

THAT YOU MAY BELIEVE

What does this chapter tell us about God?

Talk about and apply the **biblical truths** in **bold** text. Make them personal and apply them to what is happening in your family, church, community, or the world today.

Why couldn't those who disagreed with Stephen "withstand the wisdom and Spirit" with which he was speaking? Explain. What does this mean for us?

What are the main ideas in Stephen's speech (Acts 7)? Why did this make the Jews so angry? What does Stephen's speech tell you about salvation?

Talk About: *"Blessed are you when others revile you and persecute you and utter all kinds of evil against you falsely on my account. Rejoice and be glad, for your reward is great in heaven, for so they persecuted the prophets who were before you." (Matthew 5:11-12)*

How did Jesus give Stephen the grace to die well? Explain the significance or meaning of Stephen's vision.

Pray: Thank God for protecting His Church. Praise God for being a faithful and patient God. Ask Him for a bold faith and a willing heart to live for Jesus.

Think About: *Why is the covenant of salvation by grace through faith in Jesus such good news?*

CHAPTER 134
YOU WILL BE MY WITNESSES
Simon's False Faith and an Ethiopian's True Faith—Acts 8

"But you will receive power when the Holy Spirit has come upon you, and you will be my witnesses in Jerusalem and in all Judea and Samaria, and to the end of the earth." (Acts 1:8)

Do you remember what Joseph said to his brothers about the evil done to him? He said, *"As for you, you meant evil against me, but God meant it for good…"* The "good" that God was doing, was keeping His people alive during a famine. Just as God intended Joseph's suffering to bring about good, God meant the persecution of the believers in Jerusalem for good. The "good" that **God was** doing was **scattering the believers** throughout the area **so the gospel could be spread**…so the fulfillment of Jesus' Great Commission to *"Go into all the world and proclaim the gospel to the whole creation…to make disciples of all nations"* could begin.

The Jews had hated the mixed-race Samaritans, but Jesus gave His people a new heart of love. So Philip, one of Jesus' twelve disciples, went to the city of Samaria and preached to crowds of people. When they heard his message and saw the signs he did, they started paying attention! There was great joy in the city because many people were healed, and others were delivered from evil spirits.

Luke, the writer of the books of Acts, tells us what happened in the city of Samaria. But He wasn't just recording history. Luke was inspired by the Holy Spirit to write the book of Acts because God has things to tell us about true faith.

In Samaria there was a man named Simon among the people listening to Philip. Simon was a "sorcerer" or a magician who used supernatural demonic power to do magic. His magic amazed the people of Samaria but, when the people heard Philip preach "the good news about the Kingdom of God and the name of Jesus Christ," they were baptized. Simon said he, too, "believed," and he was baptized. He was amazed by the miracles he was seeing.

When the apostles in Jerusalem heard that the Samaritans were believing the word of God, they sent Peter and John to Samaria. Peter and John prayed for the Samaritans who had been baptized but had not received the Holy Spirit. They "laid their hands" on the Samaritans and prayed that they might receive the Holy Spirit. Simon wanted that power—it was stronger than his power. The signs and miracles were amazing. So he offered the apostles money saying, *"Give me this power also, so that anyone on whom I lay my hands may receive the Holy Spirit."*

> *But Peter said to him, "May your silver perish with you, because you thought you could obtain the gift of God with money! You have neither part nor lot in this matter, for your heart is not right before God. Repent, therefore, of this wickedness of yours, and pray to the Lord that, if possible, the intent of your heart may be forgiven you. For I see that you are in the gall of bitterness and in the bond of iniquity." (Acts 8:20-23)*

What is God telling us about faith through this story? **A person can "believe" without having true saving faith.** *What did Simon believe in?* He believed in signs and wonders. He believed in supernatural power. But he did not have saving faith. He did not see his own wicked, greedy, sinful heart. He did not believe in Jesus as his Lord and Savior. He did not entrust himself to Jesus. He was amazed at the miracles, but he was not amazed at the cross and Jesus' sacrifice for sinners. He was not amazed at God's willingness to forgive sinners and the good news that sinners can be made clean and free. He was not amazed at the **free gift of salvation** and the outpouring of the Holy Spirit to change hearts. His heart was not right before God. It was full of envy, greed, and pride...and there was no sorrow over his sin or humble repentance. He did not have "part or lot" in the Kingdom of God. Simon did ask the apostles to pray for him, but even that was for the wrong reasons. He didn't want God's judgment to fall on him—He didn't want punishment. **True faith produces deep heart repentance from sin and a humble turning to Jesus, trusting Him for forgiveness.**

Do you remember the Parable of the Sower? What was Simon like? Simon was like thorns. The Word of God was preached, but it was sown among thorns. Simon heard the Word, *but the cares of the world and the deceitfulness of riches* choked the Word. He said he believed, but he did not have true faith. He wanted "the gift of God" for all the wrong reasons. His heart was not right toward God.

But there was another man who did have "part or lot" in the Kingdom of God. He didn't live in Samaria; he lived hundreds of miles away. After preaching in the city of Samaria, on the way back to Jerusalem, the apostles preached in many villages of the Samaritans. But, at some point, an angel of the Lord came to Philip in a vision and told him to take the road that goes to Gaza, "a desert place." Philip obeyed the Lord, and there on the road was a man in a chariot. He was an important court official from the faraway country of Ethiopia. He was not a Jew, but as he was returning from Jerusalem along the Gaza road, he was reading the words of Isaiah, the prophet. *And the Spirit said to Philip, "Go over and join this chariot."*

So Philip ran up to him and heard him reading Isaiah. He asked the Ethiopian if he understood what he was reading. But the man said he had no one to teach him, so he really didn't understand the words he was reading. So he invited Philip to sit in his chariot with him. This is what he was reading from Isaiah:

> *"Like a sheep he was led to the slaughter and like a lamb before its shearer is silent, so he opens not his mouth. In his humiliation justice was denied him. Who can describe his generation? For his life is taken away from the earth." (Acts 8:32b-33)*

Do you know whom Isaiah was writing about? The Ethiopian man did not know, so Philip explained to him the good news about Jesus, starting with the Old Testament prophets.

When they came to some water along the road, the Ethiopian wanted to be baptized. So Philip baptized him right there. *And when they came up out of the water, the Spirit of the Lord carried Philip away, and the [man] saw him no more, and went on his way rejoicing.*

How was it that Philip happened to be at just the right place on the road to meet the Ethiopian…at just the time that he was reading these verses from Isaiah? God, who reigns over all, sovereignly placed Philip at the right place at the right time. If Philip had met the Ethiopian earlier, he might have been reading from Isaiah 52, *"My people went down at the first into Egypt to sojourn there, and the Assyrian oppressed them for nothing."* If Philip had met him later, he might have been reading from Isaiah 54, *"Sing, O barren one, who did not bear; break forth into singing and cry aloud, you who have not been in labor!"* But Philip met him just as he was reading about Jesus from Isaiah 53. God did that! **God's timing is perfect! God's plans are perfect! God is sovereign over all!**

The Ethiopian man had traveled more than 500 miles to worship in Jerusalem. He probably was a "God-fearer," but he did not know the good news that Jesus saves sinners. God sent His messenger, Philip, to tell the Ethiopian man the good news of salvation through faith in Christ. God was calling people from other nations to be part of His family!

Simon "believed" in the miracles, but he did not have true saving faith. The Ethiopian was seeking God and searching His Word for understanding. He heard the good news and put his faith in Jesus. You have heard about God and Jesus, and you probably believe the Bible…but do you have true saving faith? Have you entrusted your life and your future to Jesus? Have you deeply repented from your sin, turned in faith to Christ for the forgiveness of your sin, and accepted His grace?

…"Today, if you hear his voice, do not harden your hearts." (Hebrews 4:7b)

THAT YOU MAY BELIEVE

What does this chapter tell us about God?

Talk about and apply the **biblical truths** in **bold** text. Make them personal and apply them to what is happening in your family, church, community, or the world today.

Explain how what Satan means for evil, God turns for good. Give an example.

Talk About: …"Today, if you hear his voice, do not harden your hearts." (Hebrews 4:7b)

What is the warning in the story of Simon? What is true saving faith?

Pray: Praise God for saving people from all nations. Thank Him for the free gift of salvation and the Holy Spirit. Ask Him to give you a repentant heart and true faith.

Think About: *What am I believing in?*

CHAPTER 135
GOD'S CHOSEN INSTRUMENT
Jesus Saves Saul—Acts 9:1-31

..."he is a chosen instrument of mine to carry my name before the Gentiles and kings and the children of Israel." (Acts 9:15)

The death of Stephen was not enough for Saul, a Pharisee and persecutor of the church. He was obsessed with wiping out the followers of Jesus—and not just in Jerusalem. "Breathing threats and murder against the disciples of the Lord," Saul pursued his mission to persecute Christians. He got letters from the high priest in Jerusalem to give to the synagogues in the city of Damascus, where some of the believers had fled. This would give him permission to arrest believers there and bring them back to Jerusalem to stand trial. He would put an end to these Christ-followers who claimed Jesus is alive and reigning in heaven!

But as Saul neared Damascus, *suddenly a light from heaven flashed around him.* Saul fell to the ground, and he heard a voice from heaven saying, *"Saul, Saul, why are you persecuting me?"* And he said, *"Who are you, Lord?"* And he said, *"I am Jesus, whom you are persecuting. But rise and enter the city, and you will be told what you are to do."* Imagine Saul's shock at discovering that **Jesus is alive and reigning in heaven**! Imagine his horror that he had been persecuting Jesus Himself when he persecuted Jesus' followers!

The men traveling with Saul didn't know what to say or think. They heard the voice, but they didn't see anyone. Saul didn't see at all after seeing the glory of Christ. His eyes were open, but he was blind. Before he had been spiritually blind; now he was physically blind. So the men with Saul led him to Damascus where blind Saul did not eat or drink for three days.

But God had not forgotten Saul. Jesus came in a vision to a believer in Damascus named Ananias. God gave Ananias specific instructions in the vision: *"Rise and go to the street called Straight, and at the house of Judas look for a man of Tarsus named Saul, for behold, he is praying, and he has seen in a vision a man named Ananias come in and lay his hands on him so that he might regain his sight."*

What did Ananias think of this plan? Ananias knew who Saul was and why he was in Damascus. It was dangerous for Ananias to go to Saul. He reminded the Lord that Saul had been persecuting the saints (believers).

> *But the Lord said to him, "Go, for he is a chosen instrument of mine to carry my name before the Gentiles and kings and the children of Israel. For I will show him how much he must suffer for the sake of my name." (Acts 9:15-16)*

Saul had been an enemy of Christ. Now he was "a chosen instrument"—God's appointed messenger to the Gentiles. **God loves to turn His enemies into friends.** Before Saul had persecuted the Church of Christ; now he would suffer persecution to build the Church. **God is a God of amazing surprises and reverses!**

Ananias obeyed the Lord and, "laying his hands on" Saul, he called him "Brother Saul." **God's people forgive repentant sinners and welcome them into the community of believers.** *"Brother Saul, the Lord Jesus who appeared to you on the road by which you came has sent me so that you may regain your sight and be filled with the Holy Spirit." And immediately something like scales fell from his eyes, and he regained his sight. Then he rose and was baptized; and taking food he was strengthened.*

Saul spent several days learning from the disciples in Damascus. He knew the Old Testament well, but he did not know the teachings of Jesus. Before long Saul, now a believer in Jesus and a defender of His resurrection, started teaching in the synagogues in Damascus. He proclaimed that **Jesus is the Messiah**. The Jews who heard

227

him preach were astounded...and puzzled! Wasn't this the man who persecuted those who believed that Jesus is the Messiah? What had happened?

Saul was well-trained in Jewish beliefs and culture, and also in the Greek language, culture, and ideas. As a Pharisee, Saul knew the prophecies about the Messiah. So the Jews were unable to argue or disprove Saul's preaching proving that Jesus is the Messiah. Saul stayed in Damascus about three years, teaching about Jesus. Since the Jews could not prove Saul's teaching was wrong, they plotted to kill him. Saul found out about their evil plan, but he could not escape from Damascus because the gate to the city was guarded day and night. So one night his disciples lowered him down in a basket through an opening in the city wall! God had protected His messenger.

Saul went to Jerusalem to join the believers there. *Why would this be a problem?* The believers in Jerusalem were afraid of Saul! He had persecuted believers, causing some to flee from Jerusalem. They didn't know Saul had changed. But Barnabas brought Saul to the apostles and explained how Jesus had appeared to him on the road to Damascus and how Saul had boldly preached about Jesus. So Saul became a part of the church in Jerusalem and preached to the Greek-speaking

Jews. However, once again, the Jews were looking for a way to kill Saul because of his preaching. This time, the believers brought him to the city of Caesarea, where he left for his hometown of Tarsus.

> *So the church throughout all Judea and Galilee and Samaria had peace and was being built up. And walking in the fear of the Lord and in the comfort of the Holy Spirit, it multiplied. (Acts 9:31)*

The true story of Saul turning from being an enemy of Jesus to becoming a dedicated follower and preacher defending Jesus as the Messiah shows the power of God to change men's hearts. God changed a persecutor of the Church into someone who willingly suffered persecution so that others would know about Jesus. **There is no one God cannot save**. Do you know someone who is rejecting Jesus? Do not lose hope. Jesus is still the all-powerful Savior who loves to turn enemies into friends!

For I am not ashamed of the gospel, for it is the power of God for salvation to everyone who believes, to the Jew first and also to the Greek. (Romans 1:16)

THAT YOU MAY BELIEVE

What does this chapter tell us about God?

Talk about and apply the **biblical truths** in **bold** text. Make them personal and apply them to what is happening in your family, church, community, or the world today.

Why would Jesus ask Saul why he was persecuting Him, when Saul was persecuting the believers?

Talk About: *For I am not ashamed of the gospel, for it is the power of God for salvation to everyone who believes, to the Jew first and also to the Greek. (Romans 1:16)*

How can our family be witnesses to others? Is there some action we can take?

Pray: Praise God for His amazing grace. Thank Him for saving sinners. Pray for those you know who do not know Jesus.

Think About: Am I ashamed to tell others about Jesus' death, resurrection, and saving power?

CHAPTER 136
CHRIST WELCOMES ALL PEOPLES
God Brings Peter and Cornelius Together—Acts 9:36-10:48

"...everyone who believes in him receives forgiveness of sins through his name." (Acts 10:43b)

How did you learn to ride a two-wheel bike? You probably started by riding a tricycle first, then a two-wheel bike with training wheels. Finally, the day came when the training wheels were removed. You wobbled a little, maybe even had a few falls, but then you were riding! You learned step-by-step—one thing at a time.

God taught His Church little by little, one thing at a time, too. A baby step for Peter came when a believer in the town of Joppa named Tabitha (or Dorcas in the Greek language) became very ill and died. She was very loved and had shown great kindness sewing clothes for many poor people. Her church family sent for Peter to come immediately. When Peter arrived, he asked the weeping women to leave the room. He knelt down and prayed. Then he turned and said, "Tabitha, arise." *And she opened her eyes and when she saw Peter she sat up.* God had given her life again! Peter called the saints and showed them that Tabitha was alive! Naturally, the story of this miracle was passed around, and many people believed in the Lord because of the sign.

Peter stayed in Joppa for many days with a man named Simon, who was a tanner. A tanner is someone who works on animal skins to make leather. This was a baby step God gave Peter. Not only were there a good number of Gentiles living in Joppa, but to the Jews, tanners were "unclean" because they worked with the skins of dead animals. So this was a little uncomfortable for Peter. Peter was learning that God accepts all kinds of people—including Gentiles and "unclean" tanners.

The next step has two parts—a Cornelius part and a Peter part. Cornelius was a Roman centurion (soldier) who lived in Caesarea. He and his family were "God-fearers"—Gentiles who worshiped God. Cornelius was generous to the poor and prayed often to God. One day, Cornelius had a vision of an angel calling him by name. Cornelius was in awe and said, "What is it Lord?" The angel told him that God had heard his prayers and that his kindness was pleasing to God. But there was more...Cornelius was told to send some men to Joppa to get Peter, who was staying with Simon, a tanner living by the seaside. Immediately, Cornelius sent two servants and a soldier to Joppa.

The Peter part was this: The next day, Peter was on the rooftop praying and became hungry. While food was being cooked, Peter *fell into a trance and saw the heavens opened and something like a great sheet descending, being let down by its four corners upon the earth. In it were all kinds of animals and reptiles and birds of the air. And there came a voice to him: "Rise, Peter; kill and eat."*

Peter was being asked to eat unclean animals! *But Peter said, "By no means, Lord; for I have never eaten anything that is common or unclean." And the voice came to him again a second time, "**What God has made clean, do not call common**." This happened three times, and the thing was taken up at once to heaven. What did this vision mean?* While Peter was puzzling over the meaning, the men sent by Cornelius arrived. *And while Peter was pondering the vision,*

the Spirit said to him, "Behold, three men are looking for you. Rise and go down and accompany them without hesitation, for I have sent them."

The men told Peter about Cornelius and about the angel's message to send for Peter. So the next day, Peter and some of the believers went with them to Caesarea. In the meantime, Cornelius had gathered his relatives and close friends together at his house. When Cornelius met Peter, he fell at his feet to worship Peter. *But Peter lifted him up, saying, "Stand up; I too am a man."* How different Peter was than Simon the magician who wanted power and fame. Peter would not accept the honor and glory that belongs to God alone.

In obedience to God, Peter entered the home of a Gentile and found the house full of people gathered there. *And he said to them, "You yourselves know how unlawful it is for a Jew to associate with or to visit anyone of another nation, but God has shown me that I should not call any person common or unclean."* Little by little, God had led Peter to understand this truth. **God invites all peoples to come to Him**—not just Jews. Now Peter was in the home of a Roman soldier hearing how an angel had come to Cornelius. This was a big step! When Peter had heard the story of Cornelius's vision, Cornelius said to him, *"Now therefore we are all here in the presence of God to hear all that you have been commanded by the Lord."*

So Peter had the wonderful opportunity to preach the gospel of Jesus Christ to the Gentiles! He started by saying that **God does not have favorites—He accepts people from all nations**. Not everyone will be saved, but Peter told them about Jesus, who saves all who fear God and do what is right. Then he told them about how Jesus did good and healed people "for God was with him." Peter saw this with his own eyes. He told them about the death and the resurrection of Jesus. Again, Peter told them that he and the other disciples had witnessed this. They even ate and drank with Jesus after He rose from the dead. Peter was assuring them that **Jesus is alive**.

Peter never really ended his sermon. His last words were:

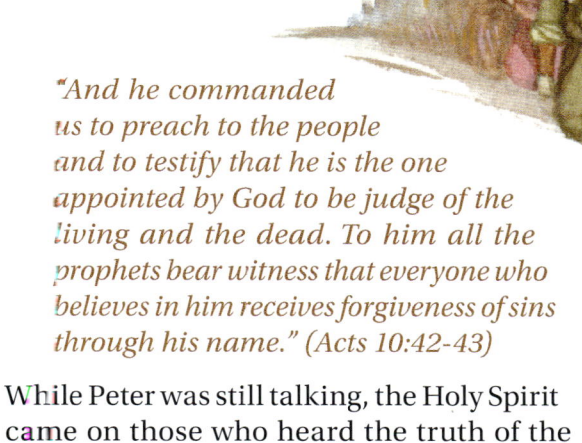

"And he commanded us to preach to the people and to testify that he is the one appointed by God to be judge of the living and the dead. To him all the prophets bear witness that everyone who believes in him receives forgiveness of sins through his name." (Acts 10:42-43)

While Peter was still talking, the Holy Spirit came on those who heard the truth of the gospel—the good news that Jesus saves. The believers who came with Peter were amazed *because* **the gift of the Holy Spirit was poured out even on the Gentiles.** *For they were hearing them speaking in tongues and extolling God.* After this, they were baptized, and Peter stayed with them for several days, teaching them.

It was an amazing thing for the Jews to accept the Gentiles. For hundreds of years, they had considered the Gentiles "unclean." They had never really understood God's words to Abraham, *"And in your offspring all the nations of the earth shall be blessed."* God's heart was for the Jews to honor and obey Him, and to be a blessing to other nations, bringing them to God. The Jewish nation had failed. But **God always accomplishes His purposes** and through Jesus, the Jewish Messiah, God was building the true Israel. **God's Church would be the people to bless all nations. God was adopting Gentiles into His family. Instead of only the Jews being God's covenant people, people from other ethnicities** (people groups) **were being added to the new multi-ethnic covenant family of God.**

Do you know any missionaries who are bringing the gospel to other nations? You do not have to wait to grow up to be a kind of missionary. You can spread the

good news of Jesus to anyone who is not a Christian. Is there someone in your neighborhood, at your school, on your sports team, or in your family with whom you can share the good news that Jesus came to make a way for sinners to belong to His family?

Know then that it is those of faith who are the sons of Abraham. And the Scripture, foreseeing that God would justify the Gentiles by faith, preached the gospel beforehand to Abraham, saying, "In you shall all the nations be blessed." So then, those who are of faith are blessed along with Abraham, the man of faith. (Galatians 3:7-9)

THAT YOU MAY BELIEVE

What does this chapter tell us about God?

Talk about and apply the **biblical truths** in **bold** text. Make them personal and apply them to what is happening in your family, church, community, or the world today.

Write a note of encouragement to a missionary you know or to a missionary your church supports. Then pray as a family for that person.

Talk About: *Know then that it is those of faith who are the sons of Abraham. (Galatians 3:7)*

Is there someone from another country or ethnic group to whom you can reach out? How can your family be like Tabitha and do acts of kindness?

Pray: Praise God that He is loving toward all people. Pray that He will send missionaries to preach the gospel to the whole world. Pray for God to save people from all the nations.

Think About: *Do I treat all people rightly? Am I prejudiced against people who are not like me? Do I dislike anyone just because that person is different?*

CHAPTER 137

TWO KINDS OF RESCUE

The Gentile Church Grows; God Rescues Peter from Prison—Acts 11-12

...And they glorified God, saying, "Then to the Gentiles also God has granted repentance that leads to life." (Acts 11:18b)

Have you ever given a report in school? What was it about? Peter had to give a report too—to people in Jerusalem who were criticizing him. The apostles and believers learned that the Gentiles had heard the word of God, and some of them weren't very excited about this. In fact, they criticized Peter for spending time with the Gentiles and eating with them. But Peter told the whole story of his vision of the great sheet and God's word to him—*"What God has made clean, do not call common."* He told them about the angel speaking to Cornelius and how he preached to Cornelius's family and his Gentile friends. He told them the Holy Spirit had come on these Gentiles—*"If then God gave the same gift to them as he gave to us when we believed in the Lord Jesus Christ, who was I that I could stand in God's way?"* Peter's listeners were silent. They had no argument. In fact, they praised God saying,

..."Then to the Gentiles also God has granted repentance that leads to life." (Acts 11:18b)

After Stephen was killed, many followers of Jesus fled from Jerusalem. Some had gone hundreds of miles away—as far as Phoenicia, Cyprus, and Antioch, spreading the gospel mostly to the Jews. Many Jews lived in Antioch, the third largest city in the Roman Empire. However, it was a city of many cultures and much wickedness. Some of the followers of Jesus who went to Antioch also preached to the Greeks about Jesus. *And the hand of the Lord was with them, and a great number who believed turned to the Lord.* This is amazing! The Greeks believed in magic and in many gods and goddesses—Zeus the king of the gods, Apollo the son of Zeus, Poseidon, Artemis, Aphrodite, Hermes, and many others. They lived in fear of their gods and were always trying to please them. For these people to turn away from their gods and worship the one true God was an incredible work of the Holy Spirit. Instead of working to keep their gods from getting angry, the Greek believers now knew the Messiah, who gave His life for them. **God rescues sinners.**

The leaders of the church in Jerusalem heard about the Greeks turning to Jesus and sent Barnabas to check on this. *When he came and saw the grace of God, he was glad, and he exhorted them all to remain faithful to the Lord with steadfast purpose, for he was a good man, full of the Holy Spirit and of faith. And a great many people were added to the Lord.*

The church in Antioch grew so large that Barnabas went to Tarsus to get Saul and bring him back to help him in Antioch. Barnabas and Saul stayed in Antioch a whole year, meeting with the believers and teaching many people. A new name for Jesus' followers was used in Antioch: Christians. They were beginning to be thought of as a distinct or separate group. Now, instead of separating Jews and Gentiles, the Church was just made up of followers of Christ, or Christians. **God was unifying His people.** He was answering Jesus' prayer to make them one.

After hearing from a prophet from Jerusalem that there would be a great famine, the Christians in Antioch sent money to Judea with Barnabas and Saul. But things weren't going well in Jerusalem. King Herod Agrippa[21] *laid violent hands on some who belonged to the church.* He killed Jesus' disciple James, the brother of John.[22] Many of the Jews hated the followers of Christ. When Herod saw that killing James pleased the Jews, he also arrested Peter and put him in prison. Four squads of four guards each were assigned to Peter—so Peter was heavily guarded at all times. *But earnest prayer for him was made to God by the church.*

Herod was planning to put Peter on trial during the Passover, but something happened during the night. *Do you know what it was?* Peter was sleeping, chained between two guards. There were also guards at the door of the prison. While Peter was sleeping, an angel of the Lord "stood next to him, and a light shone in the cell." The angel woke Peter and told him to quickly get up, dress himself, and put on his sandals. Then the angel told him to wrap his cloak around himself and follow him. Peter followed the angel, but he didn't know this was really happening. He thought it was a vision. They passed the first guard… the second guard…and got to the iron gate that led to the city. The gate…opened…by… itself…and they went out onto the street. Then the angel left Peter and Peter realized that this wasn't a vision. It was real! God had caused the chains to fall off and kept the guards from waking up! *When Peter came to himself, he said, "Now I am sure that the Lord has sent his angel and rescued me from the hand of Herod and from all that the Jewish people were expecting."* God rescued Peter from a heavily guarded prison cell. **God does the impossible. No one can stand against His plans.** God still had work for Peter to do in building His Church.

Peter went immediately to the house of Mary, the mother of John Mark, where many believers were gathered to pray. He knocked on the gate door and a servant girl named Rhoda went to answer it. She recognized Peter's voice and was so full of joy and excitement that she forgot to open the gate! Instead, she ran to tell the believers that Peter was free. He was standing at the gate. *What do you think the group did?* They told Rhoda that she had lost her mind! But she kept telling them that Peter really was at the gate…and they kept telling her that it was Peter's angel.

What would you do if you were Peter? Peter kept knocking until finally they opened the gate. When they saw Peter, they were amazed! He told them what had happened and instructed them to "tell these things to James[23] and the brothers." Then Peter left to go to a safer place.

You can imagine the surprise, confusion, and fear among the guards when they discovered in the morning that Peter was gone! Herod himself looked for Peter and couldn't find him. He must have been furious! After questioning the guards, he harshly ordered that they be put to death. Then Herod left Judea and went to Caesarea.

But things didn't go well for Herod. There had been trouble with some of the towns under his rule. But eventually, Herod had been able to work out a peace agreement. To celebrate this, he put on his royal robes, sat on his throne, and gave a speech to the people. *And the people were shouting, "The voice of a god, and not of a man!" Immediately an angel of the Lord struck him down, because he did not give God the glory, and he was eaten by worms and breathed his last.* **No one can rob God of His glory.** Herod was a proud and harsh king who could not escape the judgment of God.

But the word of God increased and multiplied. God was doing an amazing work of grace—spreading His Word beyond the Jews to people of many cultures, people groups, and nations!

God is a God of miracles. He rescued Peter from death—and He rescued Gentiles from fear, a life of sin, and eternal punishment, which is far worse than physical death. Salvation is a miracle! Barnabas and Saul were faithful servants of God, preaching and teaching with great zeal. Peter was a faithful witness who would continue to build God's Church. What part do you have in doing the work of God where you are?

> For the grace of God has appeared, bringing salvation for all people, training us to renounce ungodliness and worldly passions, and to live self-controlled, upright, and godly lives in the present age, waiting for our blessed hope, the appearing of the glory of our great God and Savior Jesus Christ, who gave himself for us to redeem us from all lawlessness and to purify for himself a people for his own possession who are zealous for good works. (Titus 2:11-14)

THAT YOU MAY BELIEVE

What does this chapter tell us about God?

Talk about and apply the **biblical truths** in **bold** text. Make them personal and apply them to what is happening in your family, church, community, or the world today.

Why is grace necessary for salvation? How has God shown grace to your family?

Talk About: *But we have this treasure in jars of clay, to show that the surpassing power belongs to God and not to us. We are afflicted in every way, but not crushed; perplexed, but not driven to despair; persecuted, but not forsaken; struck down, but not destroyed; always carrying in the body the death of Jesus, so that the life of Jesus may also be manifested in our bodies. (2 Corinthians 4:7-10)*

What good works can you do while waiting for Jesus to return?

Pray: Praise God that He is almighty and gracious. Thank Him for His grace. Ask God to show you how you can be part of building His Kingdom here.

Think About: *Do I have a concern for those who do not trust in Jesus?*

---

21 This was the grandson of Herod the Great, who ruled when Jesus was born. He was partly Jewish as a descendent of the Maccabees.
22 James and John were the sons of Zebedee and were Jesus' disciples. This is not James, the brother of Jesus, who wrote the book of James.
23 This is James, the brother of Jesus, who was the leader of the church in Jerusalem.

CHAPTER 138
GOD'S PLAN TO BLESS THE NATIONS
The First Missionary Journey—Acts 13-14

"Look, you scoffers, be astounded and perish; for I am doing a work in your days, a work that you will not believe, even if one tells it to you." (Acts 13:41)

Have you ever tried to put a large puzzle together without the completed picture? It is very hard, isn't it? You can see each individual piece, but you aren't sure how they all go together or even what the completed picture is supposed to be. God's plan for the world is something like this. He has given us many puzzle pieces...but we surely don't know what the whole picture looks like. **God is sovereign and fulfills all His plans**...but only God knows all the pieces and how they fit together in His eternal plan.

In the Bible, God has given us so many pieces, but the eternal plan of God is still a mystery to us. In Abraham's day, they had fewer "puzzle pieces." But we have so many more of those pieces in God's Word. As we put some of those pieces together, we start to see parts of **God's great and glorious plan to bring salvation to the nations.**

God made a promise to Abraham to make of him a great nation and told him, *"In you shall all the nations be blessed."* When Simeon saw baby Jesus in the temple, he said, *"my eyes have seen your salvation that you have prepared in the presence of all peoples, a light for revelation to the Gentiles, and for glory to your people Israel."* And now, in the thirteenth chapter of Acts, we see another piece of the puzzle.

While the church in Antioch was worshiping and fasting, *the Holy Spirit said, "Set apart for me Barnabas and Saul for the work to which I have called them." Then after fasting and praying [the church leaders] laid their hands on them and sent them off.* The church at Antioch sent out the first missionaries, Barnabas and Saul. Most of the places they went have names you will not recognize because they have been changed since the time of the apostles. Follow their path on the map (page 246) from Antioch to these cities: Selucia, Salamis, and Paphos on the island of Cyprus, Perga, Antioch in Pisidia (a different Antioch), Iconium, Lystra, and Derbe. Then follow their route back to Antioch.

In all these places, they preached the gospel. They first went to the Jewish synagogues in each town to preach and teach. But when the Jews rejected their message, they preached to the Gentiles. Saul and Barnabas brought John Mark to help them. They preached in the synagogue in Salamis, and then traveled across the island of Cyprus to Paphos, where they met a magician, "a Jewish false prophet." This man, Elymas, was with a Roman official who wanted to hear the word of God. Elymas resisted them, trying to turn the official away from believing in Jesus.

> *But Saul…filled with the Holy Spirit, looked intently at him and said, "You son of the devil, you enemy of all righteousness, full of all deceit and villainy, will you not stop making crooked the straight paths of the Lord? And now, behold, the hand of the Lord is upon you, and you will be blind and unable to see the sun for a time." Immediately mist and darkness fell upon him, and he went about seeking people to lead him by the hand. Then the proconsul believed, when he saw what had occurred, for he was astonished at the teaching of the Lord. (Acts 13:9-12)*

After this, John Mark left and went back to Jerusalem while Barnabas and Saul went on. Saul was a Greek-speaking Jew. His name in Hebrew was Saul; in Greek it was Paul. From this point on, Saul used his Greek name, Paul, because he was no longer teaching in Jewish territory but in the world of the Greeks and Romans. *Do you remember some of the good changes that happened during the 400 years of silence?* When Alexander the Great conquered the known world, he insisted that the people in his empire learn to speak Greek. Pompey conquered the Greek Empire and connected the Roman Empire with roads. He made laws that brought some peace to the empire. *Can you see that this was another puzzle piece?* This was part of God's plan to make it possible for Paul and Barnabas to preach and teach! The common language of Greek made it possible to preach to all peoples. Roads and "safer" travel (not safe, just safer) made it possible for them to move all around the Roman Empire. All of this happened years before during the 400 years of silence. God was preparing the world to hear the gospel. **God's plans and timing are perfect! God made a way for His message of salvation to be known to the world!**

In Antioch of Pisidia (which is modern-day Turkey), Paul preached in the synagogue. He reminded them of Israel's history, and then he told them that Jesus is the Messiah. *"Let it be known to you therefore, brothers, that through this man [Jesus] forgiveness of sins is proclaimed to you, and by him everyone who believes is freed from everything from which you could not be freed by the law of Moses."* Then he warned them not to reject the message about Jesus, reminding them of the words of the prophet Habakkuk. *"Beware, therefore, lest what is said in the Prophets should come about: "Look, you scoffers, be astounded and perish; for I am doing a work in your days, a work that you will not believe, even if one tells it to you."'* When Paul and Barnabas left the synagogue, the people encouraged them to keep teaching.

The next Sabbath "almost the whole city gathered" to hear the preaching of God's Word. *But when the Jews saw the crowds, they were filled with jealousy and began to contradict what was spoken by Paul, reviling him. And Paul and Barnabas spoke out boldly, saying, "It was necessary that the word of God be spoken first to you. Since you thrust it aside and judge yourselves unworthy of eternal life, behold, we are turning to the Gentiles. For so the Lord has commanded us, saying, 'I have made you a light for the Gentiles, that you may bring salvation to the ends of the earth.'" And when the Gentiles heard this, they began rejoicing and glorifying the word of the Lord, and as many as were appointed to eternal life believed.* The Gentiles were overjoyed at the good news of Christ, and many of them became Christians! God's Word was spreading "throughout the whole region." But the Jews complained angrily to the city leaders, stirred up persecution against Paul and Barnabas, and forced them out of the region. This experience was repeated many times in Paul's missionary ministry.

In Iconium, some believed the gospel message. Others were angry about it. But Paul and Barnabas continued to "speak boldly for the Lord" until they heard of a plot to stone them. So they fled to Lystra. At Lystra, they met a lame man who was crippled from birth. When he heard the preaching of the gospel, Paul looked at him closely, and "seeing that he had faith to be made well," he told him to stand up. And the man jumped up and started walking!

241

The people were so excited when they saw it that they said, *"The gods have come down to us in the likeness of men!"* They called Barnabas, Zeus, and Paul, Hermes. *Do you remember who Zeus and Hermes were?* They were Greek gods. *What do you think Barnabas and Paul thought of this?*

Barnabas and Paul were so upset that they tore their clothing! They were not like Herod Agrippa; they refused to take any of the glory that belongs to God! The apostles cried out, *"Men, why are you doing these things? We also are men, of like nature with you, and we bring you good news, that you should turn from these vain things to a living God, who made the heaven and the earth and the sea and all that is in them."* But, even telling the crowd this, they could hardly keep the people from offering a sacrifice to them!

Then the jealous Jews from Antioch of Pisidia and Iconium showed up in Lystra. *What did they want?* They stirred up the people against Paul and Barnabas—and the people stoned Paul! Thinking he was dead, they dragged him out of the city and left him there. But the believers gathered around Paul…and he got up! The next day, Paul and Barnabas went to Derbe to preach, and many believed in the gospel through their preaching. After this, Paul and Barnabas returned through many of the cities where they had preached. They encouraged the believers to continue believing in Jesus and to grow in faith. They also prayed and fasted, and then appointed elders (leaders) in every church. When they returned to Antioch, the church that had sent them out, they reported all that God had done "and how

He had opened a door of faith to the Gentiles." Jesus' words to the disciples were beginning to be fulfilled: *"But you will receive power when the Holy Spirit has come upon you, and you will be my witnesses in Jerusalem and in all Judea and Samaria, and to the end of the earth."*

God's plan from the very beginning was to include all peoples in His family of faith. **God always accomplishes His purposes.** *Paul and Barnabas were a puzzle piece in His plan to preach and teach to the Gentiles. Are you in this family? What part might you play in reaching the nations?*

To me, though I am the very least of all the saints, this grace was given, to preach to the Gentiles the unsearchable riches of Christ, and to bring to light for everyone what is the plan of the mystery hidden for ages in God who created all things, (Ephesians 3:8-9)

THAT YOU MAY BELIEVE

What does this chapter tell us about God?

Talk about and apply the **biblical truths** in **bold** text. Make them personal and apply them to what is happening in your family, church, community, or the world today.

Read Paul's sermon in Antioch of Pisidia in Acts 13:16-41. Summarize it in your own words.

Talk About: *To me, though I am the very least of all the saints, this grace was given, to preach to the Gentiles the unsearchable riches of Christ, and to bring to light for everyone what is the plan of the mystery hidden for ages in God who created all things, (Ephesians 3:8-9)*

What are the "unsearchable riches of Christ"?

Pray: Praise God that He is a God who always accomplishes His purposes. Thank Him for His rich grace that is given to all people. Ask God to show if you are in His family. Ask God to send His people to the nations to bring the gospel to those who have not yet heard about Jesus.

Think About: *Everyone is either a member of God's family or not. Which am I?*

CHAPTER 139
ONE FAITH, ONE PEOPLE
The Jerusalem Council; the Macedonian Call—Acts 15:1-16:15

"But we believe that we will be saved through the grace of the Lord Jesus, just as they will." (Acts 15:11)

Have you ever made a cake? How do you start? You gather the individual ingredients, like flour, sugar, eggs, vanilla, and baking powder. Then you mix these together and they make something new—a cake! Well, the Christian Church started out like the ingredients in a cake. At first, it was mostly made up of Jews who believed in Jesus. Then another "ingredient" was added—Philip preached to the Samaritans, who were part Jewish and part Gentile. Some of the Samaritans believed in Jesus and were added to the Church. Peter, Paul, and Barnabas first added Gentiles like Cornelius and the Gentiles who believed during Paul's first missionary trip. These people were from different "ethnic" backgrounds, different cultures...but together they formed the Church of Jesus. This started a whole new family group—the Church, the multi-ethnic people who follow Jesus. They were one in Christ!

But some of the Jews began to be concerned. They thought that the Gentiles needed to become more "Jewish" and follow the ceremonial law in order to be true Christians. But others, like Paul and Barnabas, disagreed with this. They were clear that **salvation is by grace alone, through faith alone, in Christ alone.** So Paul and Barnabas were appointed to go to Jerusalem from Antioch to settle the argument with the apostles and elders.

There were many different opinions given at this Jerusalem council. Some thought the Gentiles needed to keep the Sabbath laws, laws about clean and unclean foods, and other laws. Others disagreed. Peter reminded them what happened when he had preached to Cornelius and the other Gentiles, and how God had given them the gift of the Holy Spirit just as He had done with the Jewish Christians. The new covenant made the ceremonial law unnecessary. Why were the Jews now making the Gentiles keep the ceremonial law? Then Peter said something that silenced everyone. *"But we believe that we will be **saved through the grace of the Lord Jesus**, just as they will."*

Then they listened to the report from Barnabas and Paul about the "signs and wonders God had done through them among the Gentiles." Finally, James, the leader of the Jerusalem church and the half-brother of Jesus, spoke. He agreed with Peter and recommended a decision: *"Therefore my judgment is that we should not trouble those of the Gentiles who turn to God."* Then he suggested some guidelines that would help Jews and Gentiles live together peacefully. The Gentiles must keep away from practices connected to idolatry and be pure and honorable in their relationships. The council agreed that it would be good to write a letter to the church in Antioch about their decision and send it with Paul, Barnabas, and some other leaders.

The letter was read in the church in Antioch, and *they rejoiced because of its encouragement.* **Salvation does not come by works or law-keeping but by faith in Jesus.** The Church of Jesus could live together peacefully through faith in Jesus. The Bible tells Christians *to have unity of mind, sympathy, brotherly love, a tender heart, and a humble mind and to walk in a manner worthy of the calling to which you have been called, with all humility and gentleness, with patience, bearing with one another in love, **eager to maintain the unity of the Spirit** in the bond of peace.* This good decision from the council was helping the early Church to do this.

Paul and Barnabas stayed in Antioch for a while teaching and preaching, but then Paul suggested to Barnabas that they visit the believers in the cities where they had preached on their first journey. This sounded right to Barnabas. He wanted to take John Mark with them again. But Paul didn't want to bring John Mark since he had left them on the first trip. Paul and Barnabas just could not agree. So Barnabas took Mark and went one direction, and Paul took Silas and went another direction. Though at first it may not seem good that Paul and Barnabas split up, it actually made two teams going out to preach the gospel.

s second journey on the map and see all the places where he and Silas preached
When they got to Lystra, they met Timothy, a young man whose mother was
whose father was Greek. He was a faithful believer, and Paul decided to bring
him. They got to Mysia, and Paul wanted to go to Bithynia, but the Holy Spirit
stopped him. So Paul, Silas, and Timothy went to Troas. Paul had a vision in the night of a
man from Macedonia (now Greece) asking him to come and help the Macedonians. Paul
understood that God wanted the people of Macedonia to hear the gospel. So Paul and Silas
obeyed this call and got on a ship. They sailed to Macedonia and went to a city called Philippi.

Paul's Second Missionary Journey

In Philippi there was no synagogue, but they preached to the women who gathered at a place of prayer by the river. There they discovered one reason that God had sent them to Macedonia. They met a wealthy businesswoman who sold purple cloth. *Do you know her name?* Her name was Lydia, and she was "a worshiper of God." She was a Gentile who worshiped Yahweh, but she didn't know Jesus. *The Lord opened her heart to pay attention to what was said by Paul. And after [this,] she was baptized, and her household as well.* **God opens the hearts of those He is calling to come to faith in Jesus.** Lydia also gave Paul and his companions a place to stay in her house. God had led Paul, Silas, and Timothy to Philippi because they had a church to build—not a building but a community of Christians that started with Lydia and her household.

Traveling by land had been very hard. It was hot and dusty on the roads. People tried to travel in large groups because there was always the danger of robbers on the road. Not only would the robbers steal things, but sometimes they also beat travelers. Traveling by ship was not pleasant either. Passengers stayed on the deck where they were unprotected from the hot sun, wind, and rain. But Paul and his companions gladly endured these hardships in order to spread the gospel.

The Church is a bit like trail mix—a mixture of all kinds of people—Jewish, Gentile, young, old, rich, poor…but all are sinners saved by grace alone. God calls all kinds of people to be in His family and makes them one. If you are trusting in Christ alone, you, too, are part of the wonderful family of God. If you are not a child of God, you can be by putting your faith in Jesus alone for the forgiveness of your sins.

> …in Christ Jesus you are all sons of God, through faith. For as many of you as were baptized into Christ have put on Christ. There is neither Jew nor Greek, there is neither slave nor free, there is no male and female, for you are all one in Christ Jesus. (Galatians 3:26-28)

> This mystery is that the Gentiles are fellow heirs, members of the same body, and partakers of the promise in Christ Jesus through the gospel. (Ephesians 3:6)

THAT YOU MAY BELIEVE

What does this chapter tell us about God?

Talk about and apply the **biblical truths** in **bold** text. Make them personal and apply them to what is happening in your family, church, community, or the world today.

What does "salvation is by grace alone, through faith alone, in Christ alone" mean?

Talk About: *…in Christ Jesus you are all sons of God, through faith. For as many of you as were baptized into Christ have put on Christ. There is neither Jew nor Greek, there is neither slave nor free, there is no male and female, for you are all one in Christ Jesus. (Galatians 3:26-28)*

Think of the different kinds of people in your church. What makes you all one? Do you act like you are all in the same family? How can you be part of making your church like one big family?

Pray: *Praise God for being a gracious God. Thank Him for the free gift of salvation. If you are not saved, ask God to change your heart and save you by His grace. If you are saved, thank God for your salvation, the greatest gift.*

Think About: *Am I depending on my works or on Christ and His perfect work on the cross for me?*

CHAPTER 140
GREAT RESCUES!

God Rescues Paul, Silas, and a Jailer; Jesus Rescues Sinners in Greece—Acts 16:16-17:15

..."Believe in the Lord Jesus, and you will be saved, you and your household." (Acts 16:31)

How does your father or mother make money? In Philippi there were some men who made money in a strange way. They had a slave girl who had a demon that could tell the future. People would pay the men for the girl to tell them what was going to happen. And these men made a lot of money using this girl. But the girl followed Paul and his companions around Philippi yelling, *"These men are servants of the Most High God, who proclaim to you the way of salvation."* She did this for many days. Finally, Paul said to the spirit, *"I command you in the name of Jesus Christ to come out of her."* And the demon left her! She was free from it.

But her owners were very angry. *Why were they angry?* They were so mad that they couldn't make money using her that they grabbed Paul and Silas and "dragged them into the marketplace before the rulers." They complained to the rulers, *"These men are Jews, and they are disturbing our city."* Not only that, but they said that Paul and Silas were encouraging anti-Roman practices. This wasn't true, but there was a lot of Roman pride and a lot of dislike for the Jews. So the crowd around the marketplace joined in attacking them. Then everything went wild...the rulers tore off Paul and Silas' clothing and ordered them to be beaten with large sticks. After beating them many times, they threw Paul and Silas in prison. They ordered the jailer to put them in a very secure place, so he locked them into the inner prison and put their feet in stocks.

What do you think Paul and Silas were doing in prison at midnight? They weren't sleeping or complaining or groaning from their injuries. They were "praying and singing hymns to God"! Even in prison, they were witnesses of the gospel because the other prisoners were listening to them…and as they were listening, "suddenly there was a great earthquake"! The prison walls were shaking, the doors flung open, everyone's chains broke loose, the stocks broke open…it was a mighty earthquake sent by a mighty God! God sent the earthquake at the right time and the right place. **God is all-powerful and all-knowing!**

The jailer woke up and saw the open prison doors. All the prisoners must have escaped. He knew he would be in terrible trouble! He drew out his sword to kill himself, but Paul yelled to him, *"Do not harm yourself, for we are all here."* What? None of the prisoners had escaped? The jailer rushed in with lights, *and trembling with fear he fell down before Paul and Silas. Then he brought them out and said, "Sirs, what must I do to be saved?"* His awe of God was greater than his fear of the rulers. *And they said, "**Believe in the Lord Jesus, and you will be saved**, you and your household."*

Paul and Silas shared the good news of salvation with the jailer's household. Then the jailer cleaned their wounds, and he and his whole family were baptized. The greatest deliverance or rescue that night was not the rescue from prison…but the deliverance from the prison of sin and death and hell. The jailer and his whole household rejoiced in their salvation!

In the morning, the rulers sent the police to tell the jailer to let Paul and Silas go. But when the jailer reported it to Paul, Paul said, *"They have beaten us publicly, uncondemned, men who are Roman citizens, and have thrown us into prison; and do they now throw us out secretly? No! Let them come themselves and take us out."* When the police told the rulers that they had harmed Roman citizens, they were afraid because Roman citizens had special privileges. They had the right to a public hearing. It was also illegal to beat a Roman citizen unless he was guilty of a crime. The rulers had seriously broken the law, so they apologized to Paul and Silas. Maybe now the rulers might leave the Philippian church alone.

Paul and Silas left the prison and visited Lydia. They encouraged the believers in Philippi and traveled on until they got to the synagogue in Thessalonica. As usual, Paul went in and spoke to them from the Word of God. *On three Sabbath days he reasoned with them from the Scriptures, explaining and proving that it was necessary for the Christ to suffer and to rise from the dead, and saying, "This Jesus, whom I proclaim to you, is the Christ."* Paul's message over and over was **Jesus is the Christ, the Messiah, the Savior. Jesus rescues sinners!**

They stayed and preached and taught for many weeks. Again, the same pattern was repeated. Some believed; others were angry. The Jews were jealous. They stirred up a crowd of wicked men and attacked the house where Paul and the others were staying. But they couldn't find Paul, Silas, or Timothy. They did find Jason, the owner of the house, and dragged him and some other Christians before the authorities shouting, *"These men who have turned the world upside down have come here also…they are all acting against the decrees of Caesar, saying there is another king, Jesus."* The authorities asked for money from Jason and the others and let them go. Even though the crowd stopped the preaching of Paul and Silas, they could not stop the work of the Holy Spirit. People were saved, and a Church was born. **No one can stop the work of God.**

In the middle of the night, the Christians sent Paul and Silas to Berea, where a familiar pattern was repeated. Paul and Silas preached in the synagogue. The Jews of Berea "received the word with all eagerness." Many Jews and Greeks believed. The Jews from Thessalonica came and stirred up the crowd. And the Christians sent Paul off on a boat to Athens while Silas and Timothy stayed in Berea to build the church there.

In some ways, things have not changed since the time of Paul. Some people love the truth that Jesus saves sinners; others are offended and hate the truth. Where have you seen this to be true in our world today? Do you want to ask God to give you boldness to speak the truth about Jesus to others? Whom can you tell about Jesus?

So faith comes from hearing, and hearing through the word of Christ. (Romans 10:17)

THAT YOU MAY BELIEVE

What does this chapter tell us about God?

Talk about and apply the **biblical truths** in **bold** text. Make them personal and apply them to what is happening in your family, church, community, or the world today.

Since faith comes by hearing the Word of God, how important is it to be reading the Bible? Do you have a plan for reading the Bible? What can you do to be reading the Word of God more?

Talk About: *So faith comes from hearing, and hearing through the word of Christ. (Romans 10:17)*

Ask your family to pray for boldness in sharing the gospel. Share the gospel with someone this week.

Pray: Praise God for being a loving God. Thank Him for His Word and for sending Jesus, the Savior. Ask Him to give you a willing heart to suffer for the work of the Kingdom.

Think About: *What is my attitude toward the Word of God?*

CHAPTER 141
GOD IS NOT FAR
Paul Teaches in Athens and Corinth—Acts 17:16-18:22

And he made from one man every nation of mankind...that they should seek God, in the hope that they might feel their way toward him and find him. Yet he is actually not far from each one of us, (Acts 17:26-27)

Have you ever heard the expression, "Beauty is in the eye of the beholder"? What does it mean? It means that people have different ideas about what is beautiful. What is beautiful to you may not look beautiful to someone else.

This is what Paul experienced when he got to Athens. Athens was famous all over the world for its beautiful art, buildings, and design. But it wasn't beautiful to Paul. The grandest buildings were temples of the Greek gods. The sculptures were of idols, and they were everywhere. Paul was sickened and furious at the sight of all these idols and the worship of false gods. Paul understood that these gods were really demons that the people worshiped. As usual, he went to the synagogue to reason with the Jews, showing them from the Old Testament that Jesus is the Messiah. But he also went to the marketplace where ideas were discussed so he could talk with the Greeks. The people there loved to talk about and listen to new ideas.

Well, some people in the marketplace thought Paul was just a "babbler"—talking nonsense about ideas he had heard from others. Others thought he was talking about a foreign god. They couldn't understand about Jesus and the resurrection. It didn't make sense to them. Not many thought of Paul's teaching as "beautiful" or good news.

One day, Paul went to the Areopagus, the hillside outdoor meeting place of the council. He went there to preach to the people of Athens. Paul began by saying that he had noticed they were very religious, as he had seen all the "objects of [their] worship"—the statues, temples, and idols. He had also seen an altar labeled, "To the unknown god." (Because the Greeks were afraid of offending the gods, they made this altar in case there was a god they didn't know about.) Paul was there to tell them about this "god" who was unknown to them—the one true God.

> "What therefore you worship as unknown, this I proclaim to you. The God who made the world and everything in it, being Lord of heaven and earth, does not live in temples made by man, nor is he served by human hands, as though he needed anything, since he himself gives to all mankind life and breath and everything. And he made from one man every nation of mankind to live on all the face of the earth, having determined allotted periods and the boundaries of their dwelling place, that they should seek God, in the hope that they

might feel their way toward him and find him. Yet he is actually not far from each one of us, for 'In him we live and move and have our being';" (Acts 17:23b-28a)

Paul told them that God is not made of gold, silver, or stone—some piece of art made by man. **God is living and real.** God had been patient with man's ignorance, but now **He commands every man to repent**. God has appointed Jesus to rightly judge the world. God had shown that Jesus is living and able to bring judgment because He was resurrected from the dead. When the Athenians heard about the resurrection of the dead, some of them mocked; others wanted to hear more. But some saw it as beautiful—as good news—and they became believers in Jesus. God brought about repentance and faith through Paul's preaching! How beautiful are "the feet of those who bring the good news" of the gospel!

After this, Paul left Athens. *What was the next stop on this missionary journey?* (Check the map in an earlier chapter.) Paul went to Corinth where he met a Jew named Aquila. Aquila and his wife, Priscilla, had moved to Corinth because the Roman emperor Claudius Caesar had ordered all Jews to leave Rome. Aquila and Paul were both tentmakers, so Paul stayed and worked with Aquila. This was how Paul often made money so he could preach and teach for free. Paul also taught in the synagogue every Sabbath.

When Silas and Timothy arrived, Paul was still witnessing to the Jews, explaining that Jesus is the Messiah. But the Jews resisted him and mocked him. *And when they opposed and reviled him, he shook out his garments and said to them, "Your blood be on your own heads! I am innocent. From now on I will go to the Gentiles."* So Paul left and went to the house of a Gentile worshiper of God.

However, the Jewish ruler of the synagogue, Crispus, and his whole household believed in Christ. Again, God brought about repentance and faith through Paul's preaching! Many of the Corinthians who heard Paul's preaching and teaching believed and were baptized.

Do you think it would be hard—and frightening—to keep on preaching when people got so mad at you and, in the past, had even beaten you? Paul was a great apostle, but he was also a man with temptations like the rest of us. He might have been tempted to be discouraged and fearful in this situation. **God understands our weakness. He is good.** One night, in His kindness, God told Paul in a vision:

> *..."Do not be afraid, but go on speaking and do not be silent, for I am with you, and no one will attack you to harm you, for I have many in this city who are my people." (Acts 18:9b-10)*

1 & 2 THESSALONIANS

Paul wasn't just a missionary, he was also a caring pastor. He continued to keep in touch with the churches he planted and to encourage the believers there. During his second missionary journey, probably while he was in Corinth, he wrote two letters to the church in Thessalonica. The Christians there were experiencing severe persecution, so Paul wanted to encourage them by thanking God for their *work of faith and labor of love and steadfastness of hope* in Jesus. He also wanted to challenge them to stand strong in persecution and grow in faith. Some of them were confused about the return of Jesus. They were afraid that Jesus had already returned and had left them in their suffering. But Paul assures them that Jesus' return will be very obvious - everyone will know it. He will come to deliver His people and punish those who have rebelled against Him and persecuted His people. In the meantime, he encourages them that *the Lord is faithful. He will establish you and guard you against the evil one.*

Can you imagine how comforting and encouraging this must have been for Paul? So Paul stayed in Corinth a year and a half teaching the word of God. After this, the Jews accused Paul of preaching a new religion, which was against the Roman law. This was a common attack against Paul by the Jews, but this time it didn't work. Paul continued to preach and teach in Corinth, and then left with Priscilla and Aquila. *Look at the map (page 258) to see where he went next.*

Paul went to Ephesus where he taught in the synagogue. The Jews wanted him to stay longer, but Paul knew he had other places to preach. Before he left, he promised to come back: *"I will return to you if God wills."* Aquila and Priscilla stayed behind in Ephesus, but

Paul got on a ship and went to Caesarea...and then went to Jerusalem to greet the Christians in the church there... and then went back to Antioch.

Paul tirelessly taught and preached, traveling over dangerous roads and across the sea because he loved Jesus and the message of the gospel. He understood the ignorance of the people of Athens and the resistance of the Jews because Paul used to be like that himself. Later he would write this to Timothy:

I thank him who has given me strength, Christ Jesus our Lord, because he judged me faithful, appointing me to his service, though formerly I was a blasphemer, persecutor, and insolent opponent. But I received mercy because I had acted ignorantly in unbelief, and the grace of our Lord overflowed for me with the faith and love that are in Christ Jesus. The saying is trustworthy and deserving of full acceptance, that Christ Jesus came into the world to save sinners, of whom I am the foremost. (1 Timothy 1:12-15).

What about you? Have you trusted in Jesus as your Savior? If you have, are you patient with those who don't understand or accept the gospel? Do you have compassion toward them? Are you praying for those who don't know Jesus? Do you have the heart to tell others about Jesus?

[Pray] also for me, that words may be given to me in opening my mouth boldly to proclaim the mystery of the gospel, (Ephesians 6:19).

THAT YOU MAY BELIEVE

What does this chapter tell us about God?

Talk about and apply the **biblical truths** in **bold** text. Make them personal and apply them to what is happening in your family, church, community, or the world today.

There are people in many countries who have never heard about Jesus. What can your family do to support or encourage a missionary so they can bring the good news that Jesus saves to those who have never heard it?

Talk About: *[Pray] also for me, that words may be given to me in opening my mouth boldly to proclaim the mystery of the gospel, (Ephesians 6:19)*

How has God been patient with you?

Pray: Thank God for His patience. Ask Him to send people to those who have not heard about Jesus.

Think About: *Do I see the gospel as beautiful—as good news? Am I seeking God?*

LOVING LIKE JESUS LOVES

If I speak in the tongues of men and of angels, but have not love, I am a noisy gong or a clanging cymbal. ²And if I have prophetic powers, and understand all mysteries and all knowledge, and if I have all faith, so as to remove mountains, but have not love, I am nothing.

³If I give away all I have, and if I deliver up my body to be burned, but have not love, I gain nothing.

⁴Love is patient and kind; love does not envy or boast; it is not arrogant ⁵or rude. It does not insist on its own way; it is not irritable or resentful; ⁶it does not rejoice at wrongdoing, but rejoices with the truth.

⁷Love bears all things, believes all things, hopes all things, endures all things. ⁸Love never ends. As for prophecies, they will pass away; as for tongues, they will cease; as for knowledge, it will pass away. ⁹For we know in part and we prophesy in part, ¹⁰but when the perfect comes, the partial will pass away.

¹¹When I was a child, I spoke like a child, I thought like a child, I reasoned like a child. When I became a man, I gave up childish ways.

¹²For now we see in a mirror dimly, but then face to face. Now I know in part; then I shall know fully, even as I have been fully known. ¹³So now faith, hope, and love abide, these three; but the greatest of these is love.

—1 Corinthians 13:1-13

CHAPTER 142

WATCHING OVER THE FLOCK

Paul Strengthens the Church on His Final Missionary Journey—Acts 18:23–21:16

"Pay careful attention to yourselves and to all the flock, in which the Holy Spirit has made you overseers, to care for the church of God, which he obtained with his own blood." (Acts 20:28)

Paul's third missionary journey was his longest, probably about four or five years. It was also his last recorded journey. *Follow the points on the map to see what happened on that journey and discover a riot, an important letter, a dead man brought back to life, a farewell speech, and a prophecy.* Along the way, Paul visited the churches he had planted and encouraged the believers to stand strong in their faith. You will recognize those places on the map. So come along, and let's stop at the highlights of this trip.

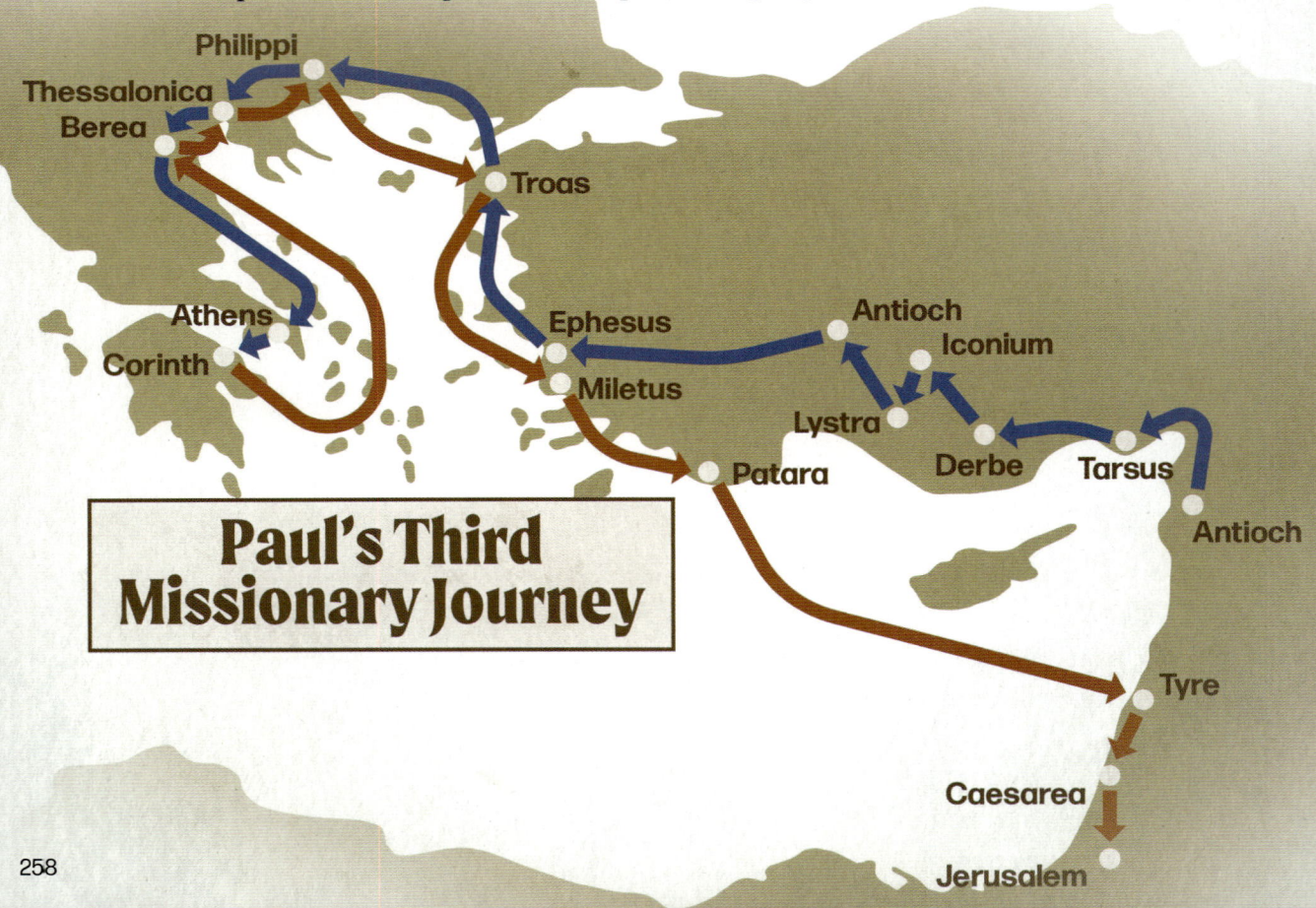

Paul's Third Missionary Journey

1. Paul stayed in Antioch about a year…and then set off to visit the churches in Galatia and Phrygia on his way to Ephesus. *Do you recognize any of these names?* (2. Derbe, Lystra, Iconium, Antioch in Psidia)

3. This is where the riot was! *What city is this?* Apollos was a believer in Jesus, and he eagerly taught the Jews in the synagogue about Jesus. He understood about water baptism but didn't understand about the coming of the Holy Spirit. So when Paul got to Ephesus, he taught the believers there about the Holy Spirit. *And when Paul had laid his hands on them, the Holy Spirit came on them.* Paul taught daily in Ephesus for two years, and his teaching was spread throughout Asia.

In Ephesus, *God was doing extraordinary miracles by the hand of Paul, so that even handkerchiefs or aprons that had touched his skin were carried away to the sick, and their diseases left them and the evil spirits came out of them.* **God's power is unlimited!** There were Jews who tried to cast out an evil spirit in a man, but they were not working in the power of the Holy Spirit. So the evil spirit overpowered them and injured them. When the people of Ephesus, both Jews and Greeks, learned about this, they were afraid. Many who practiced magic, even some believers who also wrongly practiced magic, burned their magic books.

But back to the riot…*Do you know how the riot started?* In Ephesus, there was a famous temple of the goddess Artemis. A silversmith named Demetrius made silver statues of the temple to sell. He gathered together other craftsmen who also made idols. Then he made these men upset and turned them against Paul saying, *"And you see and hear that not only in Ephesus but in almost all of Asia this Paul has persuaded and turned away a great many people, saying that gods made with hands are not gods."* He also told them that the "great goddess Artemis may be counted as nothing" if Paul continued his teaching. *What do you think these men were most concerned about?* They were losing money because fewer people were buying their idols. When these men heard what Demetrius said, *they were enraged and were crying out "Great is Artemis of the Ephesians!" So the city was filled with confusion.* They dragged Paul's friends to the officials. It was quite an uproar!

259

When an official finally got things quieted down, Paul encouraged the disciples there, said his goodbyes, and left for Macedonia (4). There he visited many of his churches. *Can you find them on the map?*

5. He traveled down to Corinth, and that is where the important letter comes in. He stayed there three months. While Paul was there, he wrote his important letter to the Romans teaching the deep truths about the salvation that is in Christ. But after hearing about a plot against him by the Jews, he went back up to Philippi (6) and across to…

7. Troas. *Do you know what happened in Troas?* Well, Paul preached…and preached…and preached until midnight. If you think your pastor preaches a long time, it is probably very short compared to Paul's preaching. Paul was preaching in an upper room where there were many lamps giving off heat, and probably fumes, too. It was late, and a young man named Eutychus was sitting in the window. Eutychus was getting drowsy…and more drowsy…and Paul kept talking…and Eutychus sank into…a…deep…sleep…and fell out the third-floor window! Poor Eutychus was dead!

But Paul went down, picked up Eutychus in his arms, and God made Eutychus alive again! **God is the Giver of Life.** It was an amazing miracle!…Then Paul went back upstairs, had the Lord's Supper with the disciples there… and taught until morning.

8. Paul left for Miletus where he asked the Ephesian elders to meet him. He told them that he would be going to Jerusalem. He didn't know what would happen there *except that the Holy Spirit testifies to me in every city that imprisonment and afflictions await me. But I do not account my life of any value nor as precious to myself, if only I may finish my course and the ministry that I received from the Lord Jesus, to testify to the gospel of the grace of God.* **Proclaiming the gospel is more precious than life itself.**

Paul warned the Ephesian elders that false teachers would try to deceive the believers. He instructed them saying, *"Pay careful attention to yourselves and to all the flock, in which the Holy Spirit has made you overseers, to care for the church of God, which he obtained with his own blood."* Then Paul prayed with them, and after many tears and hugs they went with him to see him get on a ship that brought him to...

9. Caesarea, and that is where we come to the prophecy. A prophet named Agabus came from Judea and took Paul's belt. He tied up his own feet and hands with it to give Paul a picture of what would happen. He said to Paul, *"Thus says the Holy Spirit, 'This is how the Jews at Jerusalem will bind the man who owns this belt and deliver him into the hands of the Gentiles.'"* If you were Paul's friend, what would you have told him? Paul's friends told him not to go to Jerusalem.

Then Paul answered, "What are you doing, weeping and breaking my heart? **For I am ready not only to be imprisoned but even to die** *in Jerusalem* **for the name of the Lord Jesus.**" *And since he would not be persuaded, we ceased and said, "Let the will of the Lord be done." (Acts 21:13-14)*

10. And Paul went to Jerusalem.

Paul had traveled more than 10,000 miles proclaiming the good news that Jesus is the Savior. Now he was ready to die for the name of Christ. What do you want to be written about you at the end of your life? What matters most—how many free throws you make in basketball or how many A's you make on your report cards? What matters most is this: Are you a faithful follower of Jesus? You do not need to be a great man like Paul to proclaim the gospel to a broken world. Every believer, even a child, can share the good news of Jesus with friends, neighbors, and others.

> **Him we proclaim, warning everyone and teaching everyone with all wisdom, that we may present everyone mature in Christ. For this I toil, struggling with all his energy that he powerfully works within me. (Colossians 1:28-29)**

THAT YOU MAY BELIEVE

What does this chapter tell us about God?

Talk about and apply the **biblical truths** in **bold** text. Make them personal and apply them to what is happening in your family, church, community, or the world today.

Ask your mother or father to tell you about someone who was faithful to Jesus to the end of life.

Talk About: *Him we proclaim, warning everyone and teaching everyone with all wisdom, that we may present everyone mature in Christ. For this I toil, struggling with all his energy that he powerfully works within me. (Colossians 1:28-29)*

Whom can you tell about Jesus?

Pray: Thank God for His faithfulness and for giving us faithful examples to follow. Ask God to make you a faithful follower of Jesus.

Think About: *What do I want to be said of me at the end of my life?*

CHAPTER 143
"AWAY WITH HIM!"
Paul Is Imprisoned and Escapes Death—Acts 21:17-24:26

"Take courage, for as you have testified to the facts about me in Jerusalem, so you must testify also in Rome." (Acts 23:11b)

Have you ever written a long letter? How long was it? On his third missionary journey, Paul wrote two letters to the church in Corinth that are now part of the New Testament—two long letters, twenty-nine chapters long in our Bible. Paul wrote his 1 Corinthians letter to deal with problems in the church. He had to speak pretty firmly about some sins in the church. In 2 Corinthians, we see that Paul was encouraged that the Christians in Corinth obeyed his instructions. Paul defended his right as an apostle to speak with authority and warned them that false teachers would come and tell them a different Messiah had come. He also gave them, and us, a little glimpse of the difficulties he had as a faithful messenger of the gospel.

Five times I received at the hands of the Jews the forty lashes less one. Three times I was beaten with rods. Once I was stoned. Three times I was shipwrecked; a night and a day I was adrift at sea; on frequent journeys, in danger from rivers, danger from robbers, danger from my own people, danger from Gentiles, danger in the city, danger in the wilderness, danger at sea, danger from false brothers; in toil and hardship, through many a sleepless night, in hunger and thirst, often without food, in cold and exposure. And, apart from other things, there is the daily pressure on me of my anxiety for all the churches. (2 Corinthians 11:24-28)

263

Now he was going to Jerusalem where it was prophesied that he would be imprisoned. The same God who had strengthened him in all his trials would be with him in Jerusalem. **God is always present to help His people.**

The Christians in Jerusalem welcomed Paul joyfully. But when Paul went to the temple, it was a different story. Rumors were spread that Paul had disrespected the temple—which wasn't true. People identified him as the "man who is teaching everyone everywhere against the people and the law and this place." So, of course, "then all the city was stirred up," and they dragged Paul out of the temple. They were going to kill Paul. But **God is sovereign over all things**, and the news of the confusion in Jerusalem reached an officer in the Roman army. He came with soldiers as the people were beating Paul and stopped the beating before Paul was killed. God had rescued Paul from death. Paul was arrested, but the soldiers actually had to protect him from the violent crowd of people who were crying out, "Away with him!"

What do you think Paul did in that situation? He used it as an opportunity to proclaim the gospel! He asked the officer if he could speak to the people, and then he told everyone his testimony—the story of his life as a Jew who persecuted the followers of Christ; how Jesus came to him on the Damascus road; how Ananias prayed for him, and he received his sight after being blind; how he was baptized and called to be God's messenger to the Gentiles. At this point, the Jews started screaming, "Away with such a fellow from the earth! For he should not be allowed to live." They were shouting and throwing their cloaks…so the officer took Paul inside the army building. He was going to have Paul whipped to find out from Paul why the people were accusing him of wrongdoing. But God had given Paul protection against this—Paul was a Roman citizen by birth. When Paul told the officer this, the officer was afraid because it was illegal to beat a Roman citizen without proving him guilty of a crime.

The next day, Paul was brought before the Jewish council. *And looking intently at the council, Paul said, "Brothers, I have lived my life before God in all good conscience up to this day."* At this statement, the high priest ordered Paul to be hit in the mouth. *Then Paul said to him, "God is going to strike you, you whitewashed wall! Are you sitting to judge me according to the law, and yet contrary to the law you order me to be struck?"* Now the council was really angry with Paul because he had spoken severely to the high priest. But Paul didn't realize that the man was the high priest, and Paul apologized. Paul knew what he had done was not honoring to God, and he repented immediately. But the whole council meeting turned into a big fight, and when it became violent, the officer was afraid that Paul would be "torn to pieces," so the soldiers took Paul back to the army building. *The following night the Lord stood by him and said, "Take courage, for as you have testified to the facts about me in Jerusalem, so you must testify also in Rome."* Paul had been faithful in Jerusalem; he would be faithful in Rome.

But the next day more than forty Jews plotted to kill Paul. They even took a vow or a pledge that they would not eat or drink until they had killed Paul. Their plan was to kill Paul when he was brought to the council the next day. But God put Paul's nephew in the right place at the right time to hear about their plot, and he went and told Paul about it. Paul sent his nephew to tell the officer, who made a better plan. In the middle of the night, they snuck Paul away from Jerusalem with 200 soldiers, 70 horsemen, and 200 spearmen to protect him! Paul still had gospel work to do in Rome. **Nothing can stop God's plan. God always accomplishes His purposes.**

The Roman officer sent Paul to Felix, the Roman governor of Judea, who was in Caesarea. He also sent a letter saying that Paul was a Roman citizen and that he had done nothing deserving death or imprisonment. So the Jews' evil plan was squashed! But a few days later, the Jewish council went to Caesarea to accuse Paul. Felix let Paul speak, too, and Paul told him that he had done nothing wrong. The charges weren't true. Felix knew that Paul was innocent, but Felix didn't want to cause problems with the Jews. So he said he needed more information before he could decide the case…and he kept Paul waiting in prison for two years.

Had God made a mistake? Paul was supposed to go to Rome and proclaim the gospel, but here he was sitting in Caesarea in jail for two years. Two long years just waiting for his case to be decided! But it was not a mistake. **God always knows what He is doing.**

Are there times in your life where you are tempted to wonder if God is making a mistake? God doesn't always work the way we expect Him to. Christians suffer in this broken world, and sometimes it doesn't make sense. Will you trust him even when things don't go the way you think they should?

> **And we know that for those who love God all things work together for good, for those who are called according to his purpose. (Romans 8:28)**

THAT YOU MAY BELIEVE

What does this chapter tell us about God?

Talk about and apply the **biblical truths** in **bold** text. Make them personal and apply them to what is happening in your family, church, community, or the world today.

Ask your mother or father about a time in their life when it seemed like things weren't going the way they should. How did things turn out? What did they learn?

Talk About: *And we know that for those who love God all things work together for good, for those who are called according to his purpose. (Romans 8:28)*

Why did the Jews hate Paul so much? Read John 15:18-19. *What is the good news about being hated by the world?*

Pray: Praise God for always accomplishing His purposes. Thank Him for His wisdom and love. Ask Him for faith to trust Him more.

Think About: *Is there something in my life that makes it hard to trust God's good and wise plan? How will I fight to trust God?*

CHAPTER 144
TAKE HEART AND TRUST GOD
Paul Has Confidence in God in a Storm at Sea—Acts 24:27-27:44

"...I would to God that not only you but also all who hear me this day might become such as I am—except for these chains." (Acts 26:29)

We left Paul sitting in prison...where he was until a new governor named Festus replaced Felix. The Jews immediately went to Festus to accuse Paul. Festus asked Paul if he wanted to have his trial in Jerusalem. There was no evidence against Paul, but he knew he would never get a fair trial in Jerusalem. So Paul asked to be tried in Rome. As a Roman citizen, Paul had this right. But there was a problem. Even though Festus had decided to send Paul to the emperor, he had no idea what crime to charge against Paul!

However, a king from another part of the Roman Empire named Agrippa came to visit Caesarea. Festus told Agrippa that Paul had done no crime—that the Jews were just arguing about their own religion. Agrippa and his wife Bernice were curious about Paul, so Festus brought Paul before Agrippa. Agrippa allowed Paul to defend himself, and again Paul took the opportunity to proclaim the gospel by telling Agrippa his testimony. *And Agrippa said to Paul, "In a short time would you persuade me to be a Christian?" And Paul said, "Whether short or long, I would to God that not only you but also all who hear me this day might become such as I am—except for these chains."* Paul was constantly taking opportunities to speak about Jesus. He wanted everyone to be saved.

Agrippa and Festus both agreed, *"This man is doing nothing to deserve death or imprisonment." And Agrippa said to Festus, "This man could have been set free if he had not appealed to Caesar."* Did Paul make a mistake in asking to be tried before Caesar? He could have been set free! But **God was sovereignly directing Paul.** There were people in Rome who needed to hear the good news about Jesus.

Paul and other prisoners were put on a ship along with soldiers and a centurion named Julius. Julius was very kind to Paul and even allowed him to visit friends along the coast. Eventually, they had to change ships and continued sailing toward Rome. The voyage was slow because there was not a strong wind to blow the boat along. Winter was coming soon, and the weather would be more dangerous. *Paul advised them saying, "Sirs, I perceive that the voyage will be with injury and much loss, not only of the cargo and the ship, but also of our lives."* The centurion agreed, but the owner and captain did not. So they set sail out into the open sea.

They were on the open sea when a terrible storm struck! The wind furiously whipped the ship around! The sailors couldn't control the ship, so the ship was just driven along by the raging wind. They were driven close to an island, which gave them enough protection for a little while. They were able to put ropes or cables under the ship to hold it together—kind of like making a net around the boat. But now there was a danger of crashing on the island. They "lowered the gear" so the wind would move them along. The storm raged on, and the next day they threw the cargo, the goods the ship was carrying, overboard. The third day they threw the ship's equipment overboard—probably things like ropes, cloth, and pulleys. The storm continued day after day until there was no hope of being saved.

Since they had been without food for a long time, Paul stood up among them and said, "Men, you should have listened to me and not have set sail from Crete and incurred this injury and loss. Yet now I urge you to take heart [be encouraged], for there will be no loss of life among you, but only of the ship. For this very night there stood before me an angel of the God to whom I belong

and whom I worship, and he said, 'Do not be afraid, Paul; you must stand before Caesar. And behold, God has granted you all those who sail with you.' So take heart, men, for I have faith in God that it will be exactly as I have been told. But we must run aground on some island." (Acts 27:21-26)

These men would be saved from the storm because God had appointed Paul to witness in Rome! **God rules over storms, seas, and all things. He designs all things to bring about His grand purposes.**

On the fourteenth night of the storm, the sailors realized they were nearing land. They were afraid they might crash on the rocks, so they lowered four anchors at the back of the ship "and prayed for day to come." Just before morning, the sailors lowered the ship's boat (like a lifeboat), pretending they were going to put anchors in front of the ship. But Paul knew they were just trying to save themselves and would leave the rest of them to go down with the ship. So Paul told the soldiers, *"Unless these men stay in the ship, you cannot be saved."* Agreeing with Paul, the soldiers cut the ropes to the boat.

Paul urged them again to have something to eat since they had not eaten in fourteen days—*"It will give you strength, for not a hair is going to perish from the head of any of you." And when he had said these things, he took bread, and giving thanks to God in the presence of all he broke it and began to eat.* How could Paul be so sure they would all be saved? They were all encouraged and ate some food. Then they lightened the ship more by throwing the wheat into the sea.

When day came, they saw land. They cut the anchors free, hoisted up the small guiding sail, and headed for the beach. But they hit a reef, a strip of jagged rock, coral, or sand. The front of the boat was stuck, but the back was broken up by the waves. What would happen now? The soldiers decided they were going to kill the prisoners so they wouldn't escape. *But the centurion, wishing to save Paul,*

kept them from carrying out their plan. He ordered those who could swim to jump overboard first and make for the land, and the rest on planks or on pieces of the ship. And so it was that all were brought safely to land.

Everyone on board the ship was saved! No one person was lost…just as the angel of God had told Paul. **God always does what He says He will do.** In many ways, Paul "preached" to the people on the ship. He had complete confidence in God…and they were all saved from drowning at sea.

Just as God was directing all things in Paul's life to fulfill His purposes, so God is directing everything in your life to fulfill His purpose for you. Like Paul, you can have complete confidence in God's goodness and wisdom. Will you trust Him to sovereignly watch over every detail of your life?

You keep him in perfect peace whose mind is stayed on you, because he trusts in you. (Isaiah 26:3)

THAT YOU MAY BELIEVE

What does this chapter tell us about God?

Talk about and apply the **biblical truths** in **bold** text. Make them personal and apply them to what is happening in your family, church, community, or the world today.

Ask your father or mother to tell you about a time when they recognized the goodness of God's sovereign plan in their lives.

Talk About: *You keep him in perfect peace whose mind is stayed on you, because he trusts in you. (Isaiah 26:3)*

In what kind of situations do you find it hard to trust God?

Pray: Praise God for being sovereign over all things. Praise Him that He can be trusted to keep His promises. Thank Him for His grace in your life. Ask Him to give you a greater trust in Him.

Think About: *Are God's purposes more important to me than my plans?*

CHAPTER 145

AN AMBASSADOR IN CHAINS

God's Sovereign Plan for Paul in Rome—Acts 28

...[Pray] also for me, that words may be given to me in opening my mouth boldly to proclaim the mystery of the gospel, for which I am an ambassador in chains, that I may declare it boldly, as I ought to speak. (Ephesians 6:19-20)

Everyone was saved from the shipwreck, but what would happen now? They were stranded on an island! But **God always has a plan,** and His children can trust Him completely. Even in the things that may seem like mistakes, **God works for the good of His children and for His glory**. And that is what God was doing on the island of Malta where Paul and the others were stranded. The native people who lived there showed great kindness to them. Paul and his companions were dripping wet and cold from being in the water...besides, it was raining! So the people of Malta started a fire to warm them. Paul gathered a pile of sticks for the fire...but what Paul didn't know was that hidden in the bundle of sticks there was a snake!

When Paul put the sticks on the fire, the snake wiggled out because of the heat and bit Paul on the hand. *When the native people saw the creature hanging from his hand, they said to one another, "No doubt this man is a murderer. Though he has escaped from the sea, Justice has not allowed him to live."* But Paul just shook the snake off into the fire, and Paul was fine. The native people were watching to see if Paul would swell up or drop dead from the snakebite. But nothing happened. They waited a long time, and after a while, they decided that Paul wasn't a murderer but a god! Of course, they were wrong about that, too, because **there is only one true God,** and He had protected Paul from the snakebite.

The chief leader of the island was a man named Publius. His father was very sick, and Paul went to visit the sick man. He prayed, put his hands on him, and the man was healed. So you can imagine what happened then! Many other sick people came to Paul and were healed through the power of the Holy Spirit.

Three months later, Paul and the others traveling with him boarded a ship that had stayed on Malta during the dangerous winter sailing months. The native people gave them everything they needed for the journey. This time Paul made it safely to Rome. Though he was still a prisoner, Paul was allowed to stay under "house arrest." This means that he could stay in a home with a guard instead of in a prison cell. But Paul was bound with a chain and did not have the freedom to come and go.

In our thinking, this might seem like a big mistake. Paul, the great missionary and church planter was stuck in Rome under house arrest. He could no longer travel and preach. But **God makes no mistakes.** God had much greater plans for Paul.

Because Paul could not visit the churches to encourage the believers, he wrote letters to them. Those letters—Ephesians, Philippians, and Colossians—became part of the New Testament. If Paul had visited these churches in person, his teaching would have helped the believers there, but then it may have been lost forever. But God had a plan for the New Testament to be written so that generations of Christians, including us, could have God's

Word given through Paul. Aren't God's plans better than our plans? God is still instructing His people through His words given to Paul!

Paul could also have visitors and teach people in Rome. Some of the visitors were sent by Paul's churches. Epaphroditus was sent with a gift of money for Paul from the church in Philippi. He was a great help to Paul, and when Epaphroditus went back to Philippi, he carried Paul's letter to the Philippian church with him. Timothy, who had traveled with Paul on his second missionary journey, also visited Paul in Rome. Not only was he a great help to Paul, but Paul was able to pour his wise teaching into this young man.

Paul was able to teach the Jews in Rome. Some of them believed in Jesus after hearing Paul's testimony about the Messiah, but others did not. Many of the Jews still stubbornly refused to accept Jesus as the Messiah. They became angry when Paul reminded them of the words of Isaiah.

> …"The Holy Spirit was right in saying to your fathers through Isaiah the prophet: 'Go to this people, and say, "You will indeed hear but never understand, and you will indeed see but never perceive." For this people's heart has grown dull, and with their ears they can barely hear, and their eyes they have closed; lest they should see with their eyes and hear with their ears and understand with their heart and turn, and I would heal them.' Therefore let it be known to you that this salvation of God has been sent to the Gentiles; they will listen." (Acts 28:25b-28)

Isaiah's words proved to be true—**God's Word is always true**. Paul also preached to the Roman guards, and many of these Gentiles believed in Jesus. Paul earned the respect of many Roman officials, and he spoke fearlessly to them about the gospel of Jesus. *Do you think it is easy to boldly witness about Jesus? When have you been afraid of telling others about Jesus?* Paul was afraid, too, and he wrote to the church in Ephesus, asking the believers to pray for him.

> … [Pray] also for me, that words may be given to me in opening my mouth boldly to proclaim the mystery of the gospel, for which I am an ambassador in chains, that I may declare it boldly, as I ought to speak. (Ephesians 6:19-20)

God answered this prayer and gave Paul amazing opportunities to tell others about Jesus. In fact, Paul was filled with joy because his imprisonment gave him many opportunities to preach the gospel…to people he may never have been able to preach to otherwise! This is what he wrote to the Philippian church:

> I want you to know, brothers, that what has happened to me has really served to advance the gospel, so that it has become known throughout the whole imperial guard and to all the rest that my imprisonment is for Christ. And most of the brothers, having become confident in the Lord by my imprisonment, are much more bold to speak the word without fear. (Philippians 1:12-14)

So not only did God give Paul the boldness to preach, but other Christians who saw Paul's courage also became bold rather than afraid. So God raised up many believers to tell the good news of the gospel. Paul's imprisonment wasn't a problem. It was a blessing! The gospel was preached, believers were made bold, and the letters of the New Testament were written. God's ways are "higher" or better than our ways! God had good purposes in sending Paul to Rome.

Another person Paul shared the gospel with in Rome was a Gentile slave named Onesimus. Onesimus had escaped from his master, Philemon, who was part of the church in Colossae. Onesimus could be imprisoned for running away. But Onesimus met Paul, heard the gospel, and believed in Jesus. Paul sent Onesimus back to his master with a letter. Paul asked Philemon to receive Onesimus back…not as a slave but as a beloved brother.

Do you remember what God had told Paul after he testified to the council in Jerusalem and the officer was afraid that he would be torn in pieces? His word to Paul had come true: *"Take courage, for as you have testified to the facts about me in Jerusalem, so you must testify also in Rome."* Paul had been a faithful witness in Rome…to Jews, Gentiles, soldiers, guards, a slave, and even to those in Caesar's household!

> *He lived there two whole years at his own expense, and welcomed all who came to him, proclaiming the kingdom of God and teaching about the Lord Jesus Christ with all boldness and without hindrance. (Acts 28:30-31)*

After two years, Paul was set free, and he probably made another missionary journey. But his time in Rome was not wasted. God did so much more through Paul's imprisonment than we know. Maybe in heaven we will find out more of the amazing work God did through this one faithful believer, Paul.

God may do amazing things through your life, too, if you are determined to live for Jesus and to spread His name wherever you are. Is making Jesus known to others of great importance to you? Will you trust God to work in any way He knows is best? Can you agree with Paul's words below?

But I do not account my life of any value nor as precious to myself, if only I may finish my course and the ministry that I received from the Lord Jesus, to testify to the gospel of the grace of God. (Acts 20:24)

Therefore, we are ambassadors for Christ, God making his appeal through us. We implore you on behalf of Christ, be reconciled to God. For our sake he made him to be sin who knew no sin, so that in him we might become the righteousness of God. (2 Corinthians 5:20-21)

THAT YOU MAY BELIEVE

What does this chapter tell us about God?

Talk about and apply the **biblical truths** in **bold** text. Make them personal and apply them to what is happening in your family, church, community, or the world today.

What is an ambassador? Read 2 Corinthians 5:20-21. How can you be an ambassador for Christ?

Talk About: *But I do not account my life of any value nor as precious to myself, if only I may finish my course and the ministry that I received from the Lord Jesus, to testify to the gospel of the grace of God. (Acts 20:24)*

Are you more bold or more fearful about sharing the gospel? Whom can you ask to pray for you?

Pray: Praise God for His wisdom, goodness, and sovereignty. Thank Him for the good news of the gospel and for the New Testament. Confess your fears and ask Him to give you boldness in sharing the gospel.

Think About: *Do I make Jesus and my faith most important in my life?*

DEAR CHURCH

Have you ever gotten a letter? Maybe that letter was from someone special—like your grandmother, a cousin, or a close friend. If you got a personal letter from your favorite sports star (a basketball or football player), a famous actor, or someone very important, would that letter be extra-special? You would probably read it many times and even keep it in a special place.

Well, someone very important did write you a letter. In fact, He wrote you twenty-one letters! And He isn't just someone very, very important. He is the MOST important, the Most High, the King of kings. By now, you have probably guessed who that "someone" is—God.

Do you know where to find these letters? They are in the Bible after the book of Acts, and they were written by the apostles (Peter, John, and Paul) and the brothers of Jesus (James and Jude).[24] Most of these men probably dictated the words to someone else who wrote them on a scroll. These scrolls were then sent by trusted messengers to the churches of Asia Minor or to a particular person. However, these letters were not just the words of men. God the Holy Spirit actually gave them the message in these letters. The very words were chosen by God and inspired by Him.

These churches had problems. Many of the people were new believers. Some of them weren't even Jewish and had little understanding of the Old Testament. They had to learn to turn away from their old ways to walk in the ways of Jesus. And, like all of us, they were sinners. The apostles wrote these letters to teach, correct, and encourage these believers. Paul wrote his letters to Timothy to help him to become a better leader and to give him instructions on how to help the believers grow in faith and holiness. In many ways, we are very much like the believers in the early Church. We may not have the exact same problems, but we have similar problems and need the same kind of teaching, encouragement, and even the rebukes that they did.

So these letters or "epistles" are God's message to us also—to the Church in North and South America, Africa, Asia, Australia, and Europe...the Church around the world... and to your family and you! Parts of the message of some of these letters are in *More Than a Story*. But there is so much more that God has to tell you in the New Testament letters! There are truths to learn, promises to treasure, instructions to follow, wisdom to guide you, and most of all a way for you to discover God Himself in His Word!

As you read the last eleven chapters of this book, remember that they contain just a small sliver of the truth that God wants you to know. They are just an introduction to the God you can discover in the Bible. So take out your Bible and start reading God's message to you in these precious letters!

Grace to you and peace from God our Father and the Lord Jesus Christ. (1 Corinthians 1:3)

[24] The author of the book of Hebrews is unknown.

CHAPTER 146

AN AWFUL TRADE AND A WONDERFUL GIFT

From Unrighteous to Righteous by Faith—Romans

For the wages of sin is death, but the free gift of God is eternal life in Christ Jesus our Lord. (Romans 6:23)

Do you know what the Hope Diamond is? It is one the most famous diamonds in the world. *When you think of diamonds, what color do you think of?* The Hope Diamond is different from most diamonds. It is a very rare, large, *dark blue* diamond, worth more than 250 million dollars! *Would it be appropriate to trade this diamond for a piece of candy? Or to use it when skipping rocks on the water? Or to kick it along the sidewalk?* Of course not! That would be utterly foolish! This rare and precious jewel is displayed in a museum and heavily guarded.

In Paul's letter to the Romans, he tells us about the greatest treasure, which is more precious and rare than the Hope Diamond…something that would be very foolish and terrible to trade away. *Do you know what the greatest treasure is?* **God is the greatest treasure**, perfect in righteousness; He is right in all He is and does. He is perfect in love, holiness, greatness, power, goodness, wisdom, beauty, faithfulness, truthfulness, and justice. But every person who has ever been born has failed to honor God as he should. **Every person has mistreated**

Who chose the greatest treasure?

God by ignoring, rejecting, disobeying, and disrespecting God. This is the greatest evil in the world, and every person is guilty and deserves God's wrath—God's fierce and right anger. Everyone—Jew and Gentile alike—has traded God, the greatest treasure, for other poorer treasures.

> *For the wrath of God is revealed from heaven against all ungodliness and unrighteousness of men…For although they knew God, they did not honor him as God or give thanks to him, but they became futile in their thinking, and their foolish hearts were darkened…they exchanged the truth about God for a lie and worshiped and served the creature rather than the Creator, who is blessed forever!… (Romans 1:18a, 21, 25)*

Treasuring other things like sports, possessions, money, or friends more than treasuring God is sin. When people dishonor God and are not grateful to Him, they become fools. They think they are wise, but they are really fools following a path of disobedience and evil. *What kinds of sin has spilled out of man's heart?* The Bible says that envy, murder, fighting, deceit, gossip, pride, covetousness, hate, anger, and all kinds of evil have poured out of our foolish hearts.

The first Adam rebelled against God in the Garden of Eden and brought sin, evil, and death into the world. His sin nature has been passed on to all people. *None is righteous, no, not one; no one understands; no one seeks for God. All have turned aside…no one does good, not even one.* The sinful heart of every person turns away from God and turns toward disobeying God's good commands. **The biggest problem of every person is that we are sinners** needing rescue or salvation.

But how can we be rescued? The Law cannot change sinful hearts. The Law didn't change the hearts of the Jews—God's chosen people. They had God's good Law given to them by Moses. But they could not keep God's commands, and they did not treasure Him most of all. No one can keep God's Law perfectly, so no one can be saved by law-keeping. We cannot change our own hearts. Man cannot save himself. That is really terrifying news! *Do you know why?* This is what the Bible tells us: *Because of your hard and impenitent heart you are storing up wrath for yourself on the day of wrath when God's righteous judgment will be revealed.* God will judge sinful men someday… and it will be terrifying and dreadful.

But there is good news…great news…the best news! *Do you know what it is?* God sent "a second Adam"—God's Son, Jesus, came in the form of a man and perfectly obeyed the law. He obeyed perfectly so that we can be accepted as righteous or justified in His sight. This means that those who trust in Jesus are brought into a right relationship with God; we are no longer condemned from our sin and separated from God. Jesus trades places with His people. **He took the wrath of God upon Himself on the cross**. Jesus suffered the punishment that sinners deserved! **Jesus, the Savior, took man's sin…and gives His people His perfect righteousness**! *For as by the one man's disobedience the many were made sinners, so by the one man's obedience the many will be made righteous.* But how do guilty sinners like us receive what Christ purchased on the cross?

> *Therefore, since we have been justified by faith, we have peace with God through our Lord Jesus Christ. (Romans 5:1)*

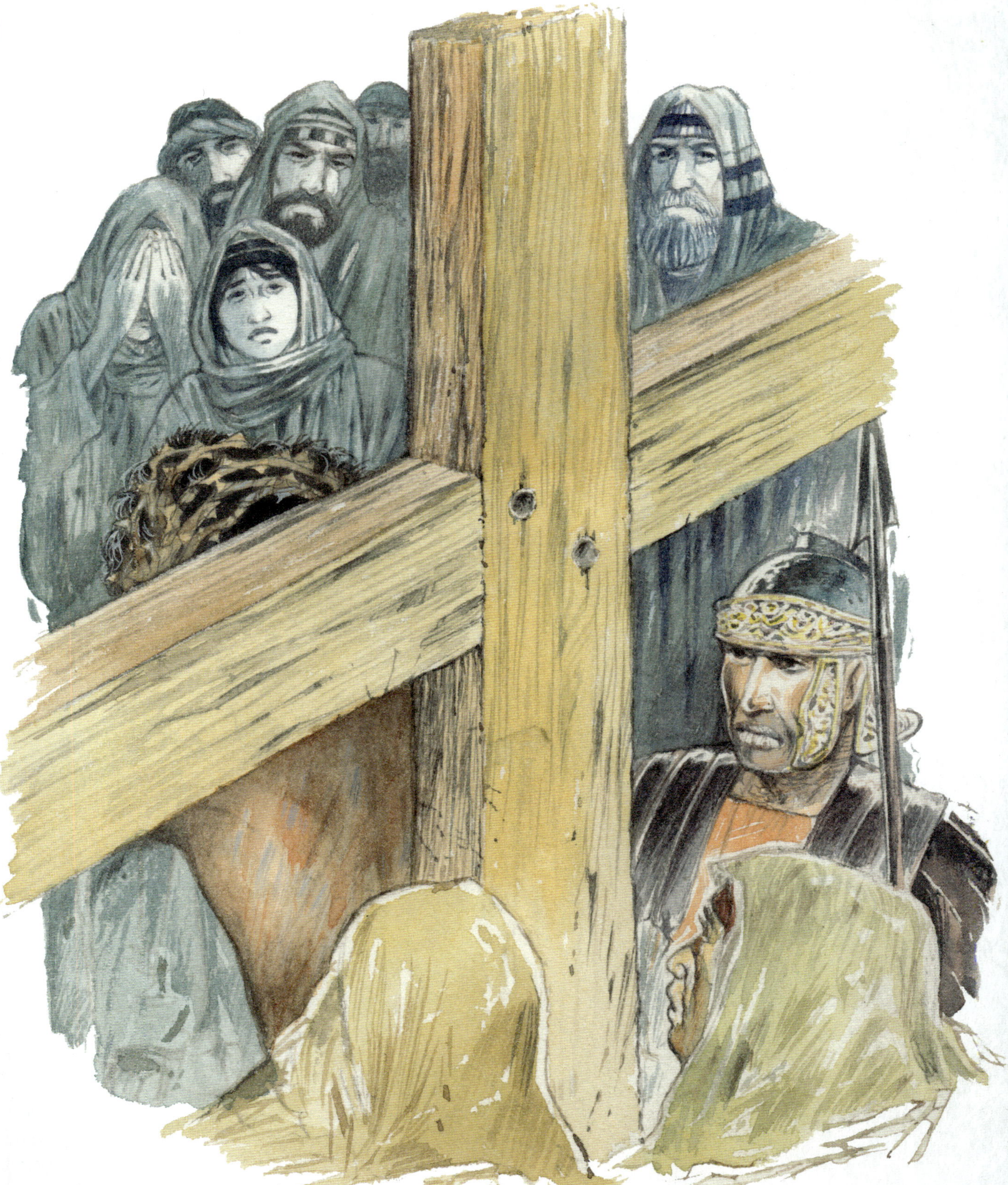

Forgiveness of sin and perfect righteousness comes through faith alone—through trusting in what Jesus did on the cross. Through trusting in Jesus, we can have peace with God. We become friends of God, receiving His love instead of His fierce anger at sin. Salvation from sin is a gift from God. It cannot be earned.

> *for all have sinned and fall short of the glory of God, and are justified by his grace as a gift, through the redemption that is in Christ Jesus. (Romans 3:23-24)*

God's grace—His kindness to undeserving sinners—leads to repentance, a deep sorrow for our sin, and a hatred of sin. God graciously gives His people faith to believe in Jesus and a new desire to follow Him. He gives His people eyes to see Jesus as the greatest treasure and the heart to love Him most of all. He also gives us the desire to obey Jesus' good commands and to please Him. We see God's Law *is holy, and the commandment is holy and righteous and good*...and we *want* to follow it. We see it as the best way to live. *Does everyone have the eyes to see Jesus as the greatest treasure?*

What family do you belong to? You belong to the family with whom you live. But those who are trusting in Jesus are adopted into another family, too. They belong to God's new covenant family. Followers of Jesus are part of the new family of Abraham, made up not just of Jews, but of believers of all nations and cultures. This is not the Smith family, the Gomez family, or the Su family. It is God's family of faith.

Those in the new family of faith turn away from their old sinful ways. God's laws could not fix the sinful human heart, but **God, the Holy Spirit, changes the heart**—He gives those who trust in Jesus a new heart. The new heart of faith gives believers the desire to love God and their neighbors as themselves. They see that God is the true treasure—much more precious than the Hope Diamond and all the temporary treasures of this world. People with hearts changed by the Holy

Spirit do not want to live like the rest of the world. They are changed by thinking differently and knowing what God loves, *what is good and acceptable and perfect.* They are becoming a people who love one another, hate what is evil, bless people who treat them unkindly, live peacefully with each other instead of fighting, and do good. They respect those in authority, care for one another, and are careful not to encourage others to sin. Christians are not perfect and don't perfectly obey Jesus' good commands, but they *want* to obey. Little by little, the Holy Spirit makes Christians more like Jesus.

A person who truly belongs to God's new covenant family will always be a part of God's family. Nothing will ever separate him from God's love. God watches over His children, and everything that happens to them will only be to bless them. *And we know that for those who love God all things work together for good, for those who are called according to his purpose.* Even suffering or danger or persecution will not win over them. God will give them victory over all things and will cause good to come to them through everything that happens to them.

Paul wrote a letter to the Christians in Rome during his third missionary trip. He wanted to make sure they understood the gospel and what it means to follow Jesus. But God did not want only the Romans to know this. He wants you to understand the gospel, too. He wants you to put your faith in Jesus and become part of His new covenant family. He wants you to love Him and your neighbor and grow to be more like Jesus. Are you part of God's new covenant family through faith in Jesus? Are you growing to be more like Jesus each day?

There is therefore now no condemnation for those who are in Christ Jesus. (Romans 8:1)

THAT YOU MAY BELIEVE

What does this chapter tell us about God?

Talk about and apply the **biblical truths** in **bold** text. Make them personal and apply them to what is happening in your family, church, community, or the world today.

What does it mean "to honor God and give thanks to Him"? What is the truth about God? What are lies about God? What does it mean to "worship and serve the creature rather than the Creator?"

Talk About: *There is therefore now no condemnation for those who are in Christ Jesus. (Romans 8:1)*

How can "all things work for good" for God's children (Romans 8:28)? Explain.

Pray: Thank God for sending Jesus to take the punishment for sinners who trust in Him. Confess the times you have worshiped other things (desired them more than you desired God). If you are not trusting in Jesus, ask God for the grace to trust in Jesus alone. Ask God to change your heart and to make you more like Jesus.

Think About: *Am I part of God's covenant family? Am I truly trusting Jesus?*

Memorize: Romans 8:1 and Romans 8:28

THE BAD NEWS IN ROMANS

The Problem

...sin came into the world through one man, and death through sin (Romans 5:12)

...for all have sinned and fall short of the glory of God (Romans 3:23)

None is righteous, no, not one...no one seeks for God. All have turned aside (Romans 3:10-12)

Man's Solution

Trusting in Religion

- Going to church
- Growing up in a Christian home
- Knowing about God and the Bible

For although they knew God they did not honor Him as God or give thanks to him, but they became futile in their thinking and their foolish hearts were darkened. (Romans 1:21)

Trusting in Good Works

- Keeping the commandments
- Doing good works with the wrong heart

You who boast in the law dishonor God by breaking the law. (Romans 2:23)

Trusting in Self

- Setting your mind on worldly things
- Following your sinful passions

For the mind that is set on the flesh is hostile to God, for it does not submit to God's law; indeed, it cannot. (Romans 8:7)

But because of your hard impenitent heart you are storing up wrath for yourself on the day of wrath when God's righteous judgment will be revealed. (Romans 2:5)

THE GOOD NEWS IN ROMANS
The Gospel
God's Solution

For while we were still weak, at the right time Christ died for the ungodly. (Romans 5:6)

Love

God shows his love for us in that while we were still sinners, Christ died for us. (Romans 5:8)

Grace

for all have sinned and fall short of the glory of God, and are justified by his grace as a gift, through the redemption that is in Christ Jesus. (Romans 3:23-24)

Children of the Promise

For as by one man's disobedience the many were made sinners, so by the one man's obedience the many will be made righteous. (Romans 5:19)

For everyone who calls on the name of the Lord will be saved. (Romans 10:13)

Salvation = Repentance + Faith

...God's kindness is meant to lead you to repentance. (Romans 2:4b)

...if you confess with your mouth that Jesus is Lord and believe in your heart that God raised him from the dead, you will be saved. (Romans 10:19)

Salvation is by GRACE alone through FAITH alone in JESUS alone!

THE GLORIOUS GIFT

Since, therefore, we have now been justified by his blood, much more shall we be saved by him from the wrath of God. (Romans 5:9)

There is therefore now no condemnation for those who are in Christ Jesus. (Romans 8:1)

Therefore, since we have been justified by faith, we have peace with God through our Lord Jesus Christ. (Romans 5:1)

For the wages of sin is death, but the free gift of God is eternal life in Christ Jesus our Lord. (Romans 6:23)

Nothing Can Separate Us from the Love of God

What then shall we say to these things? If God is for us, who can be against us? He who did not spare his own Son but gave him up for us all, how will he not also with him graciously give us all things? Who shall bring any charge against God's elect? It is God who justifies. Who is to condemn? Christ Jesus is the one who died—more than that, who was raised—who is at the right hand of God, who indeed is interceding for us. Who shall separate us from the love of Christ? Shall tribulation, or distress, or persecution, or famine, or nakedness, or danger, or sword? As it is written, "For your sake we are being killed all the day long; we are regarded as sheep to be slaughtered." No, in all these things we are more than conquerors through him who loved us. For I am sure that neither death nor life, nor angels nor rulers, nor things present nor things to come, nor powers, nor height nor depth, nor anything else in all creation, will be able to separate us from the love of God in Christ Jesus our Lord. (Romans 8:31-39)

God's Eternal Plan of Salvation is Being Fulfilled

And I will make of you a great nation, and I will bless you and make your name great, so that you will be a blessing…and in you all the families of the earth shall be blessed. (Genesis 12:2, 3b)

But it is not as though the word of God has failed. For not all who are descended from Israel belong to Israel, and not all are children of Abraham because they are his offspring, but "Through Isaac shall your offspring be named." This means that it is not the children of the flesh who are the children of God, but the children of the promise are counted as offspring…So then it depends not on human will or exertion, but on God who has mercy. (Romans 9:6-8, 16)

Jesus Welcomes All People

…because if you confess with your mouth that Jesus is Lord, and believe in your heart that God raised him from the dead, you will be saved. For with the heart one believes and is justified, and with the mouth one confesses and is saved. For the Scriptures says, "Everyone who believes in him will not be put to shame." For there is no distinction between Jew and Greek; the same Lord is Lord of all bestowing his riches on all who call on him. For "everyone who calls on the name of the Lord will be saved." (Romans 10:9-13)

CHAPTER 147
JESUS IS SUPERIOR
The Old Testament Foreshadows Jesus—Hebrews

Long ago, at many times and in many ways, God spoke to our fathers by the prophets, but in these last days he has spoken to us by his Son, whom he appointed the heir of all things, through whom also he created the world. (Hebrews 1:1-2)

Have you ever gotten a letter or phone call telling you that a grandparent or someone else special was coming to visit? Which was better—the letter or phone call, or the person actually coming and being with you? The Old Testament is like the letter or phone call announcing the coming of Jesus. But then Jesus came, and that is so much better than just the announcement!

In Old Testament times, God spoke to Israel through the prophets urging them to keep their covenant with Him. Sadly, most of Israel rebelled and turned away from God. But when Jesus came to earth, God spoke through His own Son! Jesus brought the message of salvation by grace through faith. Those who believed were adopted into God's family and given the promise of eternal life. Yet there were many who refused God's call to repent and believe. There were even those who hated Christians.

The book of Hebrews was written to Christians who were being persecuted for their faith in Jesus. Some were even put in prison. It was tempting for some to turn away from believing in Jesus and go back to the Jewish beliefs. The writer of Hebrews wanted to encourage the Christians to stand strong in their faith. He wrote to remind them that **faith in Jesus is the only way of salvation**. He did this by comparing Jesus with the Old Testament system and warning them not to turn away from the only hope of salvation.

If you went into a dark room, you might be able to see the shapes in the room, but you couldn't see the objects clearly. The Bible tells us that the Old

Testament is like looking at a shadow…or a shape in the dark. But the New Testament is like turning on the light; what was not clear becomes clear. This is what the book of Hebrews does. It turns the light on the Old Testament religious system and shows us clearly that it all points to Jesus, who is so much better. *Let's see if you can figure out how these comparisons show that Jesus is so much better. To whom is Jesus compared in these verses?*

> *He is the radiance of the glory of God and the exact imprint of his nature, and he upholds the universe by the word of his power. After making purification for sins, he sat down at the right hand of the Majesty on high, having become as much superior to angels as the name he has inherited is more excellent than theirs.* (Hebrews 1:3-4)

Jesus is superior to angels. Jesus is "superior" or far better than angels. Jesus' name is better than the angels' names—He is the "Son" of God. No angel has that position! Jesus is God the Son and is seated at the right hand of God the Father. **Jesus is the King who controls all things and will rule forever**. Angels are His servants. Even though Jesus is the King, He became a man to save others—to rescue His "brothers." Someday, King Jesus will return and defeat all His enemies.

Jesus is superior to Moses. Moses was very respected by the Hebrews. He was worthy of great honor because he was a faithful deliverer, leader, prophet, and mediator. He was the "builder" of God's people. He made them into a nation. But Jesus is far superior to Moses. **Jesus is a much greater deliverer, leader, prophet, and mediator**. *How was Jesus superior to Moses?* Jesus created Moses! Moses was the servant of God; but Jesus is the *Son of God*. Jesus didn't just "build" the nation of Israel. Jesus is the *builder of all things*—including His Church!

Jesus is a superior high priest. *What was the job of the high priest? Every high priest chosen from among men is appointed to act on behalf of men in relation to God, to offer gifts and sacrifices for sins.* But **Jesus is the perfect high priest**, superior to all priests.

> *For it was indeed fitting that we should have such a high priest, holy, innocent, unstained, separated from sinners, and exalted above the heavens. He has no need, like those high priests, to offer sacrifices daily, first for his own sins and then for those of the people, since he did this once for all when he offered up himself.* (Hebrews 7:26-27)

Why is Jesus superior to all the priests? The other priests were sinners. They had to offer sacrifices every day for their own sins and for the sins of others. But Jesus had no sin! He offered Himself as the once-and-for-all, forever sacrifice. Jesus is eternal—He rose from the dead and lives forever. **Jesus is the forever mediator between God and His people.**

> *The former priests were many in number, because they were prevented by death from continuing in office, but he holds his priesthood permanently, because he continues forever. Consequently, he is able to save to the uttermost those who draw near to God through him, since he always lives to make intercession for them. (Hebrews 7:23-25)*

Jesus is the continual intercessor for those who trust in Him. We cannot see all that is going on in the spiritual world. Satan hates God, and he hates anyone who is a true follower of Jesus. He is the accuser[25]—constantly pointing out our sin to God. But Jesus is the "intercessor" or defender for those who are trusting in Him. When Christians are accused of sin, Jesus steps in as our defender. He defends us with His blood. Because of His work on the cross, our punishment is taken care of, and we have been given His perfect righteousness. So God sees His children as "not guilty." He sees Jesus' perfect righteousness in His children.

Jesus established a superior covenant. The old covenant required people to keep God's Law, but they did not have *the heart to understand or eyes to see or ears to hear*. There was no power to obey the Law. But when Jesus came and poured out His blood on the cross, He made a new covenant between God and His people. The new covenant of faith in Jesus offers a new heart, mercy, forgiveness, and eternal life.

"…I will put my laws into their minds, and write them on their hearts, and I will be their God, and they shall be my people. And they shall not teach, each one his neighbor and each one his brother, saying, 'Know the Lord,' for they shall all know me, from the least of them to the greatest. For I will be merciful toward their iniquities, and I will remember their sins no more." (Hebrews 8:10b-12)

Warnings: After each comparison, the writer of Hebrews gives a warning. *What warnings do you think the writer of Hebrews gave to the Christians of his day and to us?* Here are some important ones to remember: *Therefore we must pay much closer attention to what we have heard, lest we drift away from it…how shall we escape if we neglect such a great salvation?*

Today, if you hear his voice, do not harden your hearts as in the rebellion. The Israelites had to wander in the wilderness for forty years because of their unbelief. The warning of Hebrews is, "Don't be like them! Don't rebel against God!"

It is impossible for those who have had their eyes opened to see who Jesus is, who have *shared in the Holy Spirit, and tasted the goodness of the word of God…if they then fall away,* to repent. Do you remember the Parable of the Sower? Hebrews is warning us not to be like the seeds that fell on the path, or in the thorns, or on the rocks. To hear the good news of the gospel of Jesus, to be taught in Sunday school and at home, and then to reject Jesus and "fall away" is to lose the promise of eternal life.

To continue to sin deliberately and turn away from Jesus brings judgment on yourself. *It is a fearful thing to fall into the hands of the living God.*

Hebrews ends with a plea to trust God, believe in Him, and receive the promised rewards of eternal life and joy forever. God's people have always found acceptance with God through faith. Even people in the Old Testament were saved by faith—Abel, Abraham, Sarah, Moses, and others died with the hope of a better life in heaven. Their faith in God should be an encouragement to us to keep on trusting God—to persevere in faith—and run from sin. God will help us to not grow tired in our faith. He will discipline us in order to train us to keep trusting Him and loving what is good and right. If we are trusting in Jesus, we can look forward to eternal life in heaven.

Therefore, since we are surrounded by so great a cloud of witnesses, let us also lay aside every weight, and sin which clings so closely, and let us run with endurance the race that is set before us, looking to Jesus, the founder and perfecter of our faith, who for the joy that was set before him endured the cross, despising the shame, and is seated at the right hand of the throne of God. (Hebrews 12:1-2)

The Old Testament shadows have disappeared! Jesus can now be clearly seen! Are you looking to Jesus in faith? Do you see Jesus as the greatest treasure, far superior to anything else? Are you listening to the warnings in Hebrews and persevering in faith?

And without faith it is impossible to please him, for whoever would draw near to God must believe that he exists and that he rewards those who seek him. (Hebrews 11:6)

THAT YOU MAY BELIEVE

What does this chapter tell us about God?

Talk about and apply the **biblical truths** in **bold** text. Make them personal and apply them to what is happening in your family, church, community, or the world today.

Explain how Jesus is superior to the Old Testament "shadows." In what way is Jesus a superior mediator and priest? Read 1 John 2:1. If you are a Christian, how did Jesus defend you this week?

Talk About: *And without faith it is impossible to please him, for whoever would draw near to God must believe that he exists and that he rewards those who seek him. (Hebrews 11:6)*

What does it mean to have faith in God? Be specific. (You may want to read Hebrews 11.)

Pray: Thank God for the New Testament, which clearly shows us who Jesus is. Ask God to give you the gift of great faith in Him and perseverance. Confess any unbelief.

Think About: *How can I draw near to God? How can I respond to the warnings in Hebrews?*

Memorize: Hebrews 11:6

---

25 The Hebrew word "Satan" and the Greek word "devil" both mean "accuser."

THE GREAT FAITH CHAPTER
HEBREWS 11[26]

Now faith is the assurance of things hoped for, the conviction of things not seen. [2] For by it the people of old received their commendation. [3] By faith we understand that the universe was created by the word of God, so that what is seen was not made out of things that are visible.

[4] By faith Abel offered to God a more acceptable sacrifice than Cain, through which he was commended as righteous, God commending him by accepting his gifts. And through his faith, though he died, he still speaks. [5] By faith Enoch was taken up so that he should not see death, and he was not found, because God had taken him. Now before he was taken he was commended as having pleased God. [6] And without faith it is impossible to please him, for whoever would draw near to God must believe that he exists and that he rewards those who seek him. [7] By faith Noah, being warned by God concerning events as yet unseen, in reverent fear constructed an ark for the saving of his household. By this he condemned the world and became an heir of the righteousness that comes by faith.

[8] By faith Abraham obeyed when he was called to go out to a place that he was to receive as an inheritance. And he went out, not knowing where he was going. [9] By faith he went to live in the land of promise, as in a foreign land, living in tents with Isaac and Jacob, heirs with him of the same promise. [10] For he was looking forward to the city that has foundations, whose designer and builder is God. [11] By faith Sarah herself received power to conceive, even

when she was past the age, since she considered him faithful who had promised. ¹²Therefore from one man, and him as good as dead, were born descendants as many as the stars of heaven and as many as the innumerable grains of sand by the seashore.

¹³These all died in faith, not having received the things promised, but having seen them and greeted them from afar, and having acknowledged that they were strangers and exiles on the earth. ¹⁴For people who speak thus make it clear that they are seeking a homeland. ¹⁵If they had been thinking of that land from which they had gone out, they would have had opportunity to return. ¹⁶But as it is, they desire a better country, that is, a heavenly one. Therefore God is not ashamed to be called their God, for he has prepared for them a city.

¹⁷By faith Abraham, when he was tested, offered up Isaac, and he who had received the promises was in the act of offering up his only son, ¹⁸of whom it was said, "Through Isaac shall your offspring be named." ¹⁹He considered that God was able even to raise him from the dead, from which, figuratively speaking, he did receive him back. ²⁰By faith Isaac invoked future blessings on Jacob and Esau. ²¹By faith Jacob, when dying, blessed each of the sons of Joseph, bowing in worship over the head of his staff. ²²By faith Joseph, at the end of his life, made mention of the exodus of the Israelites and gave directions concerning his bones.

²³By faith Moses, when he was born, was hidden for three months by his parents, because they saw that the child was beautiful, and they were not afraid of the king's edict. ²⁴By faith Moses, when he was grown up, refused to be called the son of

Pharaoh's daughter, ²⁵choosing rather to be mistreated with the people of God than to enjoy the fleeting pleasures of sin. ²⁶He considered the reproach of Christ greater wealth than the treasures of Egypt, for he was looking to the reward. ²⁷By faith he left Egypt, not being afraid of the anger of the king, for he endured as seeing him who is invisible. ²⁸By faith he kept the Passover and sprinkled the blood, so that the Destroyer of the firstborn might not touch them.

²⁹By faith the people crossed the Red Sea as on dry land, but the Egyptians, when they attempted to do the same, were drowned. ³⁰By faith the walls of Jericho fell down after they had been encircled for seven days. ³¹By faith Rahab the prostitute did not perish with those who were disobedient, because she had given a friendly welcome to the spies.

³²And what more shall I say? For time would fail me to tell of Gideon, Barak, Samson, Jephthah, of David and Samuel and the prophets— ³³who through faith conquered kingdoms, enforced justice, obtained promises, stopped the mouths of lions, ³⁴quenched the power of fire, escaped the edge of the sword, were made strong out of weakness, became mighty in war, put foreign armies to flight. ³⁵Women received back their dead by resurrection. Some were tortured, refusing to accept release, so that they might rise again to a better life. ³⁶Others suffered mocking and flogging, and even chains and imprisonment. ³⁷They were stoned, they were sawn in two, they were killed with the sword. They went about in skins of sheep and goats, destitute, afflicted, mistreated— ³⁸of whom the world was not worthy—wandering about in deserts and mountains, and in dens and caves of the earth.

³⁹And all these, though commended through their faith, did not receive what was promised, ⁴⁰since God had provided something better for us, that apart from us they should not be made perfect. (Hebrews 11:1-40)

26 Spend time talking through this chapter, perhaps in several sittings. Help your child to see how these people were living by faith, and help your child to discover the nature of true faith. How did their actions show what they truly believed? What would unbelief look like in these situations?

Therefore, since we are surrounded by so great a cloud of witnesses, let us also lay aside every weight, and sin which clings so closely, and let us run with endurance the race that is set before us, ²looking to Jesus, the founder and perfecter of our faith, who for the joy that was set before him endured the cross, despising the shame, and is seated at the right hand of the throne of God. (Hebrews 12:1-2)

CHAPTER 148
WRONG THINKING LEADS TO WRONGDOING

Paul Corrects Error in the Corinthian Church—
1 and 2 Corinthians

Therefore, if anyone is in Christ, he is a new creation. The old has passed away; behold, the new has come. (2 Corinthians 5:17)

Do you know how to play chess? If you don't understand how to play the game, you are going to make many wrong moves and probably lose the game. This is like what was happening in the church in Corinth. There was a lot that the Corinthians did not understand about the Christian life—how to think and behave as Christians. They just didn't get it...and their wrong thinking led to wrongdoing. So Paul had to correct them through letters, and even in a "painful visit" to them.

There were divisions in the church. People were fighting with each other and taking sides. Other teachers had come to teach in the church after Paul had been there. People began to choose their favorite teachers, and then to speak unkindly and disrespectfully about the other teachers. It wasn't a friendly argument about what sports team is the best, but a mean and ugly way of dividing the church. They were still living like non-Christians. So Paul had to remind them that leaders and teachers are only servants of Christ. **Jesus is the real leader of the Church**, so if they want to boast (brag), they should be united and boast about Jesus!

They were also sinning and thinking it was okay because they were "free in Christ." But Paul reminded them that *the unrighteous will not inherit the kingdom of God.* Jesus came to set them free *from* sin...not to give them the freedom *to* sin!

Corinth had many temples for Greek and Roman gods. Sometimes people offered meat to these gods. The people in the church were arguing about whether they could eat meat offered to gods or if it was sinful to eat it. But Paul told them that they were not understanding the way of Christ. They were not thinking like Christians. There is only one God, not many gods as the Greeks and Romans thought. The meat that God made is good and could be eaten because those gods weren't real.

There were so many arguments! And the Corinthians were concerned about the wrong thing. They were worried about their rights...instead of love. They should have been more concerned about loving one another. There was nothing wrong with eating meat offered to idols. But if eating the meat would offend someone or cause someone to think that worshiping other gods is okay, they shouldn't eat the meat. Loving others means giving up your rights and serving others. Paul tells them, *"So, whether you eat or drink, or whatever you do, do all to the glory of God."* They should stop thinking about themselves and what they want, and instead think about what brings glory to God—what shows His greatness and worth.

The Corinthians were just "baby Christians"—they still thought a lot like they did before they received Christ. There was a lot of fighting, pride, and envy in the church. People were disrespectful in how they took the Lord's Supper. They offended others in the church service—causing disruptions, confusion, and chaos. Again, they were not loving each other, but trying to outdo each other—to be the most important. Paul had to teach them that, though God had given them different gifts, all the gifts came from the same Holy Spirit. The Church is like the human body with many parts. *Are your hands more important than your feet? Do you need both hands and feet?* All the parts of the body are important—hands, feet, and eyes. And all work together to make one body. So each person in the "body of Christ," the Church, should do his own part, and all should work together to build up the Church. **Christians should love and serve each other.**

The church in Corinth sure had a lot of problems! Some people even said that the resurrection didn't really happen, and that it didn't matter anyway. This really upset Paul! If there was no resurrection, then Jesus would still be dead, and we would all still be stuck in our sin. But Jesus *did* rise from the dead, and He defeated death and evil!

> *For as by a man came death, by a man has come also the resurrection of the dead. For as in Adam all die, so also in Christ shall all be made alive. (1 Corinthians 15:21-22)*

Jesus' resurrection frees Christians from sin, gives power to live godly lives, and gives the promise of eternal life. It gives Christians victory in all these things!

Some people listened to Paul's scolding but, sadly, others did not. Paul had to make a very "painful visit" to them and remind them again of the gospel and what it means to truly follow Jesus. In his second letter, Paul reminded the Corinthians that it was God who sent him to preach to them. He was not a "peddler" of God's word but faithful and appointed by God. Other false teachers charged for their teaching. They were wealthy, and their teaching was impressive. But Paul didn't charge anything. He made his living by making tents. Paul wasn't trying to impress people with his abilities; he was trying to exalt Christ! Paul was merely a servant of Christ pointing them to Jesus Himself. The success of his ministry wasn't written in letters of recommendation (letters saying he did a good job) but in the changed hearts and lives done through the Holy Spirit.

Worldly success and wealth were important to the Corinthians, who lived in a large, wealthy city. But in God's Kingdom that isn't important. Jesus Himself became exalted as King through His suffering and death. Jesus died to reconcile people to God. **Suffering and self-sacrifice is the way to glory!**

> *Therefore, if anyone is in Christ, he is a new creation. The old has passed away; behold, the new has come. (2 Corinthians 5:17)*

God's people have a new way of looking at everything. Their desire is to please God and to "reconcile" others to God—to make peace between God and others through Jesus. If that means suffering, they understand that spiritual gain is more important than comfort in this life.

For this light momentary affliction is preparing for us an eternal weight of glory beyond all comparison, as we look not to the things that are seen but to the things that are unseen. For the things that are seen are transient, but the things that are unseen are eternal. (2 Corinthians 4:17-18)

Paul also encouraged the Corinthians to give generously to others. The Christians in Jerusalem were very poor because of a famine. Paul had collected money for them from other churches that were so happy to help their brothers. But the Corinthians had not helped others. Paul reminded them to follow the example of Jesus: *For you know the grace of our Lord Jesus Christ, that though he was rich, yet for your sake he became poor, so that you by his poverty might become rich.* Jesus had given up the glories of heaven and become a man to suffer for them. His suffering gave them the richness of salvation. **Followers of Christ should follow His example.**

The point is this: whoever sows sparingly will also reap sparingly, and whoever sows bountifully will also reap bountifully. Each one must give as he has decided in his heart, not reluctantly or under compulsion, for God loves a cheerful giver. And God is able to make all grace abound to you, so that having all sufficiency in all things at all times, you may abound in every good work. (2 Corinthians 9:6-8)

True Christians are "new creations" in Christ. Jesus' love and godly example changes His followers into generous people who delight to serve others. Paul himself had suffered much to preach the gospel and serve others. But other false prophets had come to lead the Corinthians away from the true gospel. The Corinthian believers had become easily deceived by these bragging, self-exalting teachers. These teachers were not at all like Paul, who boasted in his weakness *that the power of Christ may rest upon* him. He understood that the Corinthians could be deceived by these false teachers…*And no wonder, for even Satan disguises himself as an angel of light. So it is no surprise if his servants, also, disguise themselves as servants of righteousness.*

297

Paul ended his second letter by warning the Corinthians to truly look at their hearts and see if they are true followers of Jesus. This is a good thing for us to do, too. Do we truly put our confidence in Jesus? Do we live like God's Kingdom people, following Jesus' example, loving God, and loving others?

> Examine yourselves, to see whether you are in the faith. Test yourselves. Or do you not realize this about yourselves, that Jesus Christ is in you?— unless indeed you fail to meet the test! (2 Corinthians 13:5)

THAT YOU MAY BELIEVE

What does this chapter tell us about God?

Talk about and apply the **biblical truths** in **bold** text. Make them personal and apply them to what is happening in your family, church, community, or the world today.

Read about Paul's "thorn in the flesh" in 2 Corinthians 12:7-10. What can you learn from this?

Talk About: *Examine yourselves, to see whether you are in the faith. Test yourselves. Or do you not realize this about yourselves, that Jesus Christ is in you?—unless indeed you fail to meet the test! (2 Corinthians 13:5)*

What does it mean that "Satan disguises himself as an angel of light"? Why is this dangerous?

What does it mean to be a new creation in Christ? Why would we consider suffering "light and momentary"? Why would we sow bountifully? What does it mean to be an "ambassador for Christ"? (See 2 Corinthians 5:17-21)

Pray: Praise God for His Kingdom values that give life and love. Thank Jesus for "becoming poor" that you might "become rich." Confess any divisions, ungodly behavior, unloving thoughts or actions, selfishness, or pride in your heart. Ask God to make you more like Jesus.

Think About: *Am I "in the faith"? What evidence do I see in my life of faith in Jesus and living like Jesus did?*

Memorize: 2 Corinthians 5:21 or 2 Corinthians 12:9

CHAPTER 149
SALVATION BY FAITH ALONE

By Faith in Christ God's Favor Is Poured out on the Gentiles—Galatians

---

I do not nullify the grace of God, for if righteousness were through the law, then Christ died for no purpose. (Galatians 2:21)

Do you know why Paul was bold enough to speak the truth? He spoke boldly because He cared more about pleasing God than pleasing people. This is how Paul explained it, *"For am I now seeking the approval of man, or of God? Or am I trying to please man? If I were still trying to please man, I would not be a servant of Christ."* Paul was God's servant, and he spoke the truth even if people got angry with him, stoned him, or plotted to kill him. He was not afraid to point out wrong thinking and sinful living to the Corinthians. He also wrote a bold letter to the churches in Galatia. He had to tell them they were making a big mistake, too.

There were many Jewish Christians in Galatia who believed that non-Jewish Christians should follow the Laws given to Moses. They weren't talking about the Ten Commandments and Laws about right and wrong. These were laws about what to eat, laws about clean and unclean things, and laws about the nation of Israel. So instead of teaching that **salvation is by grace alone**, they were teaching that salvation is by grace *plus works*—grace plus keeping the Jewish law! They were *turning to a different gospel—not that there is another one.* The Galatians were turning away from the grace of Christ and trying to earn salvation by keeping the law! *What do you think Paul thought about that?*

Paul was angry, upset, astonished, and shocked! He was angry that the message of the true gospel was being changed. He was upset that people were actually teaching that faith in the death and resurrection of Jesus was insufficient—that more had to be added to what Jesus did in order for a person to be saved! God had appointed Paul before he was born to preach to the Gentiles the one true gospel, the gospel of salvation by grace alone. Paul reminded the Galatians that…

> **…*a person is not justified by works of the law but through faith in Jesus Christ*,** *so we also have believed in Christ Jesus, in order to be justified by faith in Christ and not by works of the law, because by works of the law no one will be justified.* (Galatians 2:16)

He was astonished and shocked that the Galatians were so foolish! They were saved by grace. Why were they so quickly becoming enslaved to the law again? The law cannot make anyone right with God. It brings death to all who cannot perfectly keep it. Why were these Galatians turning back to law-keeping, which could not give them life and freedom? Why were they insisting that the Gentiles follow the Jewish law? How could they so quickly forget the wonderful gospel of grace that was preached to them?

Just as Abraham was saved by faith alone before the Mosaic Law was even given, so God was including all people of faith in Jesus as the sons of Abraham. He reminded them that *it is those of faith who are the sons of Abraham… no one is justified before God by the law, for the righteous shall live by faith.* **God justifies—He declares righteous—all who trust in Jesus. Salvation is a gift. Salvation is by grace alone through faith alone.**

So if people are saved by faith—even Abraham and others in the Old Testament—then why did God give the Law? That is a very good question! *Do you know the answer?* The Law was just temporary. It was a way for God to help His people until Jesus came. It did two things.

Paul said that the Law was like a "guardian." *What do you think that means?* In Paul's time, the guardian was a servant who took care of the master's child, brought him to school, and made sure he was safe. The guardian guarded the child from evil and protected him from bad influences. The Law of Moses was like this, too—it protected God's people from evil and guarded them until the real teacher, Jesus, would come. The Law instructed them in God's good and right ways, showing them how to live in a way that is pleasing to God.

But the Law did something else, too. It showed the Jews that they were sinners. They couldn't keep the law. No matter how hard they tried. There was something deeply wrong with them—and with all people. We are sinners, and sin makes us all guilty before God.

The Law reveals our sin, but it cannot take away our sin. The Law shows us that we are helpless sinners, unable to keep God's Law and separated from God. It shows us we need a Savior. The Law points to Jesus, the perfect law-keeper, who fulfilled the Law, and took the guilt and punishment for sin.

> *So then, the law was our guardian until Christ came, in order that we might be justified by faith. But now that faith has come, we are no longer under a guardian, for in Christ Jesus you are all sons of God, through faith. (Galatians 3:24-26)*

Because of Jesus' work on the cross, Jews and Gentiles are all sons of Abraham through faith in Jesus. **God forgives the sins of those who trust in Jesus and makes us one family.**

> *There is neither Jew nor Greek, there is neither slave nor free, there is no male and female, for you are **all one in Christ Jesus**. And if you are Christ's, then you are Abraham's offspring, heirs according to promise. (Galatians 3:28-29)*

This new family of God is made up of people from every nation who trust in Jesus, living under a new law—the Law of love. The Holy Spirit changes those who have faith in Jesus and frees them to love and serve others.

> *For you were called to freedom, brothers. Only do not use your freedom as an opportunity for the flesh, but through love serve one another. For the whole law is fulfilled in one word: "You shall love your neighbor as yourself." (Galatians 5:13-14)*

When you look at an apple tree, what kind of fruit do you expect to see? Do you expect pears or peaches? No, apple trees produce apples. It is the same with true followers of Christ. Christians produce the same kind of "fruit" that Jesus produced. When Christians depend on the Holy Spirit, He produces the "fruit of the Spirit" in us—*love, joy, peace, patience, kindness, goodness, faithfulness, gentleness,* and *self-control*. The Holy Spirit enables His people to do good to others, to give generously, to live purely, to act wisely, and to joyfully follow God's good and right ways. This does not happen quickly, but little by little the Holy Spirit "transforms" or changes our old nature into our new Christ-like nature.

Are you trusting in what you can DO to be right with God? Or are you trusting in what Christ has DONE for you? Are you trusting in Jesus alone for salvation and growing in the fruit of the Spirit? How have you lived for Christ's glory this week?

> I have been crucified with Christ. It is no longer I who live, but Christ who lives in me. And the life I now live in the flesh I live by faith in the Son of God, who loved me and gave himself for me. (Galatians 2:20)

THAT YOU MAY BELIEVE

What does this chapter tell us about God?

Talk about and apply the **biblical truths** in **bold** text. Make them personal and apply them to what is happening in your family, church, community, or the world today.

What does "justification" mean? What does "salvation by faith alone" mean? Why is salvation a free gift? Why is salvation by grace through faith such a big deal?

Talk About: *I have been crucified with Christ. It is no longer I who live, but Christ who lives in me. And the life I now live in the flesh I live by faith in the Son of God, who loved me and gave himself for me. (Galatians 2:20)*

If we are saved by grace, do we have to obey God's Law?

Pray: Praise God for being a gracious God. Thank God for His Law, which reveals sin and protects us. Thank God for the gift of the Holy Spirit. Ask God to produce the fruit of the Spirit in you.

Think About: *Am I becoming more like Christ? Why or why not?*

CHAPTER 150
ADOPTED BY FAITH TO BE IMITATORS OF GOD
Saved by Grace through Faith, Transformed by the Spirit— Ephesians

---

But now in Christ Jesus you who once were far off have been brought near by the blood of Christ. (Ephesians 2:13)

Paul was amazed, really amazed. He was in absolute awe of God's grace poured out through His Son. *Do you remember who Paul was before he became an apostle?* Paul was a Pharisee, trying to earn God's favor by keeping the Jewish law. He was a hater of Christians and a persecutor of the Church…until Jesus, Himself, appeared to Paul on the Damascus road and poured out His grace on Paul, opened his blind eyes, and gave him a heart of faith. He forgave Paul's sins, saved Paul from eternal wrath, and promised him an eternal inheritance in heaven! That is amazing grace! It is the kind of grace Paul had to share with the Ephesian church.

*Blessed be the God and Father of our Lord Jesus Christ, who has blessed us in Christ with every spiritual blessing in the heavenly places, even as **he chose us in him before the foundation of the world, that we should be holy and blameless before him**. In love he predestined us for adoption as sons through Jesus Christ, according to the purpose of his will, to the praise of his glorious grace, with which he has blessed us in the Beloved. In him we have redemption through his blood, the forgiveness of our trespasses, according to the riches of his grace, which he lavished upon us… (Ephesians 1:3-8)*

What in these verses is so amazing to Paul? God chose His people to be saved before He ever created the world! He has declared that in Christ they are holy and blameless! Through Jesus, we can be adopted into God's family. We are saved through the blood of Jesus. Our sins are forgiven by God's grace given to us. We have a guaranteed promise of eternal life. Over and over, Paul reminded his churches of what God did in sending Jesus to die on the cross.

Paul reminded the Ephesians that they were once dead in their sins, following Satan, and were *"by nature children of wrath."* This means that they were born with a sin nature and deserved God's fierce anger at sin.

> *But God, being rich in mercy, because of the great love with which he loved us, even when we were dead in our trespasses, made us alive together with Christ—by grace you have been saved—and raised us up with him and seated us with him in the heavenly places in Christ Jesus, so that in the coming ages he might show the immeasurable riches of his grace in kindness toward us in Christ Jesus.* **For by grace you have been saved through faith.** *And this is not your own doing; it is the gift of God, not a result of works, so that no one may boast. (Ephesians 2:4-9)*

Aren't these beautiful words? Isn't God's free gift of grace amazing? Think of how much God loved sinners—sinners who rejected Him and were His enemies—and He made them His children! His grace cannot be measured!

The Ephesian Christians had once been like Paul—trapped in sin, following the evil powers of this world, children of wrath, separated from God, and without hope. But by God's grace, they were saved through faith and became part of God's new Israel, the redeemed family of Abraham, the Church. Now as a part of the family of God, Paul urged them to *walk in a manner worthy* of the children of God, *with all humility and gentleness, with patience, bearing with one another in love, eager to maintain the unity of the Spirit in the bond of peace.* The Ephesians and all Christians have been given new life in Christ.

Jesus set His people free from sin and death and gave us His Spirit, making us a new kind of people. **The Holy Spirit lives in Jesus' followers to give us a new nature.** The Holy Spirit helps us to "put off the old self" and *put on the new self, created after the likeness of God in true righteousness and holiness.*

What does the old self look like? The old self has in its heart anger, fighting, envy, jealousy, lying, stealing, gossip, revenge, bitterness, and all other kinds of evil. But listen to how beautiful the Holy Spirit is making God's children as imitators of Christ: *Walk in love, as Christ loved us and gave himself up for us; walk as children of the light and try to discern what is pleasing to the Lord; giving thanks always and for everything to God; submitting to one another out of reverence to God.*

Paul tells the Ephesians what to "put off" and what to "put on." When you read what Christians are to put off, can you figure out what they are to put on?

- Put off lying...put on speaking the truth.
- Put off anger...put on love.
- Put off stealing...put on working and sharing with anyone in need.
- Put off "corrupting" talk (unkind words)...put on only words that are good for building others up, which will give grace to those who hear you.
- Put off bitterness, wrath, anger, slander, and malice (hatred, meanness)...put on kindness toward one another, tenderheartedness, forgiveness, just as God in Christ forgave you.
- Put off filthiness, foolish talk, and crude joking...put on thanksgiving.
- Put off the "unfruitful works of darkness" (evil)...put on boldness to uncover and fight evil.

God's people are a whole new kind of people—people who walk in love and serve one another. Wives will follow their husband's leadership joyfully. Husbands will love their wives *as Christ loved the church and gave himself up for her*. Children will honor and obey their parents. Servants will obey their masters with a sincere heart. God's Kingdom people will *bear one another's burdens. If we are Christians,* we will not *grow weary in doing good* because we know there will be a reward if we do not give up. When we have the chance, we will do good to others, especially to other Christians. *For we are his workmanship, created in Christ Jesus for good works, which God prepared beforehand, that we should walk in them.*

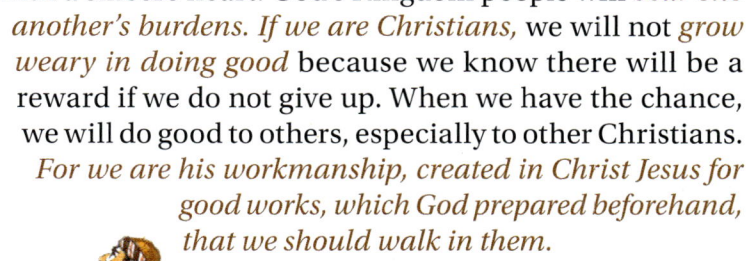

Does this seem impossible? Paul is not saying that Christians will be perfect, but Christians will be growing in becoming like Christ. He knows that there will be a battle—a battle between the old nature and the new nature. **This is a spiritual battle that calls for spiritual weapons**. It is a battle God's children cannot fight on our own, but a battle that God will help us fight if we depend on Him.

Finally, be strong in the Lord and in the strength of his might. Put on the whole armor of God, that you may be able to stand against the schemes of the devil. (Ephesians 6:10-11)

The beautiful new life of the Spirit is only possible for those who have received Jesus by faith. It is not something people can do by their own efforts and in their own strength. If you are a child of God, the Holy Spirit will help you to become more like Christ and walk in love. If you are not a child of God, you are still following your sin nature and under God's wrath. God's promises of blessing are not for you. Forgiveness is not yours. The power of the Holy Spirit is not yours. Where do you stand today? Are you in Christ, becoming more like Him through the power of the Holy Spirit? Or are you separated from God, following Satan, the prince of this world?

Now to him who is able to do far more abundantly than all that we ask or think, according to the power at work within us, to him be glory in the church and in Christ Jesus throughout all generations, forever and ever. Amen. (Ephesians 3:20-21)

THAT YOU MAY BELIEVE

What does this chapter tell us about God?

Talk about and apply the **biblical truths** in **bold** text. Make them personal and apply them to what is happening in your family, church, community, or the world today.

Talk through the "put offs" and "put ons." What does this look like in everyday life? Give specific examples. How does the Holy Spirit help us to live this new life in Christ?

Talk About: *Now to him who is able to do far more abundantly than all that we ask or think, according to the power at work within us, to him be glory in the church and in Christ Jesus throughout all generations, forever and ever. Amen. (Ephesians 3:20-21)*

Read Ephesians 1:3-14. *In how many different ways is God's grace shown in this passage?*

Pray: Praise God for His immeasurable grace. If you are not saved, ask God to give you a heart of faith. Confess the things you must put off. Ask God to give you a love for Him and for others.

Think About: *What do I need to put off? What do I need to put on?*

THE WHOLE ARMOR OF GOD

Finally, be strong in the Lord and in the strength of his might. Put on the whole armor of God, that you may be able to stand against the schemes of the devil. For we do not wrestle against flesh and blood, but against the rulers, against the authorities, against the cosmic powers over this present darkness, against the spiritual forces of evil in the heavenly places. Therefore take up the whole armor of God, that you may be able to withstand in the evil day, and having done all, to stand firm. (Ephesians 6:10-13)

- Helmet of Salvation
- Breastplate of Righteousness
- Shield of Faith
- Belt of Truth
- Sword of the Spirit
- Shoes Prepared with the Gospel of Peace

...praying at all times in the Spirit, with all prayer and supplication. To that end keep alert with all perseverance, making supplication for all the saints, (Ephesians 6:18)

CHAPTER 151
LIVING JOYFULLY AS KINGDOM PEOPLE

Pictures of Christ and His Followers—Philippians and Colossians

...work out your own salvation with fear and trembling, for it is God who works in you, both to will and to work for his good pleasure. (Philippians 2:12b-13)

Do you have a scrapbook or a photo album? Looking through a scrapbook brings back precious memories. We are going to look at the books of Philippians and Colossians as though they are a series of pictures from a scrapbook. Paul wrote both books while he was in prison in Rome. He wrote them to encourage the believers to keep following Christ and to imitate Him. They contain many precious truths. Let's look at the "pictures" in these two books and read the explanations about them!

PRAYING HANDS—Paul joyfully thanked God for the Philippians and prayed that their love would grow. He was sure that *he who began a good work in you will bring it to completion at the day of Jesus Christ.*

PRISON—Paul was joyful in prison because he had been able to preach the gospel to the Roman guards. Others had become bold in their witness because of Paul's example.

TOMBSTONE—*For to me to live is Christ, and to die is gain.* Paul couldn't really choose between life and death. He said he would love to go and be with Jesus, which would be so much better than being here. But if he lived, he could continue to encourage the Philippians and help them grow in faith. He wanted them to live in a way that shows they are followers of Jesus—*Only let your manner of life be worthy of the gospel of Christ.*

CROSS—Be unified. *Do nothing from rivalry or conceit, but in humility count others more significant than yourselves. Let each of you look not only to his own interests, but also to the interests of others.* What does this have to do with the cross?

Jesus is our example. He is God, but He gave up His position for a time. He *made himself nothing, taking the form of a servant...and being found in human form, he humbled himself by becoming obedient to the point of death, even death on a cross. Therefore God has highly exalted him and bestowed on him the name that is above every name, so that at the name of Jesus every knee should bow, in heaven and on earth and under the earth, and every tongue confess that Jesus Christ is Lord, to the glory of God the Father.*

LAMP—Shine as lights in the world, showing each day what God has done in you through the Holy Spirit. Everything you do, do without complaining or arguing.

GARBAGE—Don't put your confidence in your abilities or in the good deeds you have done, but put your confidence in Jesus. Paul had many reasons to be proud "in the flesh"—in worldly things. He was a Hebrew from the tribe of Benjamin (like Israel's first king, Saul). He was a Pharisee who knew the law. He had great energy in persecuting the Church… but none of that was really important. It is all like rubbish or garbage. Knowing Jesus is far better than all that. Paul told the Philippians, *"Indeed, I count everything as loss because of the surpassing worth of knowing Christ Jesus my Lord. For his sake I have suffered the loss of all things and count them as rubbish, in order that I may gain Christ and be found in him, not having a righteousness of my own that comes from the law, but that which comes through faith in Christ."*

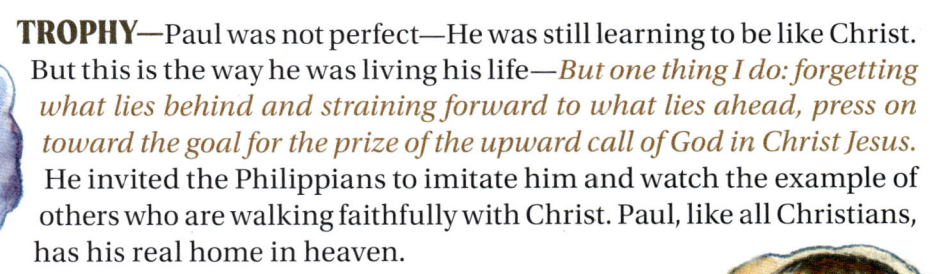

TROPHY—Paul was not perfect—He was still learning to be like Christ. But this is the way he was living his life—*But one thing I do: forgetting what lies behind and straining forward to what lies ahead, press on toward the goal for the prize of the upward call of God in Christ Jesus.* He invited the Philippians to imitate him and watch the example of others who are walking faithfully with Christ. Paul, like all Christians, has his real home in heaven.

SMILING FACE—In your photo album, what kinds of things made you smile? Well, Paul was joyful in prison! There are always reasons to rejoice in God! We don't need to worry about anything, but instead we should thank God and pray about what we need. Then we will have a peace that is very unusual in this world! We will be filled with joy if we focus on the right things.

Finally, brothers, whatever is true, whatever is honorable, whatever is just, whatever is pure, whatever is lovely, whatever is commendable, if there is any excellence, if there is anything worthy of praise, think about these things. (Philippians 4:8)

Paul had learned how to be content or happy in any situation—even in prison! It was something he had to learn; it doesn't come naturally. His secret formula for contentment is, *"I can do all things through [Christ] who strengthens me."*

We are going to put together a shorter photo album for the book of Colossians. Much of what is in Colossians you have already read about in this book...but it is a great book for you to read in your Bibles.

PRAYING HANDS—Once again, Paul started out with a prayer. He thanked God for the Colossians' faith in Jesus and love for the saints—which they had because of the hope stored up in heaven for them. *What do you think Paul prayed for them?*

And so, from the day we heard, we have not ceased to pray for you, asking that you may be filled with the knowledge of his will in all spiritual wisdom and understanding, so as to walk in a manner worthy of the Lord, fully pleasing to him, bearing fruit in every good work and increasing in the knowledge of God. May you be strengthened with all power, according to his glorious might, for all endurance and patience with joy, giving thanks to the Father, who has qualified you to share in the inheritance of the saints in light. (Colossians 1:9-12)

NUMBER 1—Jesus is the best. He is the first. The greatest praise belongs to Him.

He is the image of the invisible God, the firstborn of all creation. For by him all things were created, in heaven and on earth, visible and invisible, whether thrones or dominions or rulers or authorities—all things were created through him and for him. **And he is before all things, and in him all things hold together.** *(Colossians 1:15-17)*

Jesus made peace between God and man through His blood on the cross. At one time, all believers were far from God—rejecting Him and doing evil things. But that has changed for anyone trusting in Jesus. He will present you holy and blameless before God—*if indeed you continue in the faith, stable and steadfast, not shifting from the hope of the gospel that you heard, which has been proclaimed in all creation under heaven.*

CHURCH—Paul rejoiced in his suffering for the Church. He had the privilege of sharing what has been a mystery for many generations, for thousands of years! *Do you know what that mystery is?* It is God's plan to redeem all peoples—Jews and Gentiles—through His Son Jesus. This is why Paul was rejoicing in his suffering—he had been part of building God's worldwide Church!

Him we proclaim, warning everyone and teaching everyone with all wisdom, that we may present everyone mature in Christ. For this I toil, struggling with all his energy that he powerfully works within me. (Colossians 1:28-29)

If you made a scrapbook showing what is important in your life, what kinds of pictures would it include? Would it show that for you to live is Christ? Would others see that everything is as rubbish to you compared to knowing Christ? Would they see you making great efforts to proclaim the good news of faith in Jesus?

If then you have been raised with Christ, seek the things that are above, where Christ is, seated at the right hand of God. Set your minds on things that are above, not on things that are on earth. For you have died, and your life is hidden with Christ in God. (Colossians 3:1-3)

THAT YOU MAY BELIEVE

What does this chapter tell us about God?

Talk about and apply the **biblical truths** in **bold** text. Make them personal and apply them to what is happening in your family, church, community, or the world today.

What does it mean to "work out your salvation with fear and trembling"? How can you do that?

Talk About: *If then you have been raised with Christ, seek the things that are above, where Christ is, seated at the right hand of God. Set your minds on things that are above, not on things that are on earth. For you have died, and your life is hidden with Christ in God. (Colossians 3:1-3)*

How can you follow Philippians 4:8? What kinds of things do you fill your mind with? Is there anything you need to change in your life?

Pray: Praise Jesus using truths from Philippians 2:5-11. Thank God for His Word. Pray for someone using Colossians 1:9-12.

Think About: *Do I seek spiritual blessings and set my mind on things that are above?*

CHAPTER 152

FOLLOW THE PATTERN OF SOUND WORDS

Paul Instructs Timothy—1 and 2 Timothy

But as for you, continue in what you have learned and have firmly believed, knowing from whom you learned it and how from childhood you have been acquainted with the sacred writings, which are able to make you wise for salvation through faith in Christ Jesus. (2 Timothy 3:14-15)

Do you remember who Timothy was? Timothy's father was a Greek (Gentile), but his mother and grandmother were Jews who had become Christians. These two women had faithfully taught Timothy the Scriptures since he was a child, and Timothy became a believer. When Paul met Timothy on his second missionary journey, Timothy was a young man. Paul must have seen something special in Timothy because he invited Timothy to go with him for the rest of his trip, and again, on his third missionary trip.

Timothy became a great helper and companion to Paul during the many years they spent together. Paul became a great mentor or coach to Timothy, sharing with Timothy his understanding of the gospel and the Christian life. Paul knew that someday he would need to trust the leadership of his churches to godly younger men. When they no longer traveled together, Paul gave Timothy wise counsel by letter.

Timothy was leading the church in Ephesus when Paul wrote the letter of 1 Timothy to him. Later, Paul wrote 2 Timothy while Paul was imprisoned just before his death. Paul wanted to instruct this leader in how to lead the churches well and to carry on Paul's ministry.

First, Paul warned Timothy about false teachers. *Do you know what a false teacher is?* These are teachers who do not teach the truth about Jesus, the Bible, the Christian life, and what is true. Their teaching is false or wrong. *What kind of wrong teaching might they teach?* They are dangerous because they turn people away from the true gospel and trusting in Christ.

In order to guard the teaching and unity in the Church, Paul told Timothy to appoint leaders—both "overseers" (elders) and deacons. But these men must be carefully chosen. *What kind of qualities should a leader in a church have?*

> *Therefore an overseer must be above reproach, the husband of one wife, sober-minded, self-controlled, respectable, hospitable, able to teach, not a drunkard, not violent but gentle, not quarrelsome, not a lover of money. He must manage his own household well, with all dignity keeping his children submissive, for if someone does not know how to manage his own household, how will he care for God's church? He must not be a recent convert, or he may become puffed up with conceit and fall into the condemnation of the devil. Moreover, he must be well thought of by outsiders, so that he may not fall into disgrace, into a snare of the devil. (1 Timothy 3:2-7)*

Why are these qualities so important? Overseers or elders lead the church and teach the Bible. They are examples to other church members. If they are not godly men, they will be bad examples, and they will teach things that are not true. Deacons help serve people in the church and must also be men of good character. **To be godly is to have the character of Jesus**. *Do you see this character in the leaders in your church?*

If you participate in a sport or play a musical instrument, you must practice a lot. It is good to work hard and train yourself. Paul knew that, but he also knew there was a more important type of training, and he wanted to make sure that Timothy understood that, too.

> *Have nothing to do with irreverent, silly myths. Rather* **train yourself for godliness;** *for while bodily training is of some value, godliness is of value in every way, as it holds promise for the present life and also for the life to come. (1 Timothy 4:7-8)*

> *...***Pursue righteousness, godliness, faith, love, steadfastness, gentleness. Fight the good fight of the faith.** *Take hold of the eternal life to which you were called and about which you made the good confession in the presence of many witnesses. (1 Timothy 6:11b-12)*

*So **flee youthful passions and pursue righteousness, faith, love, and peace**, along with those who call on the Lord from a pure heart.* (2 Timothy 2:22)

Paul knew that godliness and faith are the things worth training for and fighting for because they are eternal—they last forever. *How are you training for godliness? What are you doing to develop the character of Christ? How are you fighting for your faith?*

Timothy's father was not a believer, so Paul was a spiritual father to him. *What do you think your pastor or your father would say to you if he knew he would die soon?* Paul loved Timothy like a son and wanted to encourage Timothy to stand firm in his faith. His last words to Timothy in 2 Timothy are good advice to any young person...or even older people!

First, Paul told Timothy not to be ashamed of the gospel—the truth about Jesus—but to be willing to suffer for his faith. God would give him strength to suffer for speaking the truth of the good news about Jesus and salvation. Paul had suffered persecution for his faith, and he knew that **anyone who wants to live a godly life will have hardships**. So Paul gave Timothy three examples of what it means to be faithful and hardworking, to suffer well, to persevere, and to be obedient and patient.

Share in suffering as a good soldier of Christ Jesus. No soldier gets entangled in civilian pursuits, since his aim is to please the one who enlisted him. An athlete is not crowned unless he competes according to the rules. It is the hard-working farmer who ought to have the first share of the crops. (2 Timothy 2:3-6)

Many of the people in the church were having silly arguments "about words"—not really trying to understand the Bible, but pridefully trying to show off their own particular ideas about picky points of religious beliefs. Paul called this "irreverent babble" that only led people into more and more ungodliness. The false teachers loved this kind of argument. Paul told Timothy to remind the church people of the important truths of Scripture—of what God is like, the gospel, and godly living. He told Timothy, *"Do your best to present yourself to God as one approved, a worker who has no need to be ashamed, rightly handling the word of truth."*

Paul also told Timothy something about a deposit. *Do you know what a "deposit" is?* One way to understand it is to think about making a "bank deposit." This is when you have money you want to keep, so you put it in the bank. That money is a deposit. Or, if you had some valuable jewels, you could put them in a "safety deposit box" in the bank. It takes certain signatures and keys to open a safety deposit box. Valuable things are well guarded in the bank.

Paul explained to Timothy that he had a "deposit" that he must guard well, too. Timothy's deposit was much more valuable than a lot of money or precious jewels. It was the Word of God. His mother and grandmother had taught him the Scripture. So had Paul. He had been given God's truth, which was a very precious deposit. Paul reminded Timothy of this.

> ***Follow the pattern of the sound words** that you have heard from me, in the faith and love that are in Christ Jesus. By the Holy Spirit who dwells within us, **guard the good deposit entrusted to you.** (2 Timothy 1:13-14)*

Timothy was to guard this good teaching and not be influenced by false teachers. He was to hold firm to the truth of the Word of God. Not only that, but Paul told him, *"and what you have heard from me in the presence of many witnesses entrust to faithful men who will be able to teach others also."* The sound teaching of the Word of God is very important! It is so important that Timothy was to guard the truth and train others to guard it and teach it. Why is the right understanding of the Bible so important? Why is knowing the Scripture such a treasure?

> ***All Scripture is breathed out by God and profitable for teaching, for reproof, for correction, and for training in righteousness, that the man of God may be competent, equipped for every good work.** (2 Timothy 3:16-17)*

The words in the Bible are the actual words of God! The Bible teaches us truth. It tells us everything we need for life and godly living. It points out our sin and causes our hearts to repent. It corrects us when we are wrong. It leads us to repentance and confession. It convinces us to turn from sin. It shows us how we need to change to be more like Christ. It trains us in godly living. That is a treasure worth guarding!

Even today, there are many false teachers—not only outside the church but also in the church. How will you know what to believe? How will you make sure you are not fooled into wrong thinking? You must know the Bible, God's holy and authoritative Word. You have been given a good deposit of Bible teaching—maybe through your parents, your church, and in this book. Will you treasure it, guard it, and follow it?

> Follow the pattern of the sound words that you have heard from me, in the faith and love that are in Christ Jesus. By the Holy Spirit who dwells within us, guard the good deposit entrusted to you. (2 Timothy 1:13-14)

> Let no one despise you for your youth, but set the believers an example in speech, in conduct, in love, in faith, in purity. (1 Timothy 4:12)

THAT YOU MAY BELIEVE

What does this chapter tell us about God?

Talk about and apply the **biblical truths** in **bold** text. Make them personal and apply them to what is happening in your family, church, community, or the world today.

What does it mean to be a "soldier," "athlete," and "hard-working farmer" in the Christian life? What can you learn from these examples?

Talk About: *Let no one despise you for your youth, but set the believers an example in speech, in conduct, in love, in faith, in purity. (1 Timothy 4:12)*

How can you guard the truth you know? What is your defense against wrong teaching?

Pray: Thank God for the good deposit of His Word He has given you. Ask Him to give you a love for the Bible and a desire to apply its truths in your daily life. Ask Him to guard you from wrong thinking. Confess any wrong thinking and ungodly behavior.

Think About: *Do I know the Bible well? Am I able to defend my beliefs and to tell truth from error? Am I able to spot wrong ideas and to know what the Bible says is true?*

CHAPTER 153
DOERS OF THE WORD
Learning to Live in the Wisdom from Above—James

But the wisdom from above is first pure, then peaceable, gentle, open to reason, full of mercy and good fruits, impartial and sincere. (James 3:17)

Do you know what book of the Bible talks about a mirror, a fire, deadly poison, and a farmer? If you said the book of James, that is the right answer. James was the brother of Jesus and the leader of the church in Jerusalem, and he was very wise. He wrote the book of James to pass on the wisdom God had taught him. James wrote this book shortly before he was put to death for his faith.

In a way, you could call James' wisdom "upside down." That's because the wisdom of the Kingdom of God is very different from the wisdom of this world. For example, James tells us to, *"Count it all joy, my brothers, when you meet trials of various kinds."* Why should we be joyful in troubles? That doesn't make sense—to the world, to those who only see this life on this earth. But if you are in Christ, you have a whole other life, a better life—you have a spiritual life. And this spiritual life makes everything different. There is a very good reason to be joyful in trials—*for you know that the testing of your faith produces steadfastness. Blessed is the man who remains steadfast under trial, for when he has stood the test he will receive the crown of life which God has promised to those who love him.* Christians care more about strong faith and a heavenly reward than about being comfortable in this life. True wisdom like this comes from God, so James tells us to ask God for wisdom. God is generous and will give wisdom to those who ask in faith, without doubting.

It is easy to say, "be joyful in trials," but it is a whole lot harder to actually do it—to put it into practice. *Hearing* the truth is one thing, but *doing* it is something very different! James had a strong word for us about this—*But be doers of the word, and not hearers only, deceiving yourselves.* This is where the mirror comes in. A person who only hears the word is like a man who looks in the mirror…and then walks away and forgets what he looks like. He sees, but the seeing doesn't do him any good. He isn't changed at all. He has the same attitudes, heart, and actions as the world does. *But the one who looks into the perfect law, the law of liberty, and perseveres, being no hearer who forgets but a doer who acts, he will be blessed in his doing.* The person who obeys God's Word and follows the way of Christ will receive great blessing and joy.

The upside-down wisdom of James tells us not to treat people who are rich better than other people. We are to treat all people with honor and respect. This is loving your neighbor as yourself. Sometimes people who are not smart or good at sports, or who have a disability, or who wear out-of-style clothes aren't treated kindly by others. But this is not the way of Christ. Jesus treated lepers, Samaritans, and all people with kindness. *Are you kind to those who are different from you?* True Christians care for the poor. If someone is in need and we only say, "I hope things are okay. Go in peace," without *doing* something to help, we are not helping. *So faith by itself, if it does not have works is dead.*

What does James say about a fire? How does a great forest fire start? Sometimes it is started by a campfire or a bolt of lightning. But James talks about a great forest fire started by…the tongue! The tongue is small, but it can cause great damage—just as a forest fire does. We can tame all kinds of animals, but we cannot tame or control the tongue. *It is a restless evil, full of deadly poison. With it we bless our Lord and Father, and with it we curse people who are made in the likeness of God. From the same mouth come blessing and cursing.* The tongue is very small but causes great problems. It spreads gossip, lies, arguments, and hurtful words. James tells us this shouldn't be!

Our tongues show what is in our hearts. The worldly heart is full of "bitter jealousy and selfish ambition"—fighting with others to get the best, and only thinking about yourself. It is wanting attention or glory. This is earthly wisdom. It is unspiritual and even demonic! *But the wisdom from above is first pure, then peaceable, gentle, open to reason, full of mercy and good fruits, impartial and sincere. And a harvest of righteousness is sown in peace by those who make peace.* The person who has true upside-down Kingdom wisdom and understanding will be a doer of true good works. When you truly love your neighbor as yourself, bitter jealousy and selfish ambition will not control your life, but you will be guided by Christ-like humility, kindness, and generosity. *What kind of wisdom do you want to guide you—earthly wisdom or the wisdom from above?*

Do you know what causes fights? It isn't that another person makes you angry. **Our actions come from what is in our hearts.**

> *What causes quarrels and what causes fights among you? Is it not this, that your passions are at war within you? You desire and do not have, so you murder. You covet and cannot obtain, so you fight and quarrel. You do not have, because you do not ask. You ask and do not receive, because you ask wrongly, to spend it on your passions. You adulterous people! Do you not know that friendship with the world is enmity with God? Therefore whoever wishes to be a friend of the world makes himself an enemy of God. (James 4:1-4)*

Our desires control our hearts. Everyday there are battles in our hearts—battles over what will rule our hearts and our behavior. Will we let God rule, or will we let our desires grow out of control and rule our hearts? We will either love God and His Kingdom, or we will love our own little kingdom of self. Whenever we let something else rule our hearts instead of asking God to rule our hearts, we are loving the world and making ourselves an enemy of God. True wisdom is submitting to God— obeying Him and asking Him to rule our lives. It is recognizing that we need God's help. *God opposes the proud, but gives grace to the humble." Submit yourselves therefore to God. Resist the devil, and he will flee from you. Draw near to God, and he will draw near to you. Cleanse your hands, you sinners, and purify your hearts, you double-minded.*

James reminds us that we are "double-minded." We say one thing but do another. We are hearers of the Word—knowing what is right, pure, and good—but we so often are not doers of the Word. What we say doesn't always match how we act. But God wants to make us "perfect." James does not mean that we are without sin. Perfect means whole—making our actions match what we believe. We become "whole" by recognizing that we need to be purified. We need God's help. We need to depend on Him each day to match our actions with our words—to do what is right, not just know what is right.

So how do we learn this humility? James gives us an example of pride that is surprising.

Come now, you who say, "Today or tomorrow we will go into such and such a town and spend a year there and trade and make a profit"—yet you do not know what tomorrow will bring. What is your life? For you are a mist that appears for a little time and then vanishes. Instead you ought to say, "If the Lord wills, we will live and do this or that." As it is, you boast in your arrogance. All such boasting is evil. (James 4:13-16)

Our pride makes us think we are in charge. But James reminds us that we are not in control—God is in control of all things. Living our lives understanding that God is at the center of all things makes us realize that His Kingdom is more important than ours. Everything we have comes from God, who owns all things. *Every good and perfect gift comes from above.* Life is not about us and our plans. God rules and His Kingdom purposes will come about. Until Jesus returns, we must wait patiently, as hearers *and doers* of the word. *Be patient, therefore, brothers, until the coming of the Lord. See how the farmer waits for the precious fruit of the earth, being patient about it, until it receives the early and the late rains.*

If you are a follower of Christ, you are learning the wisdom from above. You are learning to be "perfect" or whole so that your words and your actions match each other. Will you humbly ask God to help you today?

But be doers of the word, and not hearers only, deceiving yourselves. (James 1:22)

THAT YOU MAY BELIEVE

What does this chapter tell us about God?

Talk about and apply the **biblical truths** in **bold** text. Make them personal and apply them to what is happening in your family, church, community, or the world today.

Explain what the wisdom from above looks like in different situations.

Talk About: *But be doers of the word, and not hearers only, deceiving yourselves. (James 1:22)*

What is in your heart when you argue or fight with others? What is it that you want most at that moment? How is that not showing wisdom from above? (Think of a recent fight you had and examine your heart.)

Pray: Praise God for being holy, gentle, understanding, merciful, and gracious. Ask Him to give you the wisdom from above. Confess worldly wisdom and ask God for forgiveness. Thank God for patiently working in your heart.

Think About: *Am I humble? Do I depend on God to give me wisdom from above? How can I grow in "upside-down" Kingdom wisdom?*

CHAPTER 154

A LIVING HOPE

Hope for God's People in Persecution—1 and 2 Peter

Blessed be the God and Father of our Lord Jesus Christ! According to his great mercy, he has caused us to be born again to a living hope through the resurrection of Jesus Christ from the dead, (1 Peter 1:3)

Do you remember the story of Jesus walking by the Sea of Galilee where he met Simon and his brother, Andrew? Simon and Andrew were throwing their nets into the sea to catch fish. But Jesus said to them, *"Follow me, and I will make you fishers of men."* Immediately, they left their nets and followed Jesus. Both men became disciples of Jesus. Later, Jesus changed Simon's name to Peter, which means "rock." *"And I tell you, you are Peter, and on this rock I will build my church, and the gates of hell shall not prevail against it."* After Jesus died, Peter lived out this new name or new identity by building the church in Jerusalem. Later, he preached the good news beyond Israel to other parts of the Roman world. He wrote his letters of 1 and 2 Peter to encourage believers in Asia Minor (now Turkey) who were being persecuted for believing in Jesus.

Just as Jesus had given Peter a new identity or character, Peter reminded these persecuted believers of who they really were—of their new identity in Christ. He reminded them that trusting in Jesus makes a person a member of a whole new family or community.

> But **you are a chosen race, a royal priesthood, a holy nation, a people for his own possession, that you may proclaim the excellencies of him who called you out of darkness into his marvelous light.** Once you were not a people, but now you are God's people; once you had not received mercy, but now you have received mercy. (1 Peter 2:9-10)

Many of these believers were Gentiles who had been outside the covenant God made with Israel. But now through Christ they were a chosen people, part of God's royal priesthood and holy nation. They belonged to God through the new covenant of faith in Jesus. As a holy nation, **God's people are called to be holy as God is holy**—to *put away all malice and all deceit and hypocrisy and envy and slander;* to *have unity of mind, sympathy, brotherly love, a tender heart and a humble mind;* to *live as people who are free, not using [their] freedom as a cover-up for evil, but living as servants of God.* Believers are a royal priesthood—a people who *do not repay evil for evil, or reviling for reviling* (insulting), but instead bless others. **Christians are a chosen race called to be obedient and respectful to those in authority** like emperors or kings, governors, and masters—and not only rulers who are good and gentle, but also rulers who are unjust. By suffering injustice or wrong treatment with patient graciousness, believers please God by our obedience and respectful attitudes.

As God's people, we are to be a different kind of family, and the way we live shows that we are different. Peter explained to these churches what the love of Christ looks like in a family:

> *Likewise, wives, be subject to your own husbands, so that even if some do not obey the word, they may be won without a word by the conduct of their wives, when they see your*

respectful and pure conduct. Do not let your adorning be external—the braiding of hair and the putting on of gold jewelry, or the clothing you wear—but let your adorning be the hidden person of the heart with the imperishable beauty of a gentle and quiet spirit, which in God's sight is very precious. (1 Peter 3:1-4)

Likewise, husbands, live with your wives in an understanding way, showing honor to the woman as the weaker vessel, since they are heirs with you of the grace of life, so that your prayers may not be hindered. (1 Peter 3:7)

How could these persecuted Christians live like this? How can anyone live like this? It is only possible through being "born again." As Jesus told Nicodemus, this is not being born as a baby. It is being born spiritually by grace through faith in Jesus. God has given believers new life instead of judgment and wrath! **Those who are born again have the wonderful promise of eternal life in heaven**—a promise that is sure!

Blessed be the God and Father of our Lord Jesus Christ! **According to his great mercy, he has caused us to be born again to a living hope** *through the resurrection of Jesus Christ from the dead,* **to an inheritance that is imperishable, undefiled, and unfading, kept in heaven for you.** *(1 Peter 1:3-4)*

Though these Christians in Asia Minor were being persecuted, they could look forward with firm confidence that a wonderful future was waiting for them. So whatever happens in this life, all believers know that there is pure joy ahead for us in eternity. There is also blessing *in* trials.

In this you rejoice, though now for a little while, if necessary, you have been grieved by various trials, so that the tested genuineness of your faith—more precious than gold that perishes though it is tested by fire—may be found to result in praise and glory and honor at the revelation of Jesus Christ. (1 Peter 1:6-7)

What should God's children do when people are unkind to us or make fun of us? Peter reminds all believers that Jesus is our example of how to suffer and not sin.

For to this you have been called, because Christ also suffered for you, leaving you an example, so that you might follow in his steps. He committed no sin, neither was deceit found in his mouth. When he was reviled, he did not revile in return; when he suffered, he did not threaten, but continued entrusting himself to him who judges justly. He himself bore our sins in his body on the tree, that we might die to sin and live to righteousness. By his wounds you have been healed. (1 Peter 2:21-24)

Jesus was insulted, beaten, mocked, and mistreated far worse than anyone else will ever be...and He was completely innocent. Yet He was not unkind to those who mistreated

Him. He trusted that God will take care of making things right. *Do you find it hard not to react with anger when others mistreat you?* There are always temptations to pay someone back—to get even with them. But Peter reminds us that God will bless us for obeying Him. He reminds us that **our real enemy is** not that other person, but **Satan**, the accuser, who wants us to sin. But we are to resist him. Some day, suffering will end, and God will renew and strengthen His people.

> *Humble yourselves, therefore, under the mighty hand of God so that at the proper time he may exalt you, casting all your anxieties on him, because he cares for you. Be sober-minded; be watchful. Your adversary the devil prowls around like a roaring lion, seeking someone to devour. Resist him, firm in your faith, knowing that the same kinds of suffering are being experienced by your brotherhood throughout the world. And* **after you have suffered a little while, the God of all grace**, *who has called you to his eternal glory in Christ,* **will himself restore, confirm, strengthen, and establish you**. (1 Peter 5:6-10)

Peter warned the churches about false teachers who lived sinfully and said that God will not judge sin. But they were wrong! Peter reminded the Church that *God did not spare angels when they sinned, but cast them into hell and committed them to chains of gloomy darkness to be kept until the judgment.* He reminded them of those who were judged in the flood and in Sodom and Gomorrah. But God spared those who trusted in Him. He spared Noah and his family, and Lot and his family. So **God knows** *how to rescue the godly from trials.*

False teachers also taught that Jesus will not return again someday. But Peter and the other apostles were eyewitnesses of Jesus' glory. He reminded the believers that to God, one day is like a thousand years. God looks at time differently than we do. He has a gracious reason for waiting so long before sending Jesus back—*The Lord is not slow to fulfill his promise as some count slowness, but is patient toward you,* **not wishing that any should perish**, *but that all should reach repentance.* God is giving people time to repent!

But judgment will come...and the Day of the Lord will come "like a thief in the night." It will be very unexpected. For those who belong to Christ, this is not a scary thought because *according to his promise we are waiting for new heavens and a new earth in which righteousness dwells.* God is making a new world where there is no sin, no suffering, no tears—where righteousness dwells.

God's promise is sure—all believers will someday receive a wonderful inheritance in the new heavens and new earth. But God's judgment is also sure. He does not wish that any should suffer in hell, but instead repent. Have you accepted Jesus as your Savior and become God's child?

> **The Lord is not slow to fulfill his promise as some count slowness, but is patient toward you, not wishing that any should perish, but that all should reach repentance. (2 Peter 3:9)**

THAT YOU MAY BELIEVE

What does this chapter tell us about God?

Talk about and apply the **biblical truths** in **bold** text. Make them personal and apply them to what is happening in your family, church, community, or the world today.

What is the living hope Peter is talking about (1 Peter 1:3)? How is that hope gained? What do the words "imperishable," "undefiled," and "unfading" mean? Why should God be praised?

Talk About: *The Lord is not slow to fulfill his promise as some count slowness, but is patient toward you, not wishing that any should perish, but that all should reach repentance. (2 Peter 3:9)*

How would you describe yourself? Does Peter's description of the people of God fit you?

Pray: Praise God for His grace and His rescue from judgment. Thank God for His patience with sinners. Thank Him for His promises. (Name some of them.) If you have not received Jesus as your Savior, ask God for the faith to trust Jesus.

Think About: *Do I belong to God? Am I His child?*

FELLOWSHIP WITH GOD AND ONE ANOTHER

Some Verses to Think about from 1 John

THE WORD OF LIFE (JESUS)

That which was from the beginning, which we have heard, which we have seen with our eyes, which we looked upon and have touched with our hands, concerning the word of life— the life was made manifest, and we have seen it, and testify to it and proclaim to you the eternal life, which was with the Father and was made manifest to us—that which we have seen and heard we proclaim also to you, so that you too may have fellowship with us; and indeed our fellowship is with the Father and with His Son Jesus Christ. And we are writing these things that our joy may be complete. (1 John 1:1-4)

WALKING IN THE LIGHT

My little children, I am writing these things to you so that you may not sin. But if anyone does sin, we have an advocate with the Father, Jesus Christ the righteous. He is the propitiation[27] for our sins, and not for ours only but also for the sins of the whole world. And by this we know that we have come to know him, if we keep his commandments. Whoever says "I know him" but does not keep his commandments is a liar, and the truth is not in him, but whoever keeps his word, in him truly the love of God is perfected. By this we may know that we are in him: whoever says he abides in him ought to walk in the same way in which he walked. (1 John 2:1-6)

DO NOT LOVE THE WORLD

Do not love the world or the things in the world. If anyone loves the world, the love of the Father is not in him. For all that is in the world—the desires of the flesh and the desires of the eyes and pride in possessions—is not from the Father but is from the world. And the world is passing away along with its desires, but whoever does the will of God abides forever. (1 John 2:15-17)

CHILDREN OF GOD

See what kind of love the Father has given to us, that we should be called children of God; and so we are. The reason why the world does not know us is that it did not know him. Beloved, we are God's children now, and what we will be has not yet appeared; but we know that when he appears we shall be like him, because we shall see him as he is. (1 John 3:1-2)

OVERCOMERS

Little children, you are from God and have overcome them [false prophets], for he who is in you is greater than he who is in the world. (1 John 4:4)

For this is the love of God that we keep his commandments. And his commandments are not burdensome. For everyone who has been born of God overcomes the world. And this is the victory that has overcome the world—our faith. Who is it that overcomes the world except the one who believes that Jesus is the Son of God. (1 John 5:3-5)

And this is his commandment, that we believe in the name of his Son Jesus Christ and love one another, just as he has commanded us. (1 John 3:23)

---

27 "Propitiation" mean satisfaction. God is holy and must punish sin. God's wrath, His holy anger against sin must be "satisfied"—justice must be done. Instead of punishing man for his sin, God has given His people a substitute—His Son. Jesus died to take the punishment we deserve and to pay for the sins of His people.

CHAPTER 155
LET HIM HEAR

Jesus' Message to the Seven Churches and to Us—Revelation 1-3

When I saw him, I fell at his feet as though dead. But he laid his right hand on me, saying, "Fear not, I am the first and the last, and the living one. I died, and behold I am alive forevermore, and I have the keys of Death and Hades." (Revelation 1:17-18)

The Bible does not tell us what happened to most of the disciples, but history and tradition seem to suggest that most, if not all, the disciples except Judas and John were martyred or killed for their faith. Though John wasn't martyred, he was exiled to an island named Patmos in Greece. His friends had been killed, and he was alone and old. There he wrote the book of Revelation.

John wrote this letter as a message to seven churches in Asia Minor (Turkey). These churches were enduring many challenges and difficulties. John himself had been sent away as a punishment for preaching the gospel. The other disciples were dead. Life was hard, and these churches needed hope for the future. **God, who is always faithful**, gave John a vision and a message to encourage these churches and all Christians in all times.

John had a vision of Jesus as the exalted King surrounded by seven lampstands. The vision of Jesus was an awesome, glorious sight—He had a long robe and pure white hair. *His eyes were like a flame of fire*, his feet were like shiny bronze, and *his voice was like the roar of many waters...from his mouth came a sharp two-edged sword, and his face was like the sun shining in full strength.* The vision in the book of Revelation is full of symbols or pictures. This picture of Jesus shows that He is powerful and has all authority. His eyes can look into the very depth of man's heart, so He is a righteous judge.

When John saw King Jesus, he *fell at his feet as though dead.* But in his vision, John says that King Jesus *laid his right hand on me, saying, "Fear not, I am the first and the last, and the living one.* **I died, and behold I am alive forevermore***, and I have the keys of Death and Hades [hell]."*

The seven lampstands were symbols for the seven churches. Jesus had a message for each of the churches. He is a righteous King who knows their weaknesses and strengths. These churches had all suffered persecution, and some were standing strong, but others were wavering. Jesus wanted to encourage them and also to warn them. Find each of these churches on the map on the next page as you hear Jesus' warnings and promises in His message to each church.

THE CHURCH IN EPHESUS—Ephesus was a great seaport and the largest city in Asia Minor. It was a center of travel and trade. Paul had started the church there, and it became a center for evangelism. Jesus' message to the church in Ephesus was this: You are hardworking and patiently enduring persecution. Even though you are suffering, you are still faithfully serving Me. You are wisely opposing false teachers. BUT *"you have abandoned the love you had at first. Remember therefore from where you have fallen; repent, and do the works you did at first."*

The kind of love these people first had for Jesus was missing. Jesus wanted them to serve Him out of love, not just because it was a habit or the right thing to do. If they did not repent, the church would die—Jesus would "remove their lampstand." However, if they did repent, this is what Jesus promised: *"To the one who conquers I will grant to eat of the tree of life, which is in the paradise of God."*

THE CHURCH IN SMYRNA—Smyrna was a large and rich city. But the church there was poor and suffering greatly. The people were persecuted by Jews, Gentiles, and even Satan. Even so, they had been faithful, pure, and patient. In the letter to this church, Jesus said that their persecution would get *worse.* Some would be thrown in prison. But after this difficult news came a wonderful promise: *"Be faithful unto death and I will give you the crown of life."* **Faithful Christians will receive eternal life!** Suffering does come to an end...and after that, there will be an eternity of peace and joy for those who are faithful to Jesus.

THE CHURCH IN PERGAMUM—Pergamum was also a rich city, but it was very wicked. There were many worshipers of false gods, so it was a difficult place for Christians to live. Even so, Jesus said these words about the church in Pergamum: *"Yet you hold fast my name, and you did not deny my faith."* BUT they had believed some of the teaching of false teachers. If they did not repent, judgment would suddenly follow. However, Jesus gave them a promise if they repented: *"To the one who conquers I will give some of the hidden manna, and I will give him a white stone, with a new name written on the stone that no one knows except the one who receives it."* Those who remain faithful will be accepted by God, and each one will be given a special name! They will be remembered by the Lord, just like the tribes of Israel, which were written on the remembrance stones of the High Priest's ephod!

Modern Day Turkey

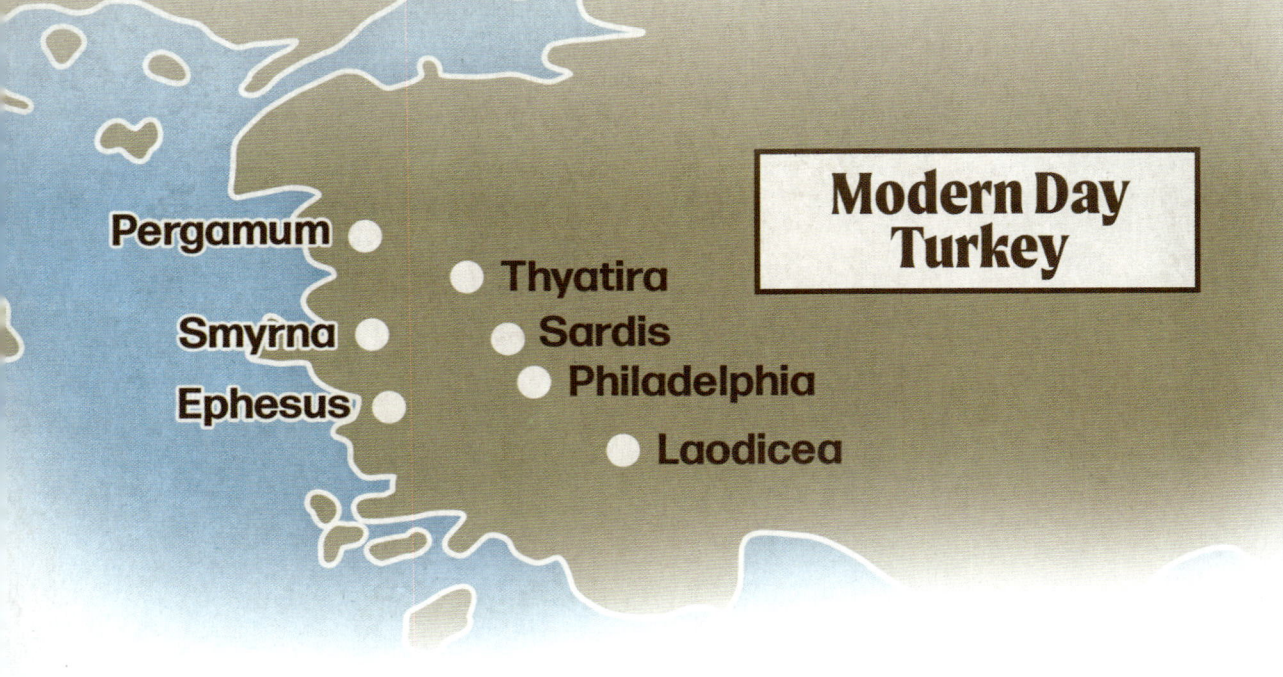

- Pergamum
- Thyatira
- Smyrna
- Sardis
- Philadelphia
- Ephesus
- Laodicea

THE CHURCH IN THYATIRA—Thyatira was a small city in a farming area. It was also known for its purple dye. The people in the church there were praised for their love, faith, service, and patient endurance in suffering. BUT they had a serious problem. Many were following a woman who claimed to be a prophetess. Her name was Jezebel, and she was evil! She had led some of the Christians into sinful living. Others refused to follow her, and Jesus' message to them was: *"Only hold fast what you have until I come."* **Jesus will return, and when He does, He will reward faithful Christians.**

THE CHURCH IN SARDIS—Sardis was an important business city that was on a busy trade route. The people there were makers of jewelry, cloth, and dye that had made the city very rich. Sadly, Sardis was also a place of false worship with a temple to a false god. The church there seemed to be alive, but it was really a place of dead faith—the people were spiritually weak. Jesus warned them: *"Remember then, what you received and heard. Keep it and repent. If you do not wake up, I will come like a thief, and you will not know at what hour I will come against you."* What should they remember? They should remember the gospel and what Jesus did for them! There were some in the Sardis church who did remember, and Jesus promised that their names will not be blotted or erased from the Book of Life. Jesus will call them His own before His Father.

THE CHURCH IN PHILADELPHIA—Philadelphia was a city in a farming area. The church there was strong and faithful. The people were very pleasing to Jesus: *"I know that you have but little power, but you have kept my word and have not denied my name."* They had patiently persevered through many trials. Jesus told them to "hold fast"—to stand firm—until He returns to fulfill this promise to the faithful: *"The one who conquers, I will make him a pillar in the temple of my God."* They will live forever with Him, and Jesus will "write His name" on them. He will be their God forever.

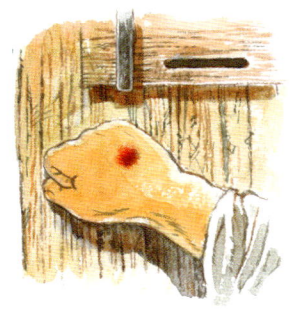

THE CHURCH IN LAODICEA—The last message was for the church in Laodicea, a rich city where wool cloth was made. This church did not receive any words of praise from Jesus.

"'I know your works: you are neither cold nor hot. Would that you were either cold or hot! So, because you are lukewarm, and neither hot nor cold, I will spit you out of my mouth. For you say, I am rich, I have prospered, and I need nothing, not realizing that you are wretched, pitiable, poor, blind, and naked." (Revelation 3:15-17)

The people of this church were so blind to their own sin that they didn't even see their spiritual darkness and need. Jesus urged them to return to Him. He was waiting for them—knocking at the door—waiting to be invited in to be with them. If they would answer Him, He would allow them to sit on His throne with Him—they would rule in Jesus' new Kingdom.

These messages of praise, rebuke, warning, and promise are not just for the churches of John's time. They are for us, too. Just as these churches did, we can become full of knowledge but lose our passion and love for Jesus. We can follow the wrong ideas and behavior of this world. We can be spiritually dead, too—following our religious practices and going to church but not really having any interest in spiritual things. We can be lazy in our faith and lukewarm, instead of seeking God with all our hearts.

After each of the messages to the seven churches, Jesus said, *"He who has an ear, let him hear what the Spirit says to the churches."* **Jesus calls us to pay attention to the Holy Spirit**, too. The Holy Spirit is calling us to hold fast to the truth, return to our first love for Jesus, persevere in suffering, and refuse to compromise—to resist following the ways of the world. He is calling us to repent and stand firm in faith. If we do, Jesus' wonderful promise of eternal life in heaven with Him will be ours. *Jesus will return some day, suddenly. Will He find you faithful?*

333

"Behold, I stand at the door and knock. If anyone hears my voice and opens the door, I will come in to him and eat with him, and he with me." (Revelation 3:20)

THAT YOU MAY BELIEVE

What does this chapter tell us about God?

Talk about and apply the **biblical truths** in **bold** text. Make them personal and apply them to what is happening in your family, church, community, or the world today.

Talk about some of the churches in Revelation 2-3 and the reasons for which Jesus rebukes them. Do you see this in the Church today?

Talk About: *"Behold, I stand at the door and knock. If anyone hears my voice and opens the door, I will come in to him and eat with him, and he with me." (Revelation 3:20)*

How can you apply these messages to your church and to your life?

Pray: Praise God for His faithfulness to His children. Thank Jesus for His wonderful promises to overcomers or conquerors. Ask Him to give you a faith that will stand strong. Confess where you fail and ask God to forgive your sin.

Think About: *What warnings to the churches do I need to listen to? What can I do to remain faithful to Jesus?*

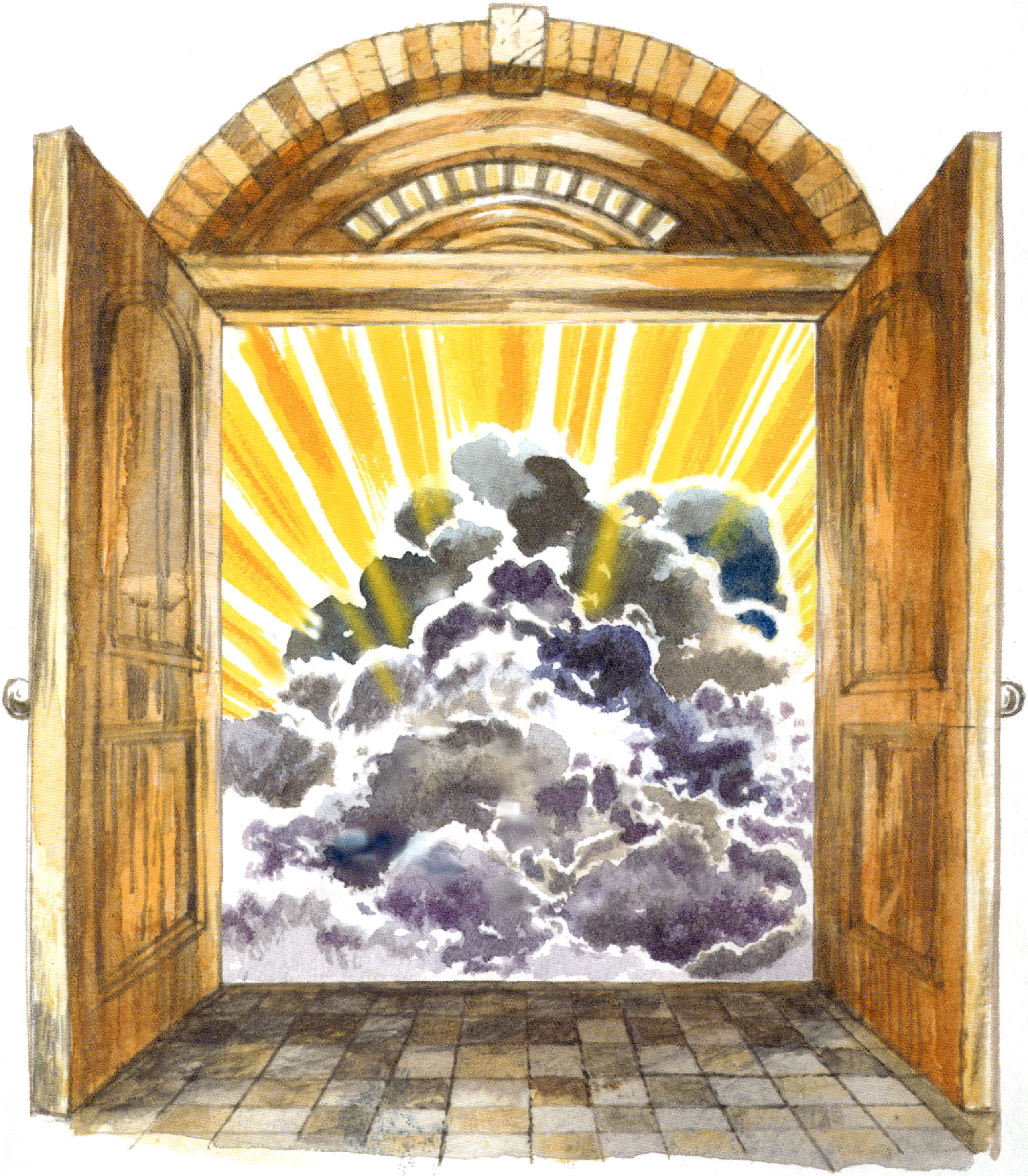

CHAPTER 156
THE KING OF KINGS REIGNS FOREVER!

Jesus Will Return to Judge and to Bless—Revelation

There is none like you among the gods, O Lord, nor are there any works like yours. All the nations you have made shall come and worship before you, O Lord, and shall glorify your name. (Psalm 86:8-9)

…"Worthy is the Lamb who was slain, to receive power and wealth and wisdom and might and honor and glory and blessing!" (Revelation 5:12)

The name of the last book of the Bible comes from a Greek word that means "revelation" or "unveiling." The future has a "veil" or a curtain over it. We can't see what is in the future. But in His Word, God has lifted the veil, "revealing" or "unveiling" what will happen at the end of time. Like Ezekiel and Daniel, Revelation is also a dream or vision of the future. Just as Daniel's statue made of four types of metal was a symbol or a picture of different kingdoms, so the book of Revelation is full of symbols.

After the messages to the churches, in his vision, John saw *a door standing open in heaven!* He heard "a voice like a trumpet" saying to him, *"Come up here, and I will show you what must take place after this."* In the vision, John was taken to the throne room of God. The throne room was glorious, filled with the glory and splendor of God. All day and all night, never stopping, "four living creatures" were praising God saying, *"Holy, holy, holy, is the Lord God Almighty, who was and is and is to come!"* We can't even begin to imagine the glory of heaven, a place of continual worship of God!

Then in the throne room of God, John was shown how God's Kingdom will fully come "on earth as it is in heaven."

Then I saw in the right hand of him who was seated on the throne a scroll written within and on the back, sealed with seven seals. And I saw a strong angel proclaiming with a loud voice, "Who is worthy to open the scroll and break its seals?" And no one in heaven or on earth or under the earth was able to open the scroll or to look into it, and I began to weep loudly because no one was found worthy to open the scroll or to look into it. And one of the elders said to me, "Weep no more; behold, the Lion of the tribe of Judah, the Root of David, has conquered, so that he can open the scroll and its seven seals." (Revelation 5:1-5)

In the vision, John is shown the seven seals and then seven trumpets. These are symbols of God's judgment during the end days. God will finally put an end to evil and Satan. But first there will be a time of great suffering and evil. There will be war, famine, disease, and death such as never has been seen before. *Do you ever get discouraged when you see the evil in the world? Do you long for justice to be done, for evil to be destroyed, and for sin and sickness and sadness to disappear forever? Do you long for life to be the way it was in the Garden of Eden before the Fall?*

We know that *"the Lion of the tribe of Judah, the Root of David, has conquered."* We know that **Jesus' death and resurrection has** *"ransomed people for God from every tribe and language and people and nation."* He has *"made them a kingdom and priests to our God, and they shall reign on the earth."* Redeemed people from all nations will be united to worship God, the Father, Son, and Holy Spirit. We will join in a great wedding feast—the marriage feast of the Lamb—where Jesus is united with His bride, the Church.

But now, when we look around, we see evil and hatred triumphing and increasing, families torn apart by sin, and Christians being killed for their faith. God has given us this vision in Revelation so we can stand firm with great confidence that good will win over evil. Jesus will conquer and reign forever! There will be a great victory! **God's Kingdom is coming!** *"Hallelujah! For the Lord our God, the Almighty reigns."* In his vision, this is what John saw:

> *Then I saw heaven opened, and behold, a white horse! The one sitting on it is called Faithful and True, and in righteousness he judges and makes war. His eyes are like a flame of fire, and on his head are many diadems, and he has a name written that no one knows but himself. He is clothed in a robe dipped in blood, and the name by which he is called is The Word of God. And the armies of heaven, arrayed in fine linen, white and pure, were following him on white horses. From his mouth comes a sharp sword with which to strike down the nations, and he will rule them with a rod of iron. He will tread the winepress of the fury of the wrath of God the Almighty. On his robe and on his thigh he has a name written, King of kings and Lord of lords. (Revelation 19:11-16)*

Jesus will come again, not as a baby or a suffering servant, but **as the King of kings and the Lord of lords! The great Day of the Lord will come, and it will bring judgment and blessing.** Jesus will defeat sin and evil and Satan forever! He will put all His enemies "under His feet." Satan will be *thrown into the lake of fire and sulfur* where he *will be tormented day and night forever and ever.* **Jesus is the victorious King who will defeat His enemies and will reign forever!**

John also saw a great white throne—the throne of judgment. *"Salvation and glory and power belong to our God, for **his judgments are true and just.**"* Everyone—great and small—will stand before the Judge of the whole earth. Then the books will be opened… *What will this be like? Will you be scared or confident in the blood of Christ?* John describes his vison, *And the dead were judged by what was written in the books, according to what they had done.* **And if anyone's name was not found written in the book of life, he was thrown into the lake of fire.** But for those whose names are written in the Book of Life, John tells us what awaits the children of God.

Then I saw a new heaven and a new earth, for the first heaven and the first earth had passed away, and the sea was no more. And I saw the holy city, new Jerusalem, coming down out of heaven from God, prepared as a bride adorned for her husband. And I heard a loud voice from the throne saying, "Behold, **the dwelling place of God is with man***. He will dwell with them, and* **they will be his people, and God himself will be with them as their God***. He will wipe away every tear from their eyes, and death shall be no more, neither shall there be mourning, nor crying, nor pain anymore, for the former things have passed away." And he who was seated on the throne said,* **"Behold, I am making all things new."** *Also he said, "Write this down, for these words are trustworthy and true." And he said to*

me, "It is done! I am the Alpha and the Omega, the beginning and the end. To the thirsty I will give from the spring of the water of life without payment. The one who conquers will have this heritage, and I will be his God and he will be my son. But as for the cowardly, the faithless, the detestable, as for murderers, the sexually immoral, sorcerers, idolaters, and all liars, their portion will be in the lake that burns with fire and sulfur, which is the second death." (Revelation 21:1-8)

Jesus will bring great blessing to His people—to those who have remained faithful to Him. They will live forever with Him in His Kingdom of love, joy, peace, patience, kindness, goodness, faithfulness, gentleness, and self-control. There will be no sadness, no evil, no tears, no unkindness, and no sickness or death. It will be a new creation and a new beginning for God's people—a new creation full of the glory of God!

And I saw no temple in the city, for its temple is the Lord God the Almighty and the Lamb. And the city has no need of sun or moon to shine on it, for the glory of God gives it light, and its lamp is the Lamb. By its light will the nations walk, and the kings of the earth will bring their glory into it, and its gates will never be shut by day—and there will be no night there. They will bring into it the glory and the honor of the nations. **But nothing unclean will ever enter it**, *nor anyone who does what is detestable or false,* **but only those who are written in the Lamb's book of life**. *Then the angel showed me the river of the water of life, bright as crystal, flowing from the throne of God and of the Lamb through the middle of the street of the city; also, on either side of the river, the tree of life with its twelve kinds of fruit, yielding its fruit each month. The leaves of the tree were for the healing of the nations. No longer will there be anything accursed, but the throne of God and of the Lamb will be in it, and his servants will worship him. They will see his face, and his name will be on their foreheads. And night will be no more. They will need no light of lamp or sun, for the Lord God will be their light, and they will reign forever and ever. (Revelation 21:22-22:5)*

"These words trustworthy and true." (Revelation 22:6a)

"And behold, I am coming soon. Blessed is the one who keeps the words of the prophecy of this book." (Revelation 22:7)

Do you believe that Jesus is coming back as King Jesus? Does this excite you or terrify you? Are you ready for the coming of the King?

And now, little children, abide in him, so that when he appears we may have confidence and not shrink from him in shame at his coming. (1 John 2:28)

Beloved, we are God's children now, and what we will be has not yet appeared; but we know that when he appears we shall be like him, because we shall see him as he is. (1 John 3:2)

THAT YOU MAY BELIEVE

What does this chapter tell us about God?

Talk about and apply the **biblical truths** in **bold** text. Make them personal and apply them to what is happening in your family, church, community, or the world today.

How can Christians remain faithful and strong in suffering? What can you do to strengthen your faith?

Do the events of Revelation make you fearful or hopeful? Explain.

Talk About: *And now, little children, abide in him, so that when he appears we may have confidence and not shrink from him in shame at his coming. (1 John 2:28)*

What will the new Kingdom be like? What will be there? And what will not be there? (Be specific as you compare it to life here and apply it personally to your life.) *What does a world of no sin and evil look like? There will be endless praise in heaven. How can you praise God now?*

Pray: Praise God for His new Kingdom. Praise Jesus for being the conquering King! Thank Jesus for His wonderful promises to those who remain faithful to Him. Ask God to show you if you are a real Christian.

Think About: *Will my name be written in the Book of Life at the last judgment?*

..."Worthy is the Lamb who was slain, to receive power and wealth and wisdom and might and honor and glory and blessing!" (Revelation 5:12)

IS HE WORTHY?

Do you feel the world is broken? We do.
Do you feel the shadows deepen? We do.
But do you know that all the dark won't stop the light
from getting through? We do.
Do you wish that you could see it all made new? We do.

Is all creation groaning? It is.
Is a new creation coming? It is.
Is the glory of the Lord to be the light within our midst? It is.
Is it good that we remind ourselves of this? It is.

Is anyone worthy? Is anyone whole?
Is anyone able to break the seal and open the scroll?
The Lion of Judah who conquered the grave
He is David's root and the Lamb who died
to ransom the slave

Is He worthy? Is He worthy?
Of all blessing and honor and glory
Is He worthy of this?
He is

Does the Father truly love us? He does.
Does the Spirit move among us? He does.
And does Jesus, our Messiah hold forever
those He loves? He does.
Does our God intend to dwell again with us? He does.

Is anyone worthy? Is anyone whole?
Is anyone able to break the seal and open the scroll?
The Lion of Judah who conquered the grave
He is David's root and the Lamb who died
to ransom the slave

From every people and tribe
Every nation and tongue
He has made us a kingdom and priests to God
To reign with the Son

Is He worthy? Is He worthy?
Of all blessing and honor and glory
Is He worthy of this?
He is!

Words and Music by Andrew Peterson and Ben Shive, © 2018 Capitol CMG Genesis (ASCAP) / Vamos Publishing (ASCAP). Used with permission.
You may want to sing along with Andrew Peterson playing "Is He Worthy" at the SING conference, youtube.com/watch?v=DMWrAqMWhWs

Come Quickly

Invitation

, Lord, Jesus!